CROCHET
CREATURES
OF MYTH & LEGEND

Advance Praise for *Crochet Creatures of Myth and Legend*

"WARNING: Crafty Intentions patterns may be ADDICTIVE! Whether you're a beginner or advanced crocheter, once you get started you won't be able to stop! If you're OK with sharing your home with all sorts of magical beasties, then you'll LOVE these designs and patterns!" **—Sarah Weinstein**

— — — — — — — —

"Every pattern is my favorite pattern! Beginner to advanced: every row is written so clearly. Crafty Intentions makes it easy to bring imagination to life. Megan Lapp is my favorite designer by a dragon's length." **—Ashley Lodge**

— — — — — — — —

"What's amazing about these patterns is how flexible they are! I love that my creativity can soar by mixing and matching from different patterns and making something that is uniquely mine without the stress of having to figure it all out on my own." **—Kari Kontoleon**

— — — — — — — —

"It all starts with that one pattern—next thing you know, Megan has you crocheting like a master, taming whatever beast you like!" **—Jasmin Parkin**

— — — — — — — —

"Megan's mastery of design, creativity, and artistry is one of a kind. The EXPERIENCE of creating a Megan Lapp pattern is worth the time and energy that goes into it. These creatures come to life one stitch after another. I come to Megan's patterns as much for the journey as I do the destination!" **—Rae Lynn Chase**

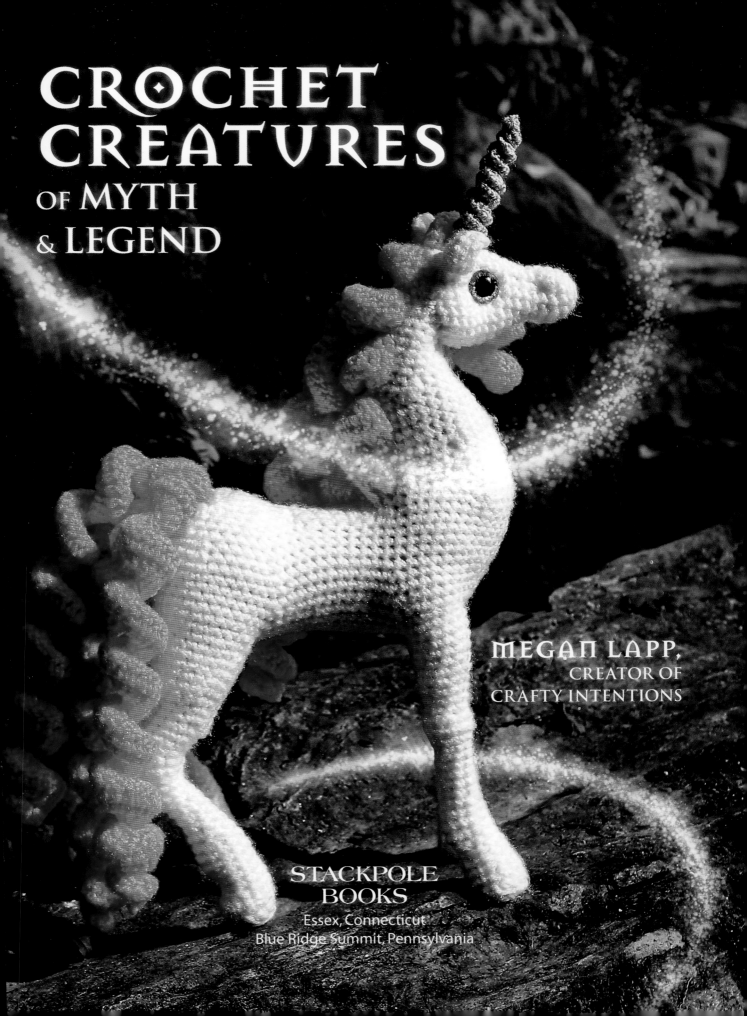

CROCHET CREATURES
OF MYTH
& LEGEND

MEGAN LAPP,
CREATOR OF
CRAFTY INTENTIONS

STACKPOLE
BOOKS
Essex, Connecticut
Blue Ridge Summit, Pennsylvania

STACKPOLE BOOKS

An imprint of The Globe Pequot Publishing Group, Inc.
64 South Main Street
Essex, CT 06426
www.globepequot.com

Distributed by NATIONAL BOOK NETWORK
800-462-6420

British Library Cataloguing in Publication Information available

Library of Congress Cataloging-in-Publication Data available

Names: Lapp, Megan, 1984– author.
Title: Crochet creatures of myth and legend / Megan Lapp.
Description: Essex, Connecticut : Stackpole Books, [2023]
Identifiers: LCCN 2022027769 (print) | LCCN 2022027770 (ebook) | ISBN
  9780811771481 (paperback) | ISBN 9780811771498 (epub)
Subjects: LCSH: Crocheting—Patterns. | Soft toy making—Patterns. |
  Stuffed animals (Toys)
Classification: LCC TT825 .L364 2023 (print) | LCC TT825 (ebook) | DDC
  746.43/4041—dc23/eng/20220819
LC record available at https://lccn.loc.gov/2022027769
LC ebook record available at https://lccn.loc.gov/2022027770

♾™ The paper used in this publication meets the minimum requirements of American National Standard for Information Sciences—Permanence of Paper for Printed Library Materials, ANSI/NISO Z39.48-1992.

First Edition

CONTENTS

STANDARD SIZE CREATURES

INTRODUCTION

Ever since I can remember, I have been making things, crafting and creating with every spare moment of my life. It may have been because of the books I read—the fairy stories, the magic and science fiction—or the art my parents displayed in our home. No matter the reason, for as long as I can remember, I have been imagining beautiful things. I see them in my mind and can turn and visualize them from all angles. Although I see them so clearly, for a time I struggled with bringing those things to life.

Over the years, I've tried my hand at nearly every imaginable artistic medium. Ample time was spent drawing in pencil and charcoal and pastels without more than passing amateurish success. More years were dedicated to painting with acrylics and oils and watercolors, loving the brilliant colors. I found that I could imitate what others made but was never able to fully realize what was in my head on paper or canvas. The first time I found some success was when, as a child, I was handed some wet clay at the end of a ceramics painting class. I had been wishing for years on pennies, dandelion fluff, and birthday candles for a puppy, so I sculpted one—and was thrilled to make the thing in my head come to life in my hands. To this day, my mother will still embarrassingly brag about the dog I sculpted as a child that prophetically looked exactly like the dog I adopted as an adult.

Finding this small measure of success sparked a long love affair with clay of all types, which eventually led me down the path of artistic education. After completing a summer program at Maryland Institute College of Art in high school, I went on to major in art and music at Lafayette College, where I received a lot of individualized attention and access to almost any art supply I could imagine. Most exciting was the preparation for my honors thesis. I took boxes and boxes of plaster rolls and cast the body of anyone who would let me, tacking them up on a wall for my final show as a roiling sea of anonymous

bodies. It was almost what I saw in my head, but not quite. That's how I felt for years. I would come so close to creating exactly what I envisioned, though never quite nailing the mark. It was frustrating, but I never wanted to stop making.

The following years brought a desk job and my marriage. The security allowed me to continue with art after hours—projects strewn about the house like half-realized dreams. I made chandeliers and packing tape sculptures. I tried wood carving and painted a mural on my bathroom wall. Nothing quite clicked, until my seeking led me to sewing.

I decided one of my first sewing projects should be a king-sized rainbow quilt. It was characteristically ambitious but far more work than I originally realized. I began to understand that tedious, detailed work was one of my strong suits. And even though I was already enjoying myself, the difficulty and slowness of the task were hampered by my lack of obvious tools. My husband broke down and researched sewing machines himself. That purchase changed everything. I finished assembling the rainbow quilt and moved on to create the most magical rainbow skirt I could imagine. Finally, things were coming together exactly as I saw them in my head.

Fiber arts, with fabric and thread, were never something I had explored before in any depth. I launched into many sewing projects, finding myself at home in them. A second bedroom became a studio. I imagined a great number of things that needed a third dimension but were difficult to realize in fabric. Children came along, and I chose to stay home with them for what I thought would be a relatively short period. My time for art was now regulated by tiny people of my own making—benevolent and inspiring as well as draining and exhausting by turns.

When my son was diagnosed with autism at the age of three, it was clear that remaining home with him was the right choice for our family. It was then a friend gifted a crocheted blanket in a rose motif, and I simply had to figure out how to make it immediately. It took me five years to move through the stages of learning stitches on YouTube, following free patterns, before I felt good enough to justify buying paid patterns. I was still sewing but doing it less and less, as crocheting felt great! It was also the most toddler-safe artistic thing I could do creatively. I began acquiring yarn in every color under the sun so I could make anything I set my mind to.

As my passion grew, the internet started to fail me. I would search for hours, or even days, for the perfect pattern, but none looked like what I wanted to create. There was no octopus pattern that looked like what was in my head. No dinosaur. No monster. And certainly no dragon! It took me a long while to even attempt making my own original items without a pattern, but once I did, it was a relief and a joy.

My ideas flowed from my hands and were realized in front of my eyes. I was making things exactly the way I imagined them. It's still a mystery to me why crochet is what clicked, but it feels like pure magic. My fingers fly and turn yarn into a three-dimensional print of what's in my mind's eye. It's hard to describe just how perfect it feels to be making things this way. And for a long time, I kept the magic to myself. It was my husband's suggestion to try writing down what I was doing, which turned out to be a lot harder than I realized. But I'm so glad I did, because it gives me so much joy to see other people make the things I've designed and see the creativity my patterns inspire. It's amazing to see my designs come to life in colors and ways I didn't predict.

Now I do this work to share the magic with others. I hope the rhythm of your stitches and the work of making these crocheted creatures slows the world and quiets anything you need it to, so you can experience the triumph of creation. It fills me with joy and is my pleasure to share this experience with you. Thank you for crocheting with me.

Megan Lapp

MATERIALS

YARN AND HOOK

I typically use a US size G (4 mm) crochet hook with a medium weight #4/ worsted weight yarn (aran works as well). Not all yarn labels are completely standard on yarn weight. Some yarns are labeled worsted but feel more bulky; some yarns are labeled worsted but feel much lighter, like a DK weight yarn. When you crochet amigurumi, it is most important for your stitches to create a fabric that is tightly woven and will not show the fiberfill stuffing. You can use any weight yarn you want, but you must adjust your hook size accordingly so that the fabric of stitches is solid. I typically think of Red Heart, Big Twist, or Impeccable yarn in basic acrylic colors as good solid medium #4/worsted weight yarns. It is also important that you use the same weight yarn throughout the pattern so that all crocheted pieces of any particular pattern are made on the same scale (unless specifically instructed to use a different weight yarn for a particular piece).

SAFETY EYES

I purchase safety eyes from two sources: Darkside Crochet and Suncatcher Craft Eyes. Darkside Crochet is UK based and Suncatcher is US based, but both ship anywhere you want. Both are also women-owned businesses.
   You can find Darkside here: https://darksidecrochet.bigcartel.com
   You can find Suncatcher here: https://suncatchercrafteyes.com

GLOSSARY OF TERMS AND STITCHES

To create the creatures in this book, you will need to learn a few possibly new-to-you stitches, particularly increases and decreases. The processes will be familiar, but where you work the stitches is important to note. Below is a list of terms and abbreviations for stitches that you should become familiar with and refer to as needed as you work the patterns.

[Brackets]	Brackets that come after BLO or FLO are used to indicate that these stitches are worked into the back loop only or front loop only. Ex.: BLO [SC 6] Brackets at the end of the row indicate the stitch count for the row. Ex.: [6]; this means there are 6 stitches in the row.
&	Located between two stitches, "&" indicates that both stitches are made into the same stitch, as an increase, but with two different types of stitches. Go here for video demonstration: https://www.youtube.com/watch?v=jGA2nAzL2cU&t=16s
< or >	Indicates the stitch will start (<) or finish (>) in the same stitch as the last stitch or the next stitch.
<Dec>	Beginning in the SAME stitch as your last stitch, make a decrease stitch into that and the next stitch, and then, into the same stitch that the decrease stitch ends in, begin your next stitch. Go here for video demonstration: https://www.youtube.com/watch?v=Ni2ZM1cXJI4
2 Dec in 3 SC	Make one decrease as normal, and then make the 2nd decrease starting in the SAME stitch as the 1st decrease and ending in the next stitch. Go here for video demonstration: https://www.youtube.com/watch?v=vWRuWd689KQ&t=4s
BLO [ ]	Back Loop Only **Pro Tip: The rows with FLO or BLO stitches will be structured with brackets [ ]. The brackets will enclose any and all stitches that the FLO or BLO instruction should apply to. Ex: "BLO [SC 3], SC 3" would mean three single crochet stitches in the BLO and then three normal single crochet.
BOLDED STITCH (F)	This particular instruction falls at the center front of the piece you are working on.
BOLDED STITCH (B)	This particular instruction falls at the center back of the piece you are working on.
Ch	Chain
Colorwork	When switching colors at the end of a row, switch to the new color when you make the slip stitch join. When you make the final yarn over to slip stitch at the end of the row, use the new color to do that final yarn over, and then chain 1; this creates a seamless transition to the new color.

DC	Double Crochet
DC Dec	YO, insert into next stitch, YO, pull up, YO, pull through 2 loops, YO, insert into next stitch, YO, pull up, YO, pull through 2 loops, YO, pull through all three loops
DC/HDC Dec	YO, insert into next stitch, YO, pull up, YO, pull through 2 loops, YO, pull through 1 loop, YO, insert into next stitch, YO, pull up, YO, pull through all four loops
Dec	Decrease: One stitch combining two spaces. All decreases are single crochet decreases unless otherwise stated.
FLO [ ]	Front Loop Only **Pro Tip: The rows with FLO or BLO stitches will be structured with brackets [ ]. The brackets will enclose any and all stitches that the FLO or BLO instruction should apply to. Ex: "FLO [SC 3], SC 3" would mean three single crochet stitches in the FLO and then three normal single crochet.
FP HDC	Front Post Half Double Crochet YO, insert hook from front to back to front around post of corresponding stitch below, YO, pull up, YO, pull through all remaining loops
Half Trip	Half Triple Crochet YO twice, insert into next stitch, YO, pull up, YO, pull through 2 loops, YO, pull through all remaining loops
Half Trip Dec	Half Triple Crochet Decrease YO twice, insert into next stitch, YO, pull up, YO, pull through 2 loops, YO twice, insert into next stitch, YO, pull up, YO, pull through 2 loops, YO, pull through all remaining loops
Half Trip Inc	Half Triple Crochet Increase Two Half Trip stitches into the same stitch
HDC	Half Double Crochet YO, insert hook into next stitch, YO, pull up, YO, pull through all three loops
HDC Dec	Half Double Crochet Decrease YO, insert into next stitch, YO, pull up, YO, pull through 2 loops, YO, insert into next stitch, YO, pull up, YO, pull through all four loops
HDC/SC Dec	Half Double Crochet and Single Crochet Decrease YO, insert into next stitch, YO, pull up, YO, pull through 2 loops, insert into next stitch, YO, pull up, YO, pull through all three loops
Inc	Increase, 2 stitches in one space Assume all increases are SC increases, unless otherwise specified.
Invisible Triple SC Decrease	Invisible Triple Single Crochet Decrease, single crochet decrease across three stitches in the front loop only Insert hook into the FLO of the 1st stitch, do not YO, insert hook into the FLO of the 2nd stitch, do not YO, insert hook into the FLO of the third stitch, YO, pull through three loops, YO, pull through remaining loops

OC	Original Chain This refers to the very first set of chain stitches you made to start the piece you're working on.
Picot	Ch 2, Sl St in the 2nd Ch from hook
Right side/ Outside vs. Wrong side/ Inside	To crochet right-side out, you will insert your hook from the outside/right side of the work to the inside/wrong side of the work, and if you are right-handed, you will be working in a clockwise direction. Here is a video on this technique: https://www.youtube.com/watch?v=beReNFWQPAs
SC	Single Crochet
SC/HDC Dec	Single Crochet/Half Double Crochet Decrease Insert into next stitch, YO, pull up, YO, insert into next stitch, YO, pull up, YO, pull through all remaining loops Here is a video on this stitch: https://www.youtube.com/watch?v=h4wkxMOMqXg&t=12s
Sk St	Skip Stitch
Sl St	Slip Stitch
Sl St to beginning stitch, Ch 1	JOINING: Most of the patterns are written with a Slip Stitch, Chain 1 joining method for each row. This DOES affect the shape of each piece, but in a minor way, as the piece was written with the seam shift in mind. If you prefer to crochet in spiral/in the round, you are welcome to try it, but I do not guarantee that all asymmetrical sections will come out exactly as shown. To end the row, after you have worked the entire row, you will slip stitch into the first stitch you worked in that row, and then Chain 1. The first stitch of the next row should be worked into the same stitch that you slip stitched into. For video demonstration, go here: https://www.youtube.com/watch?v=Qqu5N7TCt3U
St	Stitch
Triple Crochet	YO twice, insert into next stitch, YO, pull up, YO, pull through 2 loops, YO, pull through 2 loops, YO, pull through all remaining loops
Triple SC Dec	Triple Single Crochet Decrease One stitch combining three spaces using single crochet (Insert in next stitch space, YO, pull up) x 3, YO, pull through all four loops
Triple SC Inc	Triple Single Crochet Increase Three Single Crochet Stitches in one space
YO	Yarn Over

CUTE CRITTERS

The Cute Critters share many of the same anatomical pieces (body, legs, etc.). For each creature, make the parts listed in the table for that pattern, using one of the color schemes shown or creating your own, and then follow the assembly instructions to put your creature together.

ALCE WINGLESS GRIFFIN

An Alce, or Wingless Griffin, is a half-eagle, half-lion mythical creature that was often featured on family crests or shields of knights.

SIZE:

Approximately 5 to 6 in/12.5 to 15 cm tall from bottom to the top of the head, and 3 in/ 7.5 cm wide from side to side (not including wings).

MATERIALS

- » Yarn: See table on page 10 to find the yarn amounts needed for each piece. All yarn is #4 medium/ worsted weight, and all yarn amounts are approximate. Total amounts:
  - ◆ Main Color (variegated): 55 yd/50.25 m
  - ◆ Accent Color (white): 26 yd/23.75 m
  - ◆ Beak/Leg Color (gold): 10 yd/9.25 m

- » US size G (4 mm) hook

- » 15 mm black safety eyes or 15 mm or 18 mm colored iris safety eyes

- » Darning needle

- » Pins

- » Fiberfill stuffing

- » Optional: Glass gems for stability in feet and/or body

IПSTRUCTIOПS

Make the parts listed in the chart below, and then follow the Assembly instructions to complete your Alce Wingless Griffin.

PARTS TO MAKE	PAGE NUMBER	YARN COLOR	NUMBER TO MAKE	APPROX. AMOUNT
Front Leg with Rounded Foot	62	Main Color, Beak/Leg Color	2	7 yd/6.5 m Main Color, 3 yd/2.75 m Beak/Leg Color for 2 legs
Cute Critter Body	63	Main Color	1	20 yd/18.25 m
Rear Leg with Rounded Foot	65	Main Color	2	25 yd/22.75 m for 2 legs
Griffin Head	75	Accent Color, Beak/Leg Color	1	15 yd/13.75 m
Griffin Chest & Neck Piece	76	Accent Color	1	3 yd/2.75 m
Griffin Claw	78	Beak/Leg Color	2	4 yd/3.75 m for 2 claws
Griffin Ear	78	Accent Color	2	5 yd/4.5 m for 2 ears
Griffin Tail	77	Main Color, Accent Color	1	3 yd/2.75 m Main Color, 3 yd/2.75 m Accent Color
Griffin Beak	76	Beak/Leg Color	1	3 yd/2.75 m

ASSEMBLY

I. Pin the beak to the head (the Triple SC Inc on the Beak should be at the tip of the beak), sew to attach, weave in ends.

2. Pin the ears to the head, sew to attach, weave in ends.

3. Pin the rear legs to the body, sew to attach, weave in ends.

4. Pin the chest & neck piece to the body, sew to attach, weave in ends.

5. Pin the head, sew to attach, using the yarn tail to soft sculpt the head so that the eyes are inset into the head, and weave in ends.

6. Pin the claws in place along the top of the front feet, sew to attach, weave in ends. Then it is optional to pin the front legs in place against the body, sew to attach, weave in ends.

7. Pin the tail to the body, sew to attach, weave in ends.

ALICORN

The Alicorn is a winged Unicorn, or a cross between a Pegasus and Unicorn. It is found in the ancient mythology of many cultures.

SIZE:

Approximately 5 to 6 in/12.5 to 15 cm tall from bottom to the top of the head, and 3 in/ 7.5 cm wide from side to side (not including wings).

MATERIALS

» Yarn: See table on page 14 to find the yarn amounts needed for each piece. All yarn is #4 medium/ worsted weight, and all yarn amounts are approximate. Total amounts:
  • Main Color (white): 100 yd/91.5 m
  • Accent Color (various colors): 58 yd/53 m

» US size G (4 mm) hook

» 15 mm black safety eyes or 15 mm or 18 mm colored iris safety eyes

» Darning needle

» Pins

» Fiberfill stuffing

» Optional: Glass gems for stability in feet and/or body

INSTRUCTIONS

Make the parts listed in the chart below, and then follow the Assembly instructions to complete your Alicorn.

PARTS TO MAKE	PAGE NUMBER	YARN COLOR	NUMBER TO MAKE	APPROX. AMOUNT
Front Leg with Hoof	63	Main Color, Accent Color	2	12 yd/11 m Main Color, 2 yd/1.75 m Accent Color for 2 legs
Cute Critter Body	63	Main Color	1	20 yd/18.25 m
Rear Leg with Hoof	66	Main Color, Accent Color	2	25 yd/22.75 m Main Color, 3 yd/2.75 m Accent Color for 2 legs
Unicorn Head	83	Main Color	1	25 yd/22.75 m
Unicorn Ear	83	Main Color	2	5 yd/4.5 m for 2 ears
Unicorn Horn	84	Main Color or Accent Color	1	3 yd/2.75 m
Unicorn Mane	84	Accent Color	1	15 yd/13.75 m per piece
Unicorn Tail	84	Accent Color	1	25 yd/22.75 m
Griffin Wing	76	Main Color or Accent Color	2	10 yd/9 m for 2 wings

ASSEMBLY

I. Pin the rear legs to the body, sew to attach, and weave in ends.

2. Pin the head to the body, sew to attach, sew the hole in the back of the head shut, and weave in ends.

3. Pin the ears to the head, sew to attach, and weave in ends.

4. Pin the horn to the forehead, sew to attach, and weave in ends.

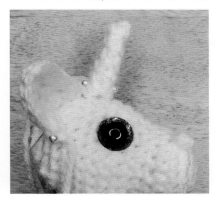

5. Pin the wings to the back, sew to attach, and weave in ends.

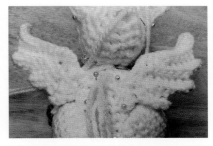

6. Pin the tail to the body, sew to attach, and weave in ends.

7. Pin the mane to attach, starting just after the horn down the center of the back of the head. There is one strand of hair at the start of the mane that is meant to fall just in front of the Alicorn's ear. Sew to attach, and weave in ends.

8. Pin the front legs down to the belly (if desired), tack in place, weave in ends.

COCKATRICE

The Cockatrice is a two-legged dragon or serpent-like creature with the head of a rooster. In some mythologies, the glance of a cockatrice is deadly.

SIZE:

Approximately 5 to 6 in/12.5 to 15 cm tall from bottom to the top of the head, and 3 in/ 7.5 cm wide from side to side (not including wings).

MATERIALS

» Yarn: See table on page 18 to find the yarn amounts needed for each piece. All yarn is #4 medium/ worsted weight, and all yarn amounts are approximate. Total amounts:
  - Main Color (dark green): 65 yd/59.5 m
  - Accent Color 1 (light taupe): 22 yd/20 m
  - Accent Color 2 (rust): 23 yd/21 m
  - Red Color: 3 yd/2.75 m

» US size G (4 mm) hook

» 15 mm black safety eyes or 18 mm colored iris safety eyes

» Darning needle

» Pins

» Fiberfill stuffing

» Optional: Glass gems for stability in feet and/or body

INSTRUCTIONS

Make the parts listed in the chart below, and then follow the Assembly instructions to complete your Cockatrice.

PARTS TO MAKE	PAGE NUMBER	YARN COLOR	NUMBER TO MAKE	APPROX. AMOUNT
Cockatrice Body	67	Main Color, Accent Color 2	1	10 yd/9 m Main Color, 20 yd/18.25 m Accent Color 2
Cockatrice Beak	67	Accent Color 1	1	1 yd/1 m
Rear Leg with Rounded Foot	65	Main Color, Accent Color 1	2	25 yd/22.75 m Main Color, 3 yd/2.75 m Accent Color 1 for 2 legs
Dragon Belly	72	Accent Color 1	1	5 yd/4.5 m
Dragon Tail	72	Main Color	1	10 yd/9 m
Dragon Leather Wing	69	Main Color, Accent Color 1	2	20 yd/18.25 m Main Color, 9 yd/8.25 m Accent Color 1 for 2 wings
Griffin Claw	78	Accent Color 1	2	4 yd/3.75 m for 2 claws
Cockatrice Wattle	68	Red Color	1	1 yd/1 m
Cockatrice Comb	68	Red Color	1	2 yd/1.75 m
Cockatrice Neck Feathers	68	Accent Color 2	1	3 yd/2.75 m

ASSEMBLY

I. Pin the belly to the body, sew to attach, weave in ends.

2. Pin the rear legs and tail to attach, check the balance and stability of the critter to sit securely on a flat surface, sew to attach, weave in ends.

3. Pin the beak piece (the seam of the beak goes along the bottom), sew to attach, weave in ends.

4. Pin the neck feathers to attach right along the edge of the color change on the body, hiding the color change, over top of the belly, sew to attach, weave in ends.

5. Pin the wattle and comb pieces. The comb is pinned as a mohawk along the top of the head with the shortest feather at the front starting just above eye level. The wattle is pinned just under the beak, without extending beyond the sides of the beak as much as possible. Sew to attach, weave in ends.

6. Pin the dragon wings to the back, sew to attach, weave in ends.

7. Pin the claws to the rear legs, sew to attach, weave in ends.

DRAGON

The Dragon is a giant winged, fire-breathing reptile with scales and a barbed tail. Many variations on this theme exist, and in different traditions, dragons may be malevolent or benevolent.

SIZE:

Approximately 5 to 6 in/12.5 to 15 cm tall from bottom to the top of the head, and 3 in/ 7.5 cm wide from side to side (not including wings).

MATERIALS

» Yarn: See table on page 24 to find the yarn amounts needed for each piece. All yarn is #4 medium/ worsted weight, and all yarn amounts are approximate. Total amounts:
  • Main Color (purple/blue variegated): 108 yd/ 98.75 m
  • Accent Color (silver): 18 yd/16.5 m

» US size G (4 mm) hook

» 12 mm or 15 mm black safety eyes or 15 mm or 18 mm colored iris safety eyes

» Darning needle

» Pins

» Fiberfill stuffing

» Optional: Glass gems for stability in feet and/or body

INSTRUCTIONS

Make the parts listed in the chart below, and then follow the Assembly instructions to complete your Dragon.

PARTS TO MAKE	PAGE NUMBER	YARN COLOR	NUMBER TO MAKE	APPROX. AMOUNT
Front Leg with Rounded Foot	62	Main Color	2	7 yd/6.5 m for 2 legs
Cute Critter Body	63	Main Color	1	20 yd/18.25 m
Rear Leg with Rounded Foot	65	Main Color	2	25 yd/22.75 for 2 legs
Dragon Head	69	Main Color	1	20 yd/18.25 m
Dragon Fin Ear	71	Main Color	2	6 yd/5.5 m for 2 ears
Dragon Tail	72	Main Color	1	10 yd/9 m
Dragon Leather Wing	69	Main Color, Accent Color	2	9 yd/8.25 m Main Color, 20 yd/18.25 m Accent Color for 2 wings
Dragon Back Scales	72	Accent Color	1	4 yd/3.75 m
Dragon Belly	72	Accent Color	1	5 yd/4.5 m

ASSEMBLY

1. Pin the belly to the body, sew to attach, weave in ends.

2. Pin the rear legs to the body, sew to attach, weave in ends.

3. Pin the head to the body, sew to attach, using the yarn tail to soft sculpt the head so that the eyes are inset into the head, and weave in ends.

4. Pin the ears to the head, sew to attach, weave in ends.

5. Stuff the tail lightly with fiberfill, pin the tail to the body, sew to attach, weave in ends.

6. Pin the back scales, sew to attach, weave in ends.

7. Pin the wings, sew to attach, weave in ends.

8. Pin the front legs down and sew in place if you desire, weave in all remaining ends.

GARGOYLE

Gargoyles, popular in Gothic architecture, are grotesque carved-stone beasts with spouts that serve to direct rainwater away from buildings.

SIZE:

Approximately 5 to 6 in/12.5 to 15 cm tall from bottom to the top of the head, and 3 in/ 7.5 cm wide from side to side (not including wings).

MATERIALS

» Yarn: See table on page 28 to find the yarn amounts needed for each piece. All yarn is #4 medium/ worsted weight, and all yarn amounts are approximate. Total amounts:
  - Main Color (gray): 146 yds/133.5 m
  - White: 2 yd/1.75 m
» US size G (4 mm) hook
» 18 mm black safety eyes
» Darning needle
» Pins
» Fiberfill stuffing
» Optional: Glass gems for stability in feet and/or body

INSTRUCTIONS

Make the parts listed in the chart below, and then follow the Assembly instructions to complete your Gargoyle.

PARTS TO MAKE	PAGE NUMBER	YARN COLOR	NUMBER TO MAKE	APPROX. AMOUNT
Front Leg with Rounded Foot	62	Main Color	2	7 yd/6.5 m for 2 legs
Cute Critter Body	63	Main Color	1	20 yd/18.25 m
Rear Leg with Rounded Foot	65	Main Color	2	25 yd/22.75 m for 2 legs
Gargoyle Bottom Jaw and Head	73	Main Color	1	30 yd/27.5 m
Gargoyle Ear	73	Main Color	2	10 yd/9 m for 2 ears
Gargoyle Horn	75	Main Color	2	5 yd/4.5 m for 2 horns
Gargoyle Teeth	74	White	1	2 yd/1.75 m
Dragon Leather Wing	69	Main Color	2	29 yd/26.5 m for 2 wings
Gargoyle Tail	75	Main Color	1	2 yd/1.75 m

ASSEMBLY

I. Tuck the teeth inside the bottom lip of the gargoyle head. The chains attaching the teeth to each other should be deep within the bottom lip, and the teeth themselves should only just peak out from underneath the lip. Sew the teeth to attach under the lip, along the bottom of the teeth and the Ch 10, weave in ends.

2. Pin the ears and horns to the head. The unfinished edge of the ears will be against the head. The final yarn tail will be at the top; fold this top corner down when pinning to the head. Sew to attach, weave in ends.

3. Pin the rear legs to attach, sew to attach, weave in ends.

4. Pin the head to attach, sew to attach, using the yarn tail to soft sculpt the head so that the eyes are inset into the head, and weave in ends.

5. Pin the front legs in place, sew to attach, weave in ends.

6. Pin the wings, sew to attach, weave in ends.

7. Pin the tail, sew to attach, weave in ends.

GRIFFIN

The Griffin is especially powerful because it is half King of the Beasts (lion) and half King of the Birds (eagle). It has the head and wings of an eagle and the body, tail, and back legs of a lion. Because of its power and majesty, it is often portrayed as a guardian of treasures.

SIZE:

Approximately 5 to 6 in/12.5 to 15 cm tall from bottom to the top of the head, and 3 in/ 7.5 cm wide from side to side (not including wings).

MATERIALS

» Yarn: See table on page 32 to find the yarn amounts needed for each piece. All yarn is #4 medium/ worsted weight, and all yarn amounts are approximate. Total amounts:
- Main Color (brown): 55 yd/50.25 m
- Accent Color 1 (white): 23 yd/21 m
- Accent Color 2 (gold or golden yellow): 13 yd/ 12 m
- Accent Color 3 (feather color/gradient): 13 yd/ 12 m

» US size G (4 mm) hook

» 12 mm or 15 mm black safety eyes or 15 mm or 18 mm colored iris safety eyes

» Darning needle

» Pins

» Fiberfill stuffing

» Optional: Glass gems for stability in feet and/or body

INSTRUCTIONS

Make the parts listed in the chart below, and then follow the Assembly instructions to complete your Griffin.

PARTS TO MAKE	PAGE NUMBER	YARN COLOR	NUMBER TO MAKE	APPROX. AMOUNT
Front Leg with Rounded Foot	62	Main Color, Accent Color 2	2	7 yd/6.5 m Main Color, 3 yd/2.75 m Accent Color 2 for 2 legs
Cute Critter Body	63	Main Color	1	20 yd/18.25 m
Rear Leg with Rounded Foot	65	Main Color	2	25 yd/22.75 m for 2 legs
Griffin Head	75	Accent Color 1, Accent Color 2	1	15 yd/13.75 m Accent Color 1, 3 yd/2.75 m Accent Color 2
Griffin Beak	76	Accent Color 2	1	3 yd/2.75 m
Griffin Chest & Neck Piece	76	Accent Color 1	1	3 yd/2.75 m
Griffin Claw	78	Accent Color 2	2	4 yd/3.75 m for 2 claws
Griffin Ear	78	Accent Color 1	2	5 yd/4.5 m for 2 ears
Griffin Tail	77	Main Color, Accent Color 3	1	3 yd/2.75 m Main Color, 3 yd/2.75 m Accent Color 3
Griffin Wing	76	Accent Color 3	2	10 yd/9 m for 2 wings

ASSEMBLY

I. Pin the rear legs to the body, sew to attach, weave in ends.

2. Pin the chest & neck piece to the body, sew to attach, weave in ends.

3. Pin the head to the chest & neck piece, sew to attach, using the yarn tail to soft sculpt the head so that the eyes are inset into the head, and weave in ends.

4. Pin the beak to the head (the Triple SC Inc should be at the tip of the beak), sew to attach, weave in ends.

5. Pin the ears to the head, sew to attach, weave in ends.

6. Pin the front legs in place, sew to attach, weave in ends. Pin the claws in place, sew to attach, weave in ends.

7. Pin the wings, sew to attach, weave in ends.

8. Pin the tail, sew to attach, weave in ends.

HIPPOGRIFF

The Hippogriff is a rare creature that is the offspring of a Griffin and a mare and therefore has the head, claws, talons, and wings of an eagle like the Griffin but the body and rear legs of a horse. Hippogriffs are prized as steeds in medieval legends, as they are easier to tame than Griffins and can fly as fast as lightning.

SIZE:

Approximately 5 to 6 in/12.5 to 15 cm tall from bottom to the top of the head, and 3 in/ 7.5 cm wide from side to side (not including wings).

MATERIALS

» Yarn: See table on page 36 to find the yarn amounts needed for each piece. All yarn is #4 medium/ worsted weight, and all yarn amounts are approximate. Total amounts:
  • Main Color (yellow): 52 yd/47.5 m
  • Accent Color 1 (light gold): 16 yd/14.75 m
  • Accent Color 2 (various): 20 yd/18.25 m
  • Accent Color 3 (various): 3 yd/2.75 m
  • Accent Color 4 (various): 25 yd/22.75 m
  • Accent Color 5 (various): 10 yd/9 m

» US size G (4 mm) hook

» 15 mm black safety eyes or 15 mm or 18 mm colored iris safety eyes

» Darning needle

» Pins

» Fiberfill stuffing

» Optional: Glass gems for stability in feet and/or body

NOTE: In the example shown in these photos, the same variagated pink/ purple yarn is used for accent colors 2–5. Individual yardages are provided for those pieces, but not because they are different colors. While you CAN make them in different colors, it is more cohesive if you make them all the same color.

INSTRUCTIONS

Make the parts listed in the chart below, and then follow the Assembly instructions to complete your Hippogriff.

PARTS TO MAKE	PAGE NUMBER	YARN COLOR	NUMBER TO MAKE	APPROX. AMOUNT
Front Leg with Rounded Foot	62	Main Color, Accent Color 1	2	7 yd/6.5 m Main Color, 3 yd/2.75 m Accent Color for 2 legs
Cute Critter Body	63	Main Color	1	20 yd/18.25 m
Rear Leg with Hoof	66	Main Color, Accent Color 1	2	25 yd/22.75 m Main Color, 3 yd/2.75 m Accent Color 1 for 2 legs
Griffin Head	75	Accent Color 1, Accent Color 2	1	3 yd/2.75 m Accent Color 1, 15 yd/13.75 m Accent Color 2
Griffin Beak	76	Accent Color 1	1	3 yd/2.75 m
Griffin Chest & Neck Piece	76	Accent Color 3	1	3 yd/2.75 m
Griffin Claw	78	Accent Color 1	2	4 yd/3.75 m for 2 claws
Griffin Ear	78	Accent Color 2	2	5 yd/4.5 m for 2 ears
Unicorn Tail	84	Accent Color 4	1	25 yd/22.75 m
Griffin Wing	76	Accent Color 5	2	10 yd/9 m for 2 wings

ASSEMBLY

I. Pin the rear legs, sew to attach, weave in ends.

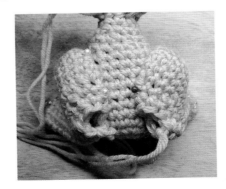

2. Pin the chest & neck piece, sew to attach, weave in ends.

3. Pin the head, sew to attach, using the yarn tail to soft sculpt the head so that the eyes are inset into the head, and weave in ends.

4. Pin the beak to the head, sew to attach, weave in ends.

5. Pin the ears to the head, sew to attach, weave in ends.

6. Pin the front legs in place, sew to attach, weave in ends. Pin the claws in place, sew to attach, weave in ends.

7. Pin the wings to the body, sew to attach, weave in ends.

8. Pin the tail, sew to attach, weave in ends.

JACKALOPE

The Jackalope is a mythical animal of North American folklore, a jackrabbit with antelope horns.

SIZE:

Approximately 5 to 6 in/12.5 to 15 cm tall from bottom to the top of the head, and 3 in/ 7.5 cm wide from side to side (not including wings).

MATERIALS

» Yarn: See table on page 40 to find the yarn amounts needed for each piece. All yarn is #4 medium/ worsted weight, and all yarn amounts are approximate. Total amounts:
  - Main Color (brown or off-white tweed): 87 yd/79.5 m
  - Accent Color (brown or white): 10 yd/9 m

» US size G (4 mm) crochet hook

» 12 mm, 15 mm, or 18 mm black safety eyes

» Darning needle

» Pins

» Fiberfill stuffing

» Optional: Glass gems for stability in feet and/or body

INSTRUCTIONS

Make the parts listed in the chart below, and then follow the Assembly instructions to complete your Jackalope.

PARTS TO MAKE	PAGE NUMBER	YARN COLOR	NUMBER TO MAKE	APPROX. AMOUNT
Front Leg with Rounded Foot	62	Main Color	2	7 yd/6.5 m for 2 legs
Cute Critter Body	63	Main Color	1	20 yd/18.25 m
Rear Leg with Rounded Foot	65	Main Color	2	25 yd/22.75 m for 2 legs
Jackalope Head	78	Main Color	1	20 yd/18.25 m
Jackalope Ear	79	Main Color	2	10 yd/9 m for 2 ears
Jackalope Antler	79	Accent Color	2	5 yd/4.5 m for 2 antlers
Jackalope Tail	80	Main or Accent Color	1	5 yd/4.5 m

ASSEMBLY

1. Pin the rear legs, sew to attach, weave in ends.

2. Pin the head, sew to attach, using the yarn tail to soft sculpt the head so that the eyes are inset into the head, and weave in ends.

3. Pin the ears and antlers, sew to attach, weave in ends.

4. Pin the tail piece, sew to attach, weave in ends.

5. Pin the front legs down (if desired), tack in place, weave in ends.

PEGASUS

Pegasus is a divine winged horse in Greek mythology, usually depicted as white. It has become one of the most recognized of mythological creatures, and there are many stories of its exploits.

SIZE:

Approximately 5 to 6 in/12.5 to 15 cm tall from bottom to the top of the head, and 3 in/ 7.5 cm wide from side to side (not including wings).

MATERIALS

» Yarn: See table on page 44 to find the yarn amounts needed for each piece. All yarn is #4 medium/ worsted weight, and all yarn amounts are approximate. Total amounts:
  • Main Color (white): 97 yd/88.75 m
  • Accent Color (purple/ blue variegated): 45 yd/41 m

» US size G (4 mm) crochet hook

» 15 mm black safety eyes or 15 mm or 18 mm colored iris safety eyes

» Darning needle

» Pins

» Fiberfill stuffing

» Optional: Glass gems for stability in feet and/or body

INSTRUCTIONS

Make the parts listed in the chart below, and then follow the Assembly instructions to complete your Pegasus.

PARTS TO MAKE	PAGE NUMBER	YARN COLOR	NUMBER TO MAKE	APPROX. AMOUNT
Front Leg with Hoof	63	Main Color, Accent Color	2	12 yd/11 m Main Color, 2 yd/1.75 m Accent Color for 2 legs
Cute Critter Body	63	Main Color	1	20 yd/18.25 m
Rear Leg with Hoof	66	Main Color, Accent Color	2	25 yd/22.75 m Main Color, 3 yd/2.75 m Accent Color for 2 legs
Unicorn Head	83	Main Color	1	25 yd/22.75 m
Unicorn Ear	83	Main Color	2	5 yd/4.5 m for 2 ears
Unicorn Mane	84	Accent Color	1	15 yd/13.75 m per piece
Unicorn Tail	84	Accent Color	1	25 yd/22.75 m
Griffin Wing	76	Main Color	2	10 yd/9 m for 2 wings

ASSEMBLY

I. Pin the rear legs to the body, sew to attach, and weave in ends.

2. Pin the head to the body, sew to attach, sew the hole in the back of the head shut, and weave in ends.

3. Pin the ears to the head, sew to attach, and weave in ends.

4. Pin the wings to the back, sew to attach, and weave in ends.

5. Pin the tail, sew to attach, and weave in ends.

6. Pin the mane, sew to attach, and weave in ends.

7. Pin the front legs down to the belly (if desired), tack in place, weave in ends.

PHOENIX

The Phoenix is a majestic bird that lives for a thousand years in Paradise and then leaves to go to the mortal world, where it sings a mournful song that makes the sun god stop and a spark of the sun fall from the sky to burn the creature up. The Phoenix is then reborn in three days from its own ashes and returns to Paradise for another thousand years.

SIZE:

Approximately 5 to 6 in/12.5 to 15 cm tall from bottom to the top of the head, and 3 in/ 7.5 cm wide from side to side (not including wings).

MATERIALS

» Yarn: See table on page 48 to find the yarn amounts needed for each piece. All yarn is #4 medium/ worsted weight, and all yarn amounts are approximate. Total amounts:
  - Main Color (red variegated): 109 yd/99.75 m
  - Accent Color (gold): 18 yd/16.5 m
» US size G (4 mm) crochet hook
» 12 mm or 15 mm black safety eyes or 15 mm or 18 mm colored iris safety eyes
» Darning needle
» Pins
» Fiberfill stuffing
» Optional: Glass gems for stability in feet and/or body

INSTRUCTIONS

Make the parts listed in the chart below, and then follow the Assembly instructions to complete your Phoenix.

PARTS TO MAKE	PAGE NUMBER	YARN COLOR	NUMBER TO MAKE	APPROX. AMOUNT
Front Leg with Rounded Foot	62	Main Color	2	7 yd/6.5 m for 2 legs
Cute Critter Body	63	Main Color	1	20 yd/18.25 m
Rear Leg with Rounded Foot	65	Main Color, Accent Color	2	25 yd/22.75 m Main Color, 3 yd/2.75 m Accent Color for 2 legs
Griffin Claw	78	Accent Color	2	4 yd/3.75 m for 2 claws
Phoenix Head	80	Main Color, Accent Color	1	18 yd/16.5 m Main Color, 3 yd/2.75 m Accent Color
Phoenix Head Feathers	82	Main Color	1	3 yd/2.75 m
Phoenix Tail	81	Main Color, Accent Color	1 or 2	11 yd/10 m Main Color, 8 yd/7.25 m Accent Color for 1 tail
Phoenix Wing	80	Main Color	2	25 yd/22.75 m for 2 wings

ASSEMBLY

1. Pin the rear legs, sew to attach, weave in ends.

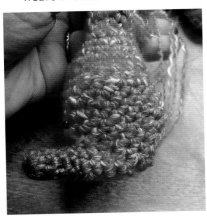

2. Pin the tail piece, sew to attach, weave in ends.

Photo below shows two layers of tail feathers. This is optional—if desired, make two tail feather pieces and layer the pieces as shown.

3. Pin the head, sew to attach, using the yarn tail to soft sculpt the head so that the eyes are inset into the head, and weave in ends.

4. Pin the claws to the rear leg feet, sew to attach, weave in ends.

5. Pin the head feathers to the head, sew to attach, weave in ends.

6. Pin the wings to the front legs, sew to attach, weave in ends.

Unicorn

The Unicorn is a legendary creature depicted in ancient art from many cultures. It is a beast, often a horse or goat-like animal, with a single large, pointed, spiraling horn on its forehead, which is said to have healing powers.

SIZE:

Approximately 5 to 6 in/12.5 to 15 cm tall from bottom to the top of the head, and 3 in/ 7.5 cm wide from side to side (not including wings).

The rounded head is the Dragon Head (page 69) with small modifications

MATERIALS

» Yarn: See table on page 52 to find the yarn amounts needed for each piece. All yarn is #4 medium/ worsted weight, and all yarn amounts are approximate. Total amounts:
  • Main Color (white): 87 yd/79.5 m
  • Accent Color 1 (gold): 3 yd/2.75 m
  • Accent Color 2 (multicolor): 45 yd/46.25 m

» US size G (4 mm) crochet hook

» 15 mm black safety eyes or 15 mm or 18 mm colored iris safety eyes

» Darning needle

» Pins

» Fiberfill stuffing

» Optional: Glass gems for stability in feet and/or body

INSTRUCTIONS

Make the parts listed in the chart below, and then follow the Assembly instructions to complete your Unicorn.

PARTS TO MAKE	PAGE NUMBER	YARN COLOR	NUMBER TO MAKE	APPROX. AMOUNT
Front Leg with Hoof	63	Main Color, Accent Color 2	2	12 yd/11 m Main Color, 2 yd/1.75 m Accent Color for 2 legs
Cute Critter Body	63	Main Color	1	20 yd/18.25 m
Rear Leg with Hoof	66	Main Color, Accent Color 2	2	25 yd/22.75 m Main Color, 3 yd/2.75 m Accent Color for 2 legs
Unicorn Head	83	Main Color	1	25 yd/22.75 m
Alternate Unicorn/ Dragon Head	69	Main Color	1	20 yd/18.25 m
Unicorn Ear	83	Main Color	2	5 yd/4.5 m for 2 ears
Unicorn Horn	84	Accent Color 1	1	3 yd/2.75 m
Unicorn Mane	84	Accent Color 2	1	15 yd/13.75 m per piece
Unicorn Tail	84	Accent Color 2	1	25 yd/22.75 m

ASSEMBLY

1. Pin the rear legs to the body, sew to attach, and weave in ends.

2. Pin the head to the body, sew the hole in the back of the head shut, sew to attach, using the yarn tail to soft sculpt the head so that the eyes are inset into the head, and weave in ends.

3. Pin the ears to the head, sew to attach, and weave in ends.

4. Pin the horn to the forehead, sew to attach, and weave in ends.

5. Pin the tail, sew to attach, and weave in ends.

6. Pin the mane, sew to attach, and weave in ends.

7. Pin the front legs down to the belly (if desired), tack in place, weave in ends.

The rounded head is the Dragon Head (page 69) with small modifications

WOLPERTINGER

The Wolpertinger is a creature of German folklore said to inhabit the forests in southern Germany. It is often depicted as having the head of a hare, the body of a squirrel, the antlers of a deer, wings, and fangs.

SIZE:

Approximately 5 to 6 in/12.5 to 15 cm tall from bottom to the top of the head, and 3 in/ 7.5 cm wide from side to side (not including wings).

MATERIALS

» Yarn: See table on page 56 to find the yarn amounts needed for each piece. All yarn is #4 medium/ worsted weight, and all yarn amounts are approximate. Total amounts:
  - Main Color (gray): 89 yd/81.5 m
  - Accent Color (white): 17 yd/15.5 m

» US size G (4 mm) crochet hook

» 12 mm, 15 mm, or 18 mm black safety eyes

» Darning needle

» Pins

» Fiberfill stuffing

» Optional: Glass gems for stability in feet and/or body

INSTRUCTIONS

Make the parts listed in the chart below, and then follow the Assembly instructions to complete your Wolpertinger.

PARTS TO MAKE	PAGE NUMBER	YARN COLOR	NUMBER TO MAKE	APPROX. AMOUNT
Front Leg with Rounded Foot	62	Main Color	2	7 yd/6.5 m for 2 legs
Cute Critter Body	63	Main Color	1	20 yd/18.25 m
Rear Leg with Rounded Foot	65	Main Color	2	25 yd/22.75 m for 2 legs
Jackalope Head	78	Main Color	1	20 yd/18.25 m
Wolpertinger Ear	85	Main Color	2	10 yd/9 m for 2 ears
Jackalope Antler	79	Accent Color	2	5 yd/4.5 m for 2 antlers
Jackalope Tail	80	Main Color	1	5 yd/4.5 m
Griffin Wing	76	Accent Color	2	10 yd/9 m for 2 wings
Wolpertinger Fang	85	Accent Color	2	2 yd/1.75 m for 2 fangs
Wolpertinger Muzzle	85	Main Color	1	2 yd/1.75 m

ASSEMBLY

1. Pin the rear legs, sew to attach, weave in ends.

2. Pin the head, sew to attach, using the yarn tail to soft sculpt the head so that the eyes are inset into the head, and weave in ends.

3. Pin the ears and antlers, sew to attach, weave in ends.

4. Pin the muzzle. Do not sew to attach yet.

5. Pin the fangs to attach as if sprouting from just under the muzzle, sew to attach, weave in ends. Sew the muzzle to attach, weave in ends.

6. Optionally, you can embroider a small nose just above the muzzle using an accent/nose color yarn.

7. Pin the tail piece, sew to attach, weave in ends.

8. Pin the front legs down (if desired), tack in place, weave in ends.

9. Pin the wings, sew to attach, weave in ends.

WYVERN

The Wyvern is a legendary dragon
with two legs instead of four.
It is rarely fire-breathing,
unlike four-legged dragons.

SIZE:

Approximately 5 to 6 in/12.5 to
15 cm tall from bottom to the
top of the head, and 3 in/
7.5 cm wide from side to side
(not including wings).

MATERIALS

➤➤ Yarn: See table on page 60
to find the yarn amounts
needed for each piece.
All yarn is #4 medium/
worsted weight, and all yarn
amounts are approximate.
Total amounts:
  ◆ Main Color (blue/teal
    variegated): 92 yd/84 m
  ◆ Accent Color (silver):
    9 yd/8.25 m

➤➤ US size G (4 mm) crochet
hook

➤➤ 12 mm or 15 mm black
safety eyes or 15 mm or
18 mm colored iris safety
eyes

➤➤ Darning needle

➤➤ Pins

➤➤ Fiberfill stuffing

➤➤ Optional: Glass gems for
stability in feet and/or body

INSTRUCTIONS

Make the parts listed in the chart below, and then follow the Assembly instructions to complete your Wyvern.

PARTS TO MAKE	PAGE NUMBER	YARN COLOR	NUMBER TO MAKE	APPROX. AMOUNT
Cute Critter Body (with no front legs)	63	Main Color	1	20 yd/18.25 m
Rear Leg with Rounded Foot	65	Main Color	2	25 yd/22.75 m for 2 legs
Wyvern Head	86	Main Color	1	20 yd/18.25 m
Dragon Leather Wing	69	Main Color (for all Parts)	2	29 yd/26.5 m for 2 wings
Dragon Tail	72	Main Color	1	10 yd/9 m
Wyvern Ear	86	Main Color	2	8 yd/7.25 m for 2 ears
Dragon Back Scales	72	Accent Color	1	4 yd//3.75 m
Gargoyle Horn	75	Accent Color	2	5 yd/4.5 m for 2 horns

ASSEMBLY

I. Pin the rear legs and the tail to attach. Verify that the critter is stable when sitting on a flat surface. Sew to attach, and weave in ends.

2. Pin the head, sew to attach, using the yarn tail to soft sculpt the head so that the eyes are inset into the head, and weave in ends.

3. Pin the ears and horns to the head. Once satisfied with placement, sew to attach, and weave in ends.

4. Pin the back scales, sew to attach, and weave in ends.

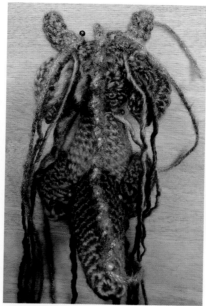

5. Pin the wings, sew to attach, and weave in ends.

CUTE CRITTER PARTS PATTERNS

Use a US size G (4 mm) hook and #4 medium weight yarn for all Cute Critter parts.

FRONT LEG WITH ROUNDED FOOT (MAKE 2)

When switching colors at the end of a row, switch to the new color when you make the slip stitch join. When you make the final yarn over to slip stitch at the end of the row, use the new color to do that final yarn over, and then chain 1; this creates a seamless transition to the new color.

NOTE: For the Alce, Hippogriff, and Griffin, work the 1st 5 rows in the Accent (Bird Foot) Color.

1. (HDC, SC, HDC) x 2 in Magic Circle, Sl St to beginning stitch, Ch 1 [6]
2–4. (3 rows of) SC 6, Sl St to beginning stitch, Ch 1 [6]
5. Dec, Inc x 2, Dec, Sl St to beginning stitch, Ch 1 [6]

NOTE: For Alce Wingless Griffin, Hippogriff, and Griffin, fasten off the Accent Color and attach the Main Color.

6. Dec, Inc x 2, Dec, Sl St to beginning stitch, Ch 1 [6]
7. SC 2, Inc x 2, SC 2, Sl St to beginning stitch, Ch 1 [8]
8. Dec, SC, Inc x 2, SC, Dec, Sl St to beginning stitch [8]

Fasten off with short yarn tail; tuck this tail into the leg. Stuff very lightly with fiberfill or not at all. The front legs in the photos are not stuffed.

Front Leg with Rounded Foot

Front Legs with Rounded Feet with color change

FRONT LEG WITH HOOF (MAKE 2)

When switching colors at the end of a row, switch to the new color when you make the slip stitch join. When you make the final yarn over to slip stitch at the end of the row, use the new color to do that final yarn over, and then chain 1; this creates a seamless transition to the new color.

Front Legs with Hooves

Starting with the Accent Hoof Color yarn:

1. DC 8 in Magic Circle, Sl St to beginning stitch, Ch 1 [8]

2. BLO [SC 8], Sl St to beginning stitch, Ch 1 [8]

3. SC 8, Sl St to beginning stitch, fasten off the Accent Hoof Color yarn, switch to the Main Body Color yarn [8]

4–12. (9 rows of) SC 8, Sl St to beginning stitch, Ch 1 [8]

Fasten off with short yarn tail. Stuff very lightly with fiberfill or not at all. The front legs in the photos are not stuffed. It is optional to include a glass gem in the hoof to fill out the shape.

CUTE CRITTER BODY

1. SC 6 in Magic Circle, Sl St to beginning stitch, Ch 1 [6]

2. Inc x 6, Sl St to beginning stitch, Ch 1 [12]

3. (SC, Inc) x 6, Sl St to beginning stitch, Ch 1 [18]

4. (SC 2, Inc) x 6, Sl St to beginning stitch, Ch 1 [24]

5–10. (6 rows of) SC 24, Sl St to beginning stitch, Ch 1 [24]

11. (SC 6, Dec) x 3, Sl St to beginning stitch, Ch 1 [21]

12. (SC 5, Dec) x 3, Sl St to beginning stitch, Ch 1 [18]

13. (SC 2, Dec, SC 2) x 3, Sl St to beginning stitch, Ch 1 [15]

14. (SC 3, Dec) x 3, Sl St to beginning stitch, Ch 1 [12]

15. SC 12, Sl St to beginning stitch, Ch 1 [12]

Stuff the body medium-firm up to this point and continue to stuff as you crochet. It is optional to include some glass gems for weight in the bottom of the body. This can make the piece more balanced and stable.

16. (SC, Dec, SC) x 3, Sl St to beginning stitch, Ch 1 [9]

NOTE: For the Wyvern, work four more rows of SC 9, Sl St to beginning stitch, Ch 1 before fastening off. The Wyvern does not have front legs.

In the following row, you will attach the front legs to the body. You will hold each front leg piece against the body so that the top (last row) is flattened against the body. You will be working through three layers of fabric for 17A and 17C (two layers from each leg and one from the body).

17A. SC 4 through the first front leg (see detailed instructions below) [4]

1st SC: Insert your hook from the outside of the work to the inside of the work through the 1st stitch of the last row on the front leg and then through the inside of the work to the outside of the work through the last stitch of the last row on the front leg, and then from the outside of the work to the inside of the work through the next available stitch on the body and complete a SC.

2nd SC: Insert your hook from the outside of the work to the inside of the work through the 2nd stitch of the last row on the front leg and then through the inside of the work to the outside of the work through the 7th stitch of the last row on the front leg, and then from the outside of the work to the inside of the work through the next available stitch on the body and complete a SC.

3rd SC: Insert your hook from the outside of the work to the inside of the work through the 3rd stitch of the last row on the front leg and then through the inside of the work to the outside of the work through the 6th stitch of the last row on the front leg, and then from the outside of the work to the inside of the work through the next available stitch on the body and complete a SC.

4th SC: Insert your hook from the outside of the work to the inside of the work through the 4th stitch of the last row on the front leg and then through the inside of the work to the outside of the work through the 5th stitch of the last row on the front leg, and then from the outside of the work to the inside of the work through the next available stitch on the body and complete a SC.

17B. SC in the next available stitch on the body [1]

17C. SC 4 through the second front leg (see detailed instructions below) [4]

1st SC: Insert your hook from the outside of the work to the inside of the work through the 5th stitch of the last row on the front leg and then through the inside of the work to the outside of the work through the 4th stitch of the last row on the front leg, and then from the outside of the work to the inside of the work through the next available stitch on the body and complete a SC.

2nd SC: Insert your hook from the outside of the work to the inside of the work through the 6th stitch of the last row on the front leg and then through the inside of the work to the outside of the work through the 3rd stitch of the last row on the front leg, and then from the outside of the work to the inside of the work through the next available stitch on the body and complete a SC.

3rd SC: Insert your hook from the outside of the work to the inside of the work through the 7th stitch of the last row on the front leg and then through the inside of the work to the outside of the work through the 2nd stitch of the last row on the front leg, and then from the outside of the work to the inside of the work through the next available stitch on the body and complete a SC.

4th SC: Insert your hook from the outside of the work to the inside of the work through the 8th stitch of the last row on the front leg and then through the inside of the work to the outside of the work through the 1st stitch of the last row on the front leg, and then from the outside of the work to the inside of the work through the next available stitch on the body and complete a SC.

Sl St to beginning stitch.

Fasten off with 18 in/46 cm yarn tail.

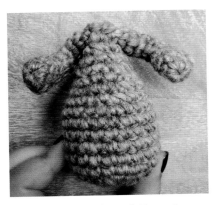

Cute Critter Body with Front Legs with Rounded Feet

Cute Critter Body with Front Legs with Hooves

Cute Critter Body with Front Legs with Rounded Feet and color change

REAR LEG WITH ROUNDED FOOT (MAKE 2)

Part 1: *Knee*

Using the Main Color yarn:

1. SC 6 in Magic Circle, Sl St to beginning stitch, Ch 1 [6]
2. Inc x 6, Sl St to beginning stitch, Ch 1 [12]
3. (SC 3, Inc) x 3, Sl St to beginning stitch [15]

Fasten off with short yarn tail.

Part 2: *Foot*

Start with the Main Color yarn for Alce, Dragon, Griffin, Hippogriff, and Wyvern.

Start with the Accent Color yarn for Cockatrice and Phoenix.

When switching colors at the end of a row, switch to the new color when you make the slip stitch join. When you make the final yarn over to slip stitch at the end of the row, use the new color to do that final yarn over, and then chain 1; this creates a seamless transition to the new color.

1. HDC, SC, HDC 5 in Magic Circle, Sl St to beginning stitch, Ch 1 [7]
2. SC 7, Sl St to beginning stitch, Ch 1 [7]
3. SC 7, Sl St to beginning stitch, Ch 1 [7]

4. SC 4, Dec, SC, Sl St to beginning stitch, Ch 1 [6]

NOTE: For the Cockatrice and the Phoenix, fasten off the Accent Color and attach the Main Color.

5. SC 5, Starting in the 1st stitch of Row 3 on the Part 1: Knee piece, SC 15 around the Part 1: Knee, SC in the same stitch as the last SC you worked on the foot before working into the Part 1: Knee piece, SC in the last stitch on the foot, Sl St to beginning stitch, Ch 1 [22]

When working into the knee, insert your hook from the outside to the inside of the work, just as you normally would. Work around the entire outside edge of the knee, and then complete your row by working the last two SC in the foot. Do not work into the "Slip Stitch, Chain 1" join space on the Knee piece.

6. SC 22, Sl St to beginning stitch, Ch 1 [22]

7. SC 4, Dec, SC 13, Dec, SC, Sl St to beginning stitch, Ch 1 [20]
8. (SC 3, Dec) x 4, Sl St to beginning stitch, Ch 1 [16]

Stuff extremely lightly with fiberfill. You may only need one tiny puff of stuffing inside the upper thigh of the leg, nothing in the foot.

9. (SC 2, Dec) x 4, Sl St to beginning stitch, Ch 1 [12]
10. (SC, Dec) x 4, Sl St to beginning stitch [8]

Fasten off with 18 in/46 cm yarn tail to use in order to sew to attach.

Rear Leg with Rounded Foot

REAR LEG WITH HOOF (MAKE 2)

Part 1: *Knee*

Using the Main Color yarn:

1. SC 6 in Magic Circle, Sl St to beginning stitch, Ch 1 [6]
2. Inc x 6, Sl St to beginning stitch, Ch 1 [12]
3. (SC 3, Inc) x 3, Sl St to beginning stitch [15]

Fasten off with short yarn tail.

Part 2: *Hoof*

Start with the Accent Hoof Color yarn for all.

When switching colors at the end of a row, switch to the new color when you make the slip stitch join. When you make the final yarn over to slip stitch at the end of the row, use the new color to do that final yarn over, and then chain 1; this creates a seamless transition to the new color.

1. DC 8 in Magic Circle, Sl St to beginning stitch, Ch 1 [8]
2. BLO [SC 8], Sl St to beginning stitch, Ch 1 [8]
3. SC 8, Sl St to beginning stitch, fasten off Accent Hoof Color yarn, switch to Main Body Color yarn [8]

4–5. (2 rows of) SC 8, Sl St to beginning stitch, Ch 1 [8]
6. SC 3, Dec, SC 3, Sl St to beginning stitch, Ch 1 [7]
7. SC 2, 2 Dec in 3 SC, SC 2, Sl St to beginning stitch, Ch 1 [6]
8. SC 3, Starting in the 1st stitch of Row 3 on the Part 1: Knee piece, SC 15 around the Part 1: Knee, SC in the same stitch as the last SC you worked on the foot before working into the Part 1: Knee piece; starting in the next available stitch on the bottom part of the leg, SC 3, Sl St to beginning stitch, Ch 1 [22]

When working into the knee, insert your hook from the outside to the inside of the work, just as you normally would. Work around the entire outside edge of the knee, and then complete your row by working the last four SC in the leg.

9. SC 22, Sl St to beginning stitch, Ch 1 [22]
10. SC 2, Dec, SC 14, Dec, SC 2, Sl St to beginning stitch, Ch 1 [20]

11. (SC 3, Dec) x 4, Sl St to beginning stitch, Ch 1 [16]

Stuff extremely lightly with fiberfill. You may only need one tiny puff of stuffing inside the upper thigh of the leg, nothing in the hoof. It is optional to include a glass gem in the hoof to fill out the shape.

12. (SC 2, Dec) x 4, Sl St to beginning stitch, Ch 1 [12]
13. (SC, Dec) x 4, Sl St to beginning stitch [8]

Fasten off with 18 in/46 cm yarn tail to use in order to sew to attach.

Rear Leg with Hoof

COCKATRICE BODY

1. Start with the Main Color yarn, SC 6 in Magic Circle, Sl St to beginning stitch, Ch 1 [6]
2. Inc x 6, Sl St to beginning stitch, Ch 1 [12]
3. (SC, Inc) x 6, Sl St to beginning stitch, Ch 1 [18]
4. (SC 2, Inc) x 6, Sl St to beginning stitch, Ch 1 [24]
5. SC 24, Sl St to beginning stitch, Ch 1 [24]
6. (SC 5, Inc) x 4, Sl St to beginning stitch, Ch 1 [28]
7–10. (4 rows of) SC 28, Sl St to beginning stitch, Ch 1 [28]
11. (SC 6, Dec, SC 6) x 2, Sl St to beginning stitch, Ch 1 [26]
12. (SC 11, Dec) x 2, Sl St to beginning stitch, Ch 1 [24]
13. (SC 5, Dec, SC 5) x 2, Sl St to beginning stitch, Ch 1 [22]
14. (SC 9, Dec) x 2, Sl St to beginning stitch, Ch 1 [20]
15. (SC 4, Dec, SC 4) x 2, Sl St to beginning stitch, Ch 1 [18]

Fasten off the Main Body color yarn here and switch to Accent Color 1 yarn. See Glossary for tips on colorwork.

16–23. (8 rows of) SC 18, Sl St to beginning stitch, Ch 1 [18]

Insert 15 mm black safety eyes or 18 mm colored iris safety eyes between Row 20 and Row 21 with 4 stitch spaces between the posts. Begin stuffing the body medium-firm, and continue to stuff as you work.

24. (SC 2, Dec, SC 2) x 3, Sl St to beginning stitch, Ch 1 [15]
25. (SC, Dec) x 5, Sl St to beginning stitch, Ch 1 [10]
26. Dec x 5, Sl St to beginning stitch [5]

Fasten off with 12 in/30 cm yarn tail to use to sew hole shut.

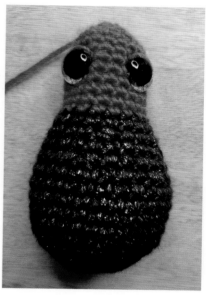

Cockatrice Body

COCKATRICE BEAK

1. SC 4 in Magic Circle, Sl St to beginning stitch, Ch 1 [4]
2. SC 3, Inc, Sl St to beginning stitch [5]

Fasten off with long enough yarn tail to sew to attach.

Cockatrice Beak

COCKATRICE WATTLE

1. Starting with a long enough yarn tail to weave in later, Ch 4, starting in the 2nd Ch from hook, HDC Dec, SC, Ch 4, Turn [2]

2. Starting in the 2nd Ch from hook, HDC Dec, SC [2]

Fasten off with 12 in/30 cm yarn tail.

Cockatrice Wattle

COCKATRICE COMB

1. Starting with a long enough yarn tail to weave in later, Ch 5, starting in the 2nd Ch from hook, SC 3, HDC, Ch 1, Turn [4]

2. SC 2, Ch 3, Turn [2]

3. Starting in the 2nd Ch from hook, SC 3, HDC, Ch 1, Turn [4]

4. SC 2, Ch 3, Turn [2]

5. Starting in the 2nd Ch from hook, SC 3, HDC, Ch 1, Turn [4]

6. SC, Ch 2, Turn [1]

7. Starting in the 2nd Ch from hook, SC 2 [2]

Fasten off with 12 in/30 cm yarn tail.

Cockatrice Comb

COCKATRICE NECK FEATHERS

1. Starting with a long enough yarn tail to weave in later, Ch 4, working into the 4th Ch from hook, HDC [1]

2–10. (9 rows of) Ch 4, Working into the 4th Ch from hook, HDC [1]

Fasten off with 24 in/61 cm yarn tail.

Cockatrice Neck Feathers

DRAGON HEAD

This piece is worked in spiral; do not Sl St, Ch 1.

I. SC 8 in Magic Circle [8]

2. SC, Inc x 2, SC 2, Inc x 2, SC [12]

3. SC, Inc x 3, SC, Ch 2, SC in the 2nd Ch from hook, SC in the same stitch as your last SC into the head, SC 2, SC, Ch 2, SC in the 2nd Ch from hook, SC in the same stitch as your last SC into the head, Inc x 3, SC [20]

Pro Tip: These [Ch 2, SC in 2nd Ch from hook] instructions create nostrils. In the following row, ignore the nostrils; do not stitch into them. They are not counted in the stitch count. Skip these nostrils if you are making the Dragon Head as a Unicorn Head.

4–5. (2 rows of) SC 20 [20]

6. SC 4, Inc, SC, Inc, SC 6, Inc, SC, Inc, SC 4 [24]

7. SC 24 [24]

8. (SC 3, Inc) x 6 [30]

9–12. (4 rows of) SC 30 [30]

If you are using colorful iris safety eyes, insert 18 mm eyes (if using black safety eyes, 15 mm will work) between Row 8 and Row 9 with 8 stitch spaces between the posts. The SC 6 in Row 6 will be at the top center of the head. Begin stuffing the head medium-firm, and continue to stuff as you work.

13. (SC 3, Dec) x 6 [24]

14. (SC 2, Dec) x 6 [18]

15. (SC, Dec) x 6 [12]

16. Dec x 6 [6]

Fasten off with 24 in/61 cm yarn tail to use to sew hole shut, soft sculpt the eyes/head to be slightly more inset and use to sew to attach. You can use the yarn tail from the body to sew to attach as well if you run out of the head's yarn tail length.

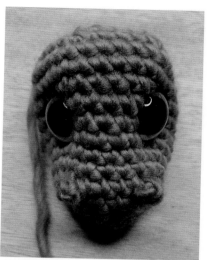

Dragon Head

DRAGON LEATHER WING (MAKE 2—1 RIGHT WING AND 1 LEFT WING)

Left and Right Wings are worked the same except in Rows 11 and 17 in Part 1, and Rows 2 and 3 in Part 2. Follow the notes in those rows to make 1 Left and 1 Right Wing.

NOTE: For the Cockatrice, I recommend using the Main Color yarn for Part 1 and Accent Color 2 yarn for Part 2. For the Dragon, use Accent Color for Part 1 and Main Color for Part 2. For the Wyvern, the Main Color is used for all parts.

Part 1: Using the Main Color:

I. Starting with a long enough yarn tail to weave in later, Ch 7, starting in the 2nd Ch from hook, SC 4, Dec, Ch 1, Turn [5]

2. Dec, SC 3, Ch 1, Turn [4]

3. SC 2, Dec, Ch 1, Turn [3]

4. SC 2, Inc, Ch 5, Turn [4]

5. Working back along the Ch stitches and then the other stitches from Row 4 and starting in the 2nd Ch from hook, SC 8, Ch 1, Turn [8]

6. SC 6, Ch 1, Turn [6]

In this and following rows, you will not always use all of the available stitches/chains. These unworked stitches will be used in a later row to create the diagonal wing edge.

7. SC 5, Inc, Ch 1, Turn [7]

8. SC 4, Ch 1, Turn [4]

9. SC 3, Inc, Ch 1, Turn [5]

10. SC 4, SC/HDC Dec & HDC, SC, SC/HDC Dec & HDC, Sl St, Ch 1, Turn [10]

> The SC/HDC Dec in this row are worked down the "steps" made by leaving stitches unworked in previous rows. Work only into the stitches as normal; do not work into the sides of stitches.

11. Skip the Slip Stitch, BLO (Right Wing) or FLO (Left Wing) [SC 7, Dec], Ch 1, Turn [8]

> All indicated stitches should be worked as BLO for the Right Wing and FLO for the Left Wing.

12. SC 6, Ch 1, Turn [6]
13. SC 5, Inc, Ch 1, Turn [7]
14. SC 4, Ch 1, Turn [4]
15. SC 3, Inc, Ch 1, Turn [5]
16. SC 4, SC/HDC Dec & HDC, SC, SC/HDC Dec & HDC, SC, Sl St in the same stitch you slip stitched into at the end of Row 10, Ch 1, Turn [11]
17. Skip the Slip Stitch, BLO (Right Wing) or FLO (Left Wing) [SC 7, Dec], Ch 1, Turn [8]

> All indicated stitches should be worked as BLO for the Right Wing and FLO for the Left Wing.

18. SC 6, Ch 1, Turn [6]
19. SC 5, Inc, Ch 1, Turn [7]
20. SC 4, Ch 1, Turn [4]
21. SC 3, Inc, Ch 1, Turn [5]
22. SC 4, SC/HDC Dec & HDC, SC, SC/HDC Dec & HDC, SC, Sl St in the same stitch you slip stitched into at the end of Row 10 and Row 16 [11]

Fasten off with a long enough yarn tail to weave in later.

Part 2

> The stiffer the yarn you use for Part 2, the more the wings will hold themselves up. You do not need to use the same yarn as for Part 1—you can substitute a stiffer/bulkier yarn for this part. You can also size down your hook size to make your stitches a little bit tighter to increase the stiffness of this piece. These techniques will all help the wings stand up on their own. If you like, you can use wire in this row to give the wings pose-ability and strength and ensure that they stand up on their own. If this is an item intended as a toy, do not use wire. If you use wire, use a light 18-gauge cloth-wrapped wire, hold it along the edge of the wing, and crochet all stitches around the wire as you go along the edge. Pipe cleaners are not strong enough.

1. Starting with a long enough yarn tail to weave in later, attach the yarn to the side of the last SC from Row 1 of Part 1 opposite the starting yarn tail, working along the edge of the wing toward where you fastened off Part 1 (this point is the elbow of the wing), SC along the edge until you reach that point, work an Inc in that point, SC to the end of the wing edge, Ch 1, Turn

Right Wing

Left Wing

If you use optional wire, hold the wire against the edge of the wing so that 1 to 2 in/2.5 to 5 cm of wire extend beyond the base of the wing; crochet Row 1 around the wire.

As you reach the elbow of the wing, fold the wire over on itself so that it will not extend beyond the end point of the wing. Trim the wire so that it does not extend beyond where your current stitches are. Then continue to crochet to the end, encasing the wire in your crochet work. In order to secure the wire where it is, I recommend putting a small dab of glue on the end of the wire and then pulling it slightly inside the crochet work. This should anchor the wire at the end of the wing.

2. Sl St back along the stitches from Part 2, Row 1 until you reach the 1st ridge of BLO or FLO stitches, SC along the BLO or FLO stitches to the end, and then Ch 1, Turn

Right Wing

Left Wing

3. Sl St back along the SC stitches from Part 2, Row 2, Sl St again in the elbow of the wing, and then SC along the next BLO or FLO ridge of stitches to the end, then Ch 1, Turn

4. Sl St back along the SC stitches from Part 2, Row 3, Sl St again in the elbow of the wing, and then Sl St back along the edge of the wing to where you started Part 2

Fasten off with 18 in/46 cm yarn tail.

Dragon Leather Wings

DRAGON FIN EAR (MAKE 2)

1. Starting with a long enough yarn tail to weave in later, Ch 7, starting in the 2nd Ch from hook, Sl St 2, Ch 2, DC/HDC Dec, HDC, SC, Ch 1, Turn [5]

2. BLO [SC, HDC, DC & Half Trip], Ch 3, Turn [4]

3. Starting in the 2nd Ch from hook, Sl St 2, Ch 2, BLO [DC/HDC Dec, HDC, SC], Ch 1, Turn [5]

4. BLO [SC, HDC, DC & Half Trip], Ch 3, Turn [4]

5. Starting in the 2nd Ch from hook, Sl St 6 [6]

Fasten off with 12 in/30 cm yarn tail.

Dragon Fin Ear

DRAGON TAIL

This piece is worked in spiral; do not Sl St, Ch 1.

1. SC 5 in Magic Circle [5]
2. SC 2, Inc, SC 2 [6]
3. SC 3, <Dec>, SC 3 [7]
4. SC 3, Inc, SC 3 [8]
5. SC 4, <Dec>, SC 4 [9]
6. SC 4, Inc, SC 4 [10]
7. SC 5, <Dec>, SC 5 [11]
8. SC 5, Inc, SC 5 [12]
9. SC 6, <Dec>, SC 6 [13]
10. SC 6, Inc, SC 6 [14]
11. SC 7, <Dec>, SC 7 [15]
12. SC 7, Inc, SC 7 [16]
13. SC 8, <Dec>, SC 8 [17]
14. SC 8, Inc, SC 8 [18]

Fasten off with 24 in/61 cm yarn tail.

Stuff medium-firm with fiberfill.

Dragon Tail

DRAGON BACK SCALES

1. Start with a long enough yarn tail to weave in later, Ch 3, starting in the 2nd Ch from hook, Sl St, SC [2]

Repeat this row until you have a piece long enough to stretch from the forehead of the dragon to the tip of the tail (approximately 16 times).

Fasten off with 18 in/46 cm yarn tail.

Dragon Back Scales

DRAGON BELLY

1. Start with a long enough yarn tail to weave in later, Ch 5, starting in the 2nd Ch from hook, SC 4, Ch 1, Turn [4]
2. BLO [Inc, SC 2, Inc], Ch 1, Turn [6]
3-5. (3 rows of) BLO [SC 6], Ch 1, Turn [6]
6. BLO [Dec, SC 2, Dec], Ch 1, Turn [4]
7. BLO [SC 4], Ch 1, Turn [4]
8. BLO [SC, Dec, SC], Ch 1, Turn [3]
9. BLO [SC 3], Ch 1, reorient the work (see next row) [3]
10. Starting by working around the side of the last SC stitch in Row 9, SC 8 down the side of the rows to the OC, make an Inc in the OC, and then SC 2 across the next 2 stitches and Inc again in the last corner, then SC about 8 back up to the 1st stitch you made in Row 9 [~22]

Fasten off with 24 in/61 cm yarn tail.

Dragon Belly

GARGOYLE EAR (MAKE 2)

1. Starting with a long enough yarn tail to weave in, Ch 8, Turn, starting in the 2nd Ch from hook, SC 7, Ch 1, Turn [7]
2. SC 5, Dec, Ch 1, Turn [6]
3. SC 6, Ch 1, Turn [6]
4. SC 4, Dec, Ch 1, Turn [5]
5. SC 5, Ch 1, Turn [5]
6. SC 3, Dec, Ch 1, Turn [4]
7. SC 4, Ch 1, Turn [4]
8. SC 2, Dec, Ch 1, Turn [3]
9. SC 3, Ch 1, Turn [3]
10. SC, Dec, Ch 1, Turn [2]
11. Dec, Ch 1, reorient work to work back up the unfinished edge to the OC [1]
12. SC about 13 back to OC 1st available corner, Triple SC Inc in the corner, SC 6 back to the end of the final ear edge [22]

Fasten off with 12 in/30 cm yarn tail.

Gargoyle Ear

GARGOYLE BOTTOM JAW AND HEAD

Part 1: Bottom Jaw

1. SC 6 in Magic Circle, Sl St to beginning stitch, Ch 1 [6]
2. Inc x 6, Sl St to beginning stitch, Ch 1 [12]
3. (SC, Inc) x 6, Sl St to beginning stitch, Ch 1 [18]
4. (SC 2, Inc) x 6, Sl St to beginning stitch, Ch 1 [24]
5. (SC 3, Inc) x 6, Sl St to beginning stitch, Ch 1 [30]
6. SC 30, Sl St to beginning stitch, Ch 1 [30]
7. SC 10, Inc, SC 8, Inc, SC 10, Sl St to beginning stitch, Ch 1 [32]
8. SC 14, HDC 4, SC 14, Sl St to beginning stitch [32]

Fasten off with a long enough yarn tail to weave in.

Gargoyle Bottom Jaw

Part 2: Head

1. SC 6 in Magic Circle, Sl St to beginning stitch, Ch 1 [6]

> The Magic Circle will be the bottom/center stitches on the head. You will be positioning the Magic Circle over the neck opening of the body when you sew to attach.

2. Inc x 6, Sl St to beginning stitch, Ch 1 [12]
3. (SC, Inc) x 6, Sl St to beginning stitch, Ch 1 [18]
4. (SC 2, Inc) x 6, Sl St to beginning stitch, Ch 1 [24]
5. (SC 3, Inc) x 6, Sl St to beginning stitch, Ch 1 [30]
6. SC 30, Sl St to beginning stitch, Ch 1 [30]
7. SC 10, Inc, SC 8, Inc, SC 10, Sl St to beginning stitch, Ch 1 [32]

8. Holding the bottom jaw against the bottom/outside of this head piece you're working on, and working through the 1st stitch of both (inserting the crochet hook from the outside/right side of the work to the inside/wrong side of the work on both pieces), SC 10; then working ONLY into the current head and NOT into the bottom jaw, SC, Dec, SC 6, Dec, SC; then skip 12 stitches on the bottom jaw and working through both pieces at the same time, SC 10 to the end, Sl St to beginning stitch, Ch 1 [30]

9. Working around the head stitches only, SC 6, (SC, Dec) x 6, SC 6, Sl St to beginning stitch, Ch 1 [24]

10–12. (3 rows of) SC 24, Sl St to beginning stitch, Ch 1 [24]

13. (SC, Dec, SC) x 6, Sl St to beginning stitch, Ch 1 [18]

> Insert 18 mm black safety eyes between Row 10 and Row 11 with 3 or 4 stitch spaces between the posts—whatever looks best centered over the mouth. Stuff medium-firm with fiberfill and continue to stuff as you finish the piece to fill out the shape.

14. (SC, Dec) x 6, Sl St to beginning stitch, Ch 1 [12]

15. Dec x 6, Sl St to beginning stitch [6]

Fasten off with 24 in/61 cm yarn tail to use to sew hole shut.

Gargoyle Head

GARGOYLE TEETH

1. Start with a 12 in/30 cm yarn tail, Ch 4, starting in the 2nd Ch from hook, Sl St, SC 2, Ch 10, Turn [3]

2. Starting in the 2nd Ch from hook, Sl St, SC 2 [3]

Fasten off with 12 in/30 cm yarn tail.

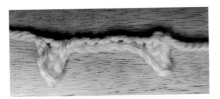

Gargoyle Teeth

GARGOYLE HORN (MAKE 2)

1. SC 5 in Magic Circle, Sl St to beginning stitch, Ch 1 [5]
2. SC 3, Inc, SC, Sl St to beginning stitch, Ch 1 [6]
3. Inc, SC 2, Dec, SC, Sl St to beginning stitch, Ch 1 [6]
4. Inc, SC 2, Dec, SC, Sl St to beginning stitch, Ch 1 [6]
5. SC, Inc, SC 4, Sl St to beginning stitch [7]

Fasten off with 12 in/30 cm yarn tail.

Gargoyle Horn

GARGOYLE TAIL

1. Starting with a long enough yarn tail to weave in later, Ch 20, Turn, starting in the 2nd Ch from hook, Sl St, HDC, Half Trip, Ch 1, Skip 1 Ch stitch, Sl St 15 all the way back to the base of the tail [18]

Fasten off with 12 in/30 cm yarn tail.

Gargoyle Tail

GRIFFIN HEAD

1. Starting with the Beak/Foot Color yarn, SC 6 in Magic Circle, Sl St to beginning stitch, Ch 1 [6]
2. (SC, Inc, SC) x 2, Sl St to beginning stitch, Ch 1 [8]
3. (SC 3, Inc) x 2, Sl St to beginning stitch, Ch 1 [10]
4. (SC 2, Inc, SC 2) x 2, Sl St to beginning stitch [12]

Fasten off with short yarn tail, switch yarn color to the Accent Feather Color.

5. BLO [SC, Inc x 4, SC 2, Inc x 4, SC], continue in spiral [20]
6. SC 20 [20]
7. SC 4, Inc, SC, Inc, SC 6, Inc, SC, Inc, SC 4 [24]
8. (SC 3, Inc) x 6 [30]

9–12. (4 rows of) SC 30 [30]

If you are using colorful iris eyes, use 15 mm or 18 mm eyes (if using black safety eyes, 15 mm will work) between Row 7 and Row 8, with 7 stitch spaces between the posts. The "SC 6" in Row 7 will be at the top center of the head.

13. (SC 3, Dec) x 6 [24]
14. (SC 2, Dec) x 6 [18]
15. (SC, Dec) x 6 [12]

At this point, stuff the head medium-firm with fiberfill.

16. Dec x 6 [6]

Fasten off with 24 in/61 cm yarn tail to use to sew hole shut, soft sculpt the eyes/head to be slightly more

inset and use to sew to attach. You can use the yarn tail for the body to sew to attach as well if you run out of the head's yarn tail length.

Griffin Head

GRIFFIN BEAK

1. Starting with a long enough yarn tail to weave in later, Ch 2, starting in the 2nd Ch from hook, Inc, Ch 1, Turn [2]
2. SC, <Dec>, SC, Ch 1, Turn [3]
3. Inc, SC, Inc, Ch 1, Turn [5]
4. SC 2, Inc, SC 2, Ch 1, reorient so that you will be working along the unfinished edge of the rows toward the OC [6]
5. Starting by working around the side of the last SC stitch you made in Row 4, SC 4, Triple SC Inc in the OC, SC 4 [11]

Fasten off with 12 in/30 cm yarn tail to use to sew to attach.

Griffin Beak

GRIFFIN CHEST & NECK PIECE

> In this piece, the Chain stitches are not included in the stitch count.

1. Start with 12 in/30 cm yarn tail to use to weave in later, Ch 4, starting in the 3rd Ch from hook, HDC, SC, Ch 1, Turn [2]
2. BLO [SC 2], Ch 4, Turn [2]
3. Starting in the 3rd Ch from hook, DC, HDC, BLO [SC 2], Ch 1, Turn [4]
4. BLO [SC 3], Ch 5, Turn [3]
5. Starting in the 3rd Ch from hook, DC, HDC 2, BLO [SC 3], Ch 1, Turn [6]
6. BLO [SC 3], Ch 3, Turn [3]
7. Stating in 3rd Ch from hook, DC, BLO [HDC, SC 2], Ch 1, Turn [4]
8. BLO [SC 2], Ch 2, Turn [2]
9. Skip the Ch stitches, BLO [HDC, SC] [2]

Fasten off with 18 in/46 cm yarn tail to use to sew to attach.

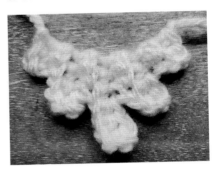

Griffin Chest & Neck Piece

GRIFFIN WING (MAKE 2)

1. Starting with a long enough yarn tail to weave in later, Ch 4, starting in the 2nd Ch from hook, HDC 3, Ch 1, Turn [3]
2. BLO [Inc, SC], Ch 3, Turn [3]
3. Starting in the 2nd Ch from hook, HDC 2, BLO [HDC, SC], Ch 1, Turn [4]

> In this and following rows, you will not always use all of the available stitches/chains. These unworked stitches will be used in a later row.

4. BLO [SC 3], Ch 4, Turn [3]
5. Starting in the 2nd Ch from hook, HDC 3, BLO [HDC, SC, SC/HDC Dec & HDC], Ch 1, Turn [7]

> The SC/HDC Dec in this row is worked down the "steps" made by leaving stitches unworked in previous rows. Work only into the stitches as normal; do not work into the sides (or around the posts) of stitches. The SC/HDC Dec is defined in the Glossary (page 4), as is the "&" symbol.

6. BLO [SC 6], Ch 4, Turn [6]
7. Starting in the 2nd Ch from hook, HDC 3, BLO [HDC, SC 3], Ch 1 Turn [7]
8. BLO [SC 6], Ch 4, Turn [6]
9. Starting in the 2nd Ch from hook, HDC 3, BLO [HDC 3, SC 2, SC/HDC Dec & HDC, HDC], Ch 1 [11]

10. Reorient work and start by working into the same stitch you last Half Double Crocheted into in Row 9, SC along the unfinished wing edge back to the OC (approximately 5 SC) [~5]

Fasten off with 24 in/61 cm yarn tail.

Griffin Wing

GRIFFIN TAIL

Part 1: *Starting with the Accent Color yarn:*

1. Starting with a long enough yarn tail to weave in later, Ch 5, starting in the 2nd Ch from hook, Sl St, SC, HDC, SC, Ch 1, Turn [4]

2. BLO [SC 2], Ch 5, Turn [2]

3. Starting in the 2nd Ch from hook, Sl St, SC, HDC 2, BLO [HDC, SC], Ch 1, Turn [6]

4. BLO [SC 2], Ch 3, Turn [2]

5. Starting in the 2nd Ch from hook, Sl St, SC, BLO [HDC, SC] [4]

Fasten off with a long enough yarn tail to weave in later.

Part 2: *Starting with the Main Color yarn:*

1. Starting with a long enough yarn tail to weave in later, Ch 22, insert the hook through the starting Ch and then the final SC of Part 1 of this tail and make a Sl St, Ch 1, Turn [1]

> This row attaches Part 1 (Tail Feather Accent) to Part 2 (Tail); the Tail Feather Accent will be folded, so the Sl St is made through 2 layers of fabric from Part 1 (see photos below).

2. Working back along Row 1's Ch stitches and encasing Part 1's yarn tails as you go, SC about 21 [~21]

Fasten off with 12 in/30 cm yarn tail.

Griffin Tail

GRIFFIN EAR (MAKE 2)

1. Start with 12 in/30 cm long yarn tail, make a Magic Circle, Ch 4, starting in the 2nd Ch from hook, HDC, SC 2, Sl St in Magic Circle, Ch 1, Turn [4]

> In this piece, the Chain stitches are not included in the stitch count.

2. Skip the Slip Stitch, BLO [SC 2], Ch 3, Turn [2]

3. Starting in the 2nd Ch from hook, HDC, SC, BLO [SC 2], Sl St in Magic Circle, Ch 1, Turn [5]

4. Skip the Slip Stitch, BLO [SC 2, Inc], Ch 3, Turn [4]

5. Starting in the 2nd Ch from hook, HDC, SC, BLO [SC 4], Sl St in Magic Circle and tighten Magic Circle [7]

Fasten off with 12 in/30 cm yarn tail.

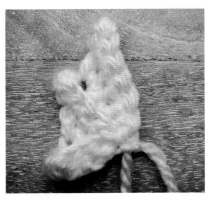

Griffin Ear

GRIFFIN CLAW (MAKE 2)

1. Starting with a 12 in/30 cm yarn tail, Ch 5, Starting in the 2nd Ch from hook, Sl St 2, SC 2, Ch 5, Turn [4]

> In this piece, the Chain stitches are not included in the stitch count.

2. Starting in the 2nd Ch from hook, Sl St 2, SC 2, Ch 5, Turn [4]

3. Starting in the 2nd Ch from hook, Sl St 2, SC 2, Ch 1, reorient the work so that you will work

across the flat top unfinished edge of all 3 rows [4]

4. Dec (working into the top of the 3rd Row and the 2nd Row), and then make another Dec (working

into the same stitch your last Dec ended in and the top of the 1st Row) [2]

Fasten off with 24 in/61 cm yarn tail.

Griffin Claw

JACKALOPE HEAD

> This piece is worked in spiral; do not Sl St, Ch 1.

1. SC 8 in Magic Circle [8]
2. SC, Inc x 2, SC 2, Inc x 2, SC [12]
3. SC, Inc x 4, SC 2, Inc x 4, SC [20]
4. SC 20 [20]
5. SC 4, Inc, SC, Inc, SC 6, Inc, SC, Inc, SC 4 [24]

> This SC 6 in Row 5 is the front center of the forehead.

6. (SC 3, Inc) x 6 [30]
7–10. (4 rows of) SC 30 [30]

Insert 12 mm, 15 mm, or 18 mm black safety eyes between Row 6 and 7, with 8 stitch spaces between the posts. 18 mm black safety eyes are used in the photos of the light-colored Jackalope (page 41). 12 mm safety eyes are used in the photos of the brown Jackalope (page 40). Begin stuffing the head medium-firm, and continue to stuff as you work.

11. (SC 3, Dec) x 6 [24]
12. (SC 2, Dec) x 6 [18]
13. (SC, Dec) x 6 [12]
14. Dec x 6 [6]

Fasten off with 24 in/61 cm yarn tail to use to sew hole shut and to do more when you assemble.

Jackalope Head

JACKALOPE EAR (MAKE 2)

1. Starting with a long enough yarn tail to weave in later, Ch 11, starting in the 2nd Ch from hook, HDC 5, SC 4, Inc in the last Ch, continuing along the opposite side of the OC, SC 4, HDC 5, Ch 1, Turn [20]
2. SC 9, Inc x 2, SC 9, Ch 1, Turn [22]
3. SC 10, Inc x 2, SC 10, Slip Stitch into the 1st stitch of this row [24]

Fasten off with 12 in/30 cm yarn tail.

Jackalope Ear

JACKALOPE ANTLER (MAKE 2)

1. SC 4 in Magic Circle, Sl St to beginning stitch, Ch 1 [4]
2-4. (3 rows of) SC 4, Sl St to beginning stitch, Ch 1 [4]
5. SC, Bobble, Inc, SC, Sl St to beginning stitch, Ch 1 [5]

6-7. (2 rows of) SC 5, Sl St to beginning stitch, Ch 1 [5]
8. SC, HDC, DC, HDC & SC, Sl St [6]

Fasten off with 12 in/30 cm yarn tail. Stuff with a tiny bit of fiberfill if desired; the antlers in the photos are not stuffed.

A Bobble in this row is made like this: YO, insert your hook into the next available stitch, YO, pull up, YO, pull through 2 loops, YO, insert your hook into the same stitch, YO, pull up, YO, pull through 2 loops, YO, insert your hook into the same stitch, YO, pull up, YO, pull through 2 loops, YO, pull through all 4 remaining loops.

Jackalope Antler

JACKALOPE TAIL

1. SC 6 in Magic Circle, Sl St to beginning stitch, Ch 1 [6]
2. (SC, Inc, SC) x 2, Sl St to beginning stitch, Ch 1 [8]
3. (SC 3, Inc) x 2, Sl St to beginning stitch, Ch 1 [10]
4. (SC 2, Inc, SC 2) x 2, Sl St to beginning stitch, Ch 1 [12]
5. SC 12, Sl St to beginning stitch, Ch 1 [12]
6. (SC, Dec) x 4, Sl St to beginning stitch, Ch 1 [8]
7. Dec x 4, Sl St to beginning stitch [4]

Fasten off with 12 in/30 cm yarn tail.

The Jackalope tail is not stuffed with fiberfill.

Jackalope Tail

PHOENIX HEAD

Starting with the Accent Color yarn:

1. SC 6 in Magic Circle, Sl St to beginning stitch, Ch 1 [6]
2. (SC, Inc, SC) x 2, Sl St to beginning stitch, Ch 1 [8]
3. (SC 3, Inc) x 2, Sl St to beginning stitch, Ch 1 [10]
4. (SC 2, Inc, SC 2) x 2, Sl St to beginning stitch, Ch 1 [12]

Switch to the Main Color yarn:

5. BLO [SC, Inc x 4, SC 2, Inc x 4, SC], continue in spiral, do not Sl St, Ch 1 [20]
6. SC 20 [20]
7. SC 4, Inc, SC, Inc, SC 6, Inc, SC, Inc, SC 4 [24]
8. (SC 3, Inc) x 6 [30]
9−12. (4 rows of) SC 30 [30]

For the Phoenix, if you are using colorful iris eyes, use 15 mm or 18 mm eyes (if using black safety eyes, 15 mm will work) between Row 5 and Row 6, with 7 stitch spaces between the posts. The SC 6 in Row 7 will be at the top center of the head. Begin to stuff the piece medium-firm with fiberfill, and continue to stuff as you finish crocheting.

13. (SC 3, Dec) x 6 [24]
14. (SC 2, Dec) x 6 [18]
15. (SC, Dec) x 6 [12]
16. Dec x 6 [6]

Fasten off with 24 in/61 cm yarn tail to use to sew hole shut and to do more in the assembly section.

Phoenix Head

PHOENIX WING (MAKE 2)

1. Starting with a long enough yarn tail to weave in later, Ch 4, starting in the 2nd Ch from hook, HDC 3, Ch 1, Turn [3]
2. BLO [Inc, SC], Ch 3, Turn [3]
3. Starting in the 2nd Ch from hook, HDC 2, BLO [HDC, SC], Ch 1, Turn [4]

In this and following rows, you will not always use all of the available stitches/chains. These unworked stitches will be used in a later row.

4. BLO [SC 3], Ch 4, Turn [3]
5. Starting in the 2nd Ch from hook, HDC 3, BLO [HDC, SC, SC/HDC Dec & HDC], Ch 1, Turn [7]

The SC/HDC Dec in this row is worked down the "steps" made by leaving stitches unworked in previous rows. Work only into the stitches as normal; do not work into the sides of stitches.

6. BLO [SC 6], Ch 4, Turn [6]
7. Starting in the 2nd Ch from hook, HDC 3, BLO [HDC, SC 3], Ch 1, Turn [7]

8. BLO [SC 6], Ch 4, Turn [6]
9. Starting in the 2nd Ch from hook, HDC 3, BLO [HDC 3, SC 2, SC/HDC Dec & HDC, HDC], Ch 1, Turn [11]
10. BLO [SC 8], Ch 5, Turn [8]

11. Starting in the 2nd Ch from hook, HDC 4, BLO [HDC 2, SC 3], Ch 1, Turn [9]
12. BLO [SC 6], Ch 3, Turn [6]
13. Starting in the 2nd Ch from hook, HDC 2, BLO [HDC 4, SC, SC/HDC Dec & HDC, HDC, SC], Ch 1, Turn [11]

14. Reorient work and start by working into the same stitch you last Single Crocheted into in Row 13, SC along the unfinished wing edge back to the OC (approximately 10 SC) [~10]

Fasten off with 24 in/61 cm yarn tail.

Phoenix Wing

PHOENIX TAIL

Starting with the Main Color yarn and a long enough yarn tail to weave in later:

1. Ch 16, Turn, starting in the 2nd Ch from hook, Sl St, SC, HDC, DC 5, HDC 4, SC 3, Ch 1, Turn [15]
2. BLO [SC 12], Ch 7, Turn [12]
3. Starting in the 2nd Ch from hook, Sl St, SC, HDC, DC 3, BLO [DC 3, HDC 5, SC 4], Ch 1, Turn [18]
4. BLO [SC 15], Ch 7, Turn [15]

5. Starting in the 2nd Ch from hook, Sl St, SC, HDC, DC 3, BLO [DC 4, HDC 6, SC 5], Ch 1, Turn [21]

6. BLO [SC 15], Ch 4, Turn [15]
7. Starting in the 2nd Ch from hook, Sl St, SC, HDC, BLO [DC 6, HDC 5, SC 4], Ch 1, Turn [18]

8. BLO [SC 12], Ch 4, Turn [12]
9. Starting in the 2nd Ch from hook, Sl St, SC, HDC, BLO [DC 5, HDC 4, SC 3] [15]

Fasten off with 12 in/30 cm yarn tail.

Phoenix Tail without Accent Color

Optional Part 2: This is an optional way to add an accent color to the tail.

Starting with an Accent Color and a long enough yarn tail to weave in later:

1. Attach the yarn to the 1st Ch stitch you made in Row 1, SC 15 along that edge, Inc in top of first feather, FLO [SC 3], SC 12 along the leftover FLO stitches from Row 1 (created by the BLO stitches from Row 2 of Part 1), Ch 1, Turn [32]

2. Sl St 12, SC 6, Inc in the top of the second feather, FLO [SC 3], SC 15 along the leftover FLO stitches from Row 4 (created by the BLO stitches from Row 5 of Part 1), Ch 1, Turn [38]

3. Sl St 15, SC 6, Inc in the top of the third feather, FLO [SC 6], SC 15 along the leftover FLO stitches from Row 6 (created by the BLO stitches from Row 7 of Part 1), Ch 1, Turn [44]

4. Sl St 15, SC 3, Inc in the top of the fourth feather, FLO [SC 6], SC 12 along the leftover FLO stitches from Row 8 (created by the BLO stitches from Row 9 of Part 1), Ch 1, Turn [38]

5. Sl St 12, SC 3, Inc in the top of the fifth feather, FLO [SC 15] [32]

Fasten off with 12 in/30 cm yarn tail.

Phoenix Tail with Accent Color

PHOENIX HEAD FEATHERS

Starting with a long enough yarn tail to weave in later:

1. Ch 7, Starting in the 2nd Ch from hook, Sl St, SC, HDC, DC, HDC, SC, Ch 1, Turn [6]
2. BLO [SC 3], Ch 5, Turn [3]
3. Starting in the 2nd Ch from hook, Sl St, SC, HDC, DC, BLO [DC, HDC, SC], Ch 1, Turn [7]
4. BLO [SC 3], Ch 4, Turn [3]
5. Starting in the 2nd Ch from hook, Sl St, SC, HDC, BLO [DC, HDC, SC] [6]

Fasten off with 18 in/46 cm yarn tail to use to sew to attach.

NOTE: It is optional for you to create a border edge around this feather set the same way you can for the tail (see Phoenix Tail instructions on the preceding page for details).

Phoenix Head Feathers

UNICORN EAR (MAKE 2)

1. Starting with a long enough yarn tail to weave in later, Ch 2, starting in the 2nd Ch from hook, Inc, Ch 1, Turn [2]
2. SC, <Dec>, SC, Ch 1, Turn [3]
3. SC, Inc, SC, Ch 1, Turn [4]
4. SC 2, <Dec>, SC 2, Ch 1, Reorient so that you will be working up the unfinished edge of the work toward Row 1 [5]
5. Start by working around the side of the last stitch you made in Row 4, SC 4, working in the OC, SC & HDC & SC (this is the tip of the ear), SC 4 down the other side [11]

Fasten off with 12 in/30 cm yarn tail.

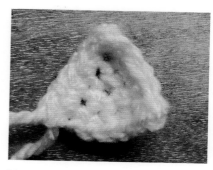

Unicorn Ear

UNICORN HEAD

> This piece is worked in spiral; do not Sl St, Ch 1.

1. SC 6 in Magic Circle [6]
2. Inc x 2, SC, Inc x 2, SC [10]
3. Inc x 3, Ch 3, Inc, SC, Inc, Ch 3, Inc x 3, SC [18]

> These [Ch 3] instructions create nostrils. In the following row, do not work into the stitches that make up the nostrils; keep them oriented to the right side/ outside of the work.

4. SC 18 [18]
5. (SC 2, Dec, SC 2) x 3 [15]
6. SC 15 [15]
7. (SC 2, Inc, SC 2) x 3 [18]
8. (SC 5, Inc) x 3 [21]
9. (SC 3, Inc, SC 3) x 3 [24]
10–13. (4 rows of) SC 24 [24]

> Insert 18 mm color safety eyes (or 15 mm black safety eyes) between Row 9 and Row 10, with 8 stitch spaces between the posts.

14. (SC 4, Dec) x 4 [20]
15. (SC 2, Dec) x 5 [15]
16. (SC, Dec) x 5 [10]

> Stuff the head medium-lightly with fiberfill.

17. Dec x 5 [5]

Fasten off with 24 in/61 cm yarn tail to use to sew hole shut and to do more during assembly.

Unicorn Head

UNICORN HORN

I. SC 5 in Magic Circle [5]
2. BLO [SC 5] [5]
3. BLO [Inc, SC 4] [6]
4. BLO [SC 6] [6]

5. BLO [Inc, SC 5] [7]
6. BLO [SC 7] [7]

Fasten off with 12 in/30 cm yarn tail to use to sew to attach. You do not need to stuff the horn.

Unicorn Horn

UNICORN MANE (MAKE 1 OR 2)

NOTE: For tight curls (as shown in photos), keep your chain stitches and general tension fairly tight.

I. Starting with a long enough yarn tail to weave in later, Ch 13, Turn, starting in the 2nd Ch from hook, (SC, Inc) x 6 [18]
2. Ch 25, Turn, starting in the 2nd Ch from hook, (SC, Inc) x 12, Ch 1, Turn [36]

3. BLO [SC 2], Ch 25, Turn, starting in the 2nd Ch from hook, (SC, Inc) x 12, BLO [SC 2], Ch 1, Turn [40]
4. BLO [SC 3], Ch 25, Turn, starting in the 2nd Ch from hook, (SC, Inc) x 12, BLO [SC 3], Ch 1, Turn [42]
5. BLO [SC 3], Ch 25, Turn, starting in the 2nd Ch from hook, (SC, Inc) x 12, BLO [SC 3] [42]

Fasten off with 24 in/61 cm yarn tail.

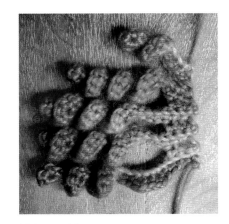

Unicorn Mane

UNICORN TAIL

NOTE: For tight curls (as shown in photos), keep your chain stitches and general tension fairly tight.

I. Starting with a long enough yarn tail to weave in later, Ch 36, Turn, starting in the 2nd Ch from hook, (SC, Inc) x 17, SC, Ch 36, Turn [52]
2-5. (4 rows of) Starting in the 2nd Ch from hook, (SC, Inc) x 17, SC, SC in the OC from Row 1, Ch 36, Turn [53]
6. Starting in the 2nd Ch from hook, (SC, Inc) x 17, SC, SC in the OC from Row 1 [53]

Fasten off with 24 in/61 cm yarn tail.

Unicorn Tail

WOLPERTINGER FANG (MAKE 2)

1. Starting with a long enough yarn tail to weave in later, Ch 4, starting in the 2nd Ch from hook, Sl St 2, SC [3]

Fasten off with 12 in/30 cm yarn tail.

Wolpertinger Fang

WOLPERTINGER EAR (MAKE 2)

1. Starting with a long enough yarn tail to weave in later, Ch 16, starting in the 2nd Ch from hook, HDC 5, SC 9, Inc in the last Ch, continuing along the opposite side of the OC, SC 9, HDC 5, Ch 1, Turn [30]

2. SC 14, Inc x 2, SC 14, Ch 1, Turn [32]

3. SC 10, HDC 5, HDC Inc x 2, HDC 5, SC 10, Slip Stitch into the 1st stitch of this row [34]

Fasten off with 12 in/30 cm yarn tail.

Wolpertinger Ear

WOLPERTINGER MUZZLE

Part 1

1. Starting with a long enough yarn tail to weave in later, SC 6 in Magic Circle, Sl St to beginning stitch [6]

Fasten off with a long enough yarn tail to weave in.

Part 2

1. Starting with a long enough yarn tail to weave in later, SC 6 in Magic Circle, Sl St to beginning stitch, Ch 1 [6]

2. (SC, Inc) x 3, continue by working into the 1st available stitch on Part 1 and continuing around the stitches on Part 1, (SC, Inc) x 3, SC in the same stitch as where you worked the 1st SC into Part 1, SC into the same stitch as where you worked the last stitch in Part 2, Sl St to beginning stitch [20]

Fasten off with 18 in/46 cm yarn tail.

Wolpertinger Muzzle

WYVERN HEAD

1. SC 6 in Magic Circle, Sl St to beginning stitch, Ch 1 [6]
2. Inc x 6, Sl St to beginning stitch, Ch 1 [12]
3. (SC, Inc) x 6, Sl St to beginning stitch, Ch 1 [18]
4. SC 7, Bobble, SC, <Dec>, SC, Bobble, SC 7, Sl St to beginning stitch, Ch 1 [19]

> Bobble is worked as follows: YO, insert your hook into the next available stitch, YO, pull up, YO, pull through 2 loops, YO, insert your hook into the same stitch, YO, pull up, YO, pull through 2 loops, YO, pull through all remaining loops.

5–7. (3 rows of) SC 19, Sl St to beginning stitch, Ch 1 [19]
8. SC 8, Inc, SC 2, Inc, SC 7, Sl St to beginning stitch, Ch 1 [21]
9. (SC 3, Inc, SC 3) x 3, Sl St to beginning stitch, Ch 1 [24]
10–13. (4 rows of) SC 24, Sl St to beginning stitch, Ch 1 [24]
14. (SC, Dec, SC) x 6, Sl St to beginning stitch, Ch 1 [18]

> Insert 15 mm black safety eyes or 18 mm colored iris safety eyes between Row 9 and Row 10, with about 7 stitch spaces between the posts. Stuff medium-firm with fiberfill.

15. (SC, Dec) x 6, Sl St to beginning stitch, Ch 1 [12]
16. Dec x 6, Sl St to beginning stitch [6]

Fasten off with 18 in/46 cm yarn tail to use to sew the hole shut and to do more during assembly.

Wyvern Head

WYVERN EAR (MAKE 2)

1. Starting with a long enough yarn tail to weave in later, Ch 2, SC 6 in the 2nd Ch from hook, Ch 1, Turn [6]
2. Inc x 6, Ch 1, Turn [12]
3. SC, Inc, HDC, HDC Inc, DC, DC & Half Trip, Ch 2, Sl St in the 2nd Ch from hook, Half Trip & DC, DC, HDC Inc, HDC, Inc, SC, Sl St to the 1st stitch in this row [18]

Fasten off with 12 in/30 cm yarn tail.

Wyvern Ear

STANDARD SIZE CREATURES

DRAGON

In Eastern mythology, dragons are powerful and benevolent, with power over storms and water. In the West, Dragons are more often viewed as evil, bringing darkness and death on their wings. They are always portrayed as huge, magnificent flying reptiles.

SIZE:

Approximately 12 in/30 cm tall from head to toe, 18 in/ 46 cm long from nose to tail, 24 in/61 cm wingtip to wingtip.

MATERIALS

» Yarn: See table on page 90 to choose the parts you will make for your Dragon and find the yarn amounts needed for each piece. All yarn amounts are approximate.

» US size G (4 mm) crochet hook

» 18 mm to 24 mm safety eyes

» Wire strong enough to support posing the dragon and supporting the wings. I recommend six 18 in/46 cm pieces of 18-gauge paper-wrapped wire (found in the faux floral arrangement section of any craft store; if this exact wire cannot be found, please use 14- to 16-gauge wire—hanger wire works—err on the side of heavier wire).

» Fiberfill stuffing

» Duct tape

» Darning needle

» Pins

» Scissors

» Stitch markers

» Pliers

» Optional: Four standard-sized glass gems, one for the bottom of each foot

InstructIons

Look at the Gallery beginning on page 92, the chart below, and the pages and photos of the various Dragon Parts to choose the pieces you will make for your Dragon. Because there are so many options available, specific color suggestions are not made. Approximate amounts of yarn needed for each piece are given, so you can plan your Dragon and gather the amounts needed of your chosen colors. Crochet all the parts of your Dragon following the instructions on pages 95–138, and then proceed to Dragon Assembly on page 139 to put them all together.

PARTS TO MAKE	PAGE NO.	YARN COLOR	NUMBER TO MAKE	APPROX. AMOUNT
Dragon Head	95	Main Color	1	20 yd/18.25 m
Dragon Body	96	Main Color	1	125 yd/114.25 m
Front Legs: Choose one of the following				
Standing/Straight	99	Main Color	2	27 yd/24.75 m per leg
Laying Down (Make Lower and Upper)	100 and 104	Main Color	2	34 yd/31 m total per leg (17 yd/15.5 m for lower and 17 yd/15.5 m for upper)
Begging (Make Lower and Upper)	102 and 104	Main Color	2	34 yd/31 m total per leg (17 yd/15.5 m for lower and 17 yd/15.5 m for upper)
Rear Legs: Choose one of the following				
Sitting, Laying, or Begging (Make Upper and Lower)	104 and 105	Main Color	2	62 yd/56.75 m total for 2 legs (48 yd/44 m for upper and 14 yd/12.75 m for lower)
Standing/Straight	106	Main Color	2	54 yd/49.5 m for 2 legs
Horns: Choose one of the following				
Simple	108	Accent Color	2	8 yd/7.25 m for 2 horns
Spiral	108	Accent Color	2	8 yd/7.25 m for 2 horns
Large Spiral	109	Main Color, Accent Color	2	14 yd/12.75 m Main Color, 12 yd/11 m Accent Color for 2 horns
Face Ornamentation: Choose from options following				
Long Cheek Frill	110	Main or Accent Color	2	8 yd/7.25 m for 2 frills
Short Cheek Frill	110	Main or Accent Color	2	8 yd/7.25 m for 2 frills

PARTS TO MAKE	PAGE NO.	YARN COLOR	NUMBER TO MAKE	APPROX. AMOUNT
Head Plate	111	Main Color	1	9 yd/8.25 m
Fancy Head Plate	111	Main Color	1	14 yd/12.75 m
Curly Eyelid	113	Main or Accent Color	2	3 yd/2.75 m for 2 eyelids
Simple Eyelid	113	Main or Accent Color	2	4 yd/3.75 m for 2 eyelids
Heart Eyelid	113	Two Accent Colors	2	7 yd/6.5 m for 2 eyelids
Ears: Choose one of the following				
Folded Ear, Style 1	114	Main or Accent Color	2	10 yd/9 m for 2 ears
Folded Ear, Style 2	115	Main or Accent Color	2	8 yd/7.25 m for 2 ears
Fin Ear	115	Main Color, Accent Color	2	8 yd/7.25 m Main Color, 10 yd/9 m Accent Color for 2 ears
Long Droopy Ear	117	Main Color	2	7 yd/6.5 m for 2 ears
Back Scales: Choose one of the following				
One Color	118	Accent Color	1	16 yd/14.75 m
Three Color	119	3 Accent Colors	1	20 yd/18.25 m Accent Color 1, 11 yd/10 m Accent Color 2, 11 yd/10 m Accent Color 3
Circles	120	Accent Color	1	14 yd/12.75 m
Triangles	121	Accent Color	1	11 yd/10 m
Full Hearts	121	Accent Color	1	24 yd/22 m
Curved	121	Accent Color	1	12 yd/11 m
Belly: Choose one of the following				
Classic	121	Accent Color	1	60 yd/54.75 m
Classic with Ornamented Edging	123	2 Accent Colors	1	23 yd/21 m Accent Color 1, 20 yd/18.25 m Accent Color 2
Hearts	124	Accent Color	1	22 yd/20 m

PARTS TO MAKE	PAGE NO.	YARN COLOR	NUMBER TO MAKE	APPROX. AMOUNT
Neck Ornamentation	125	Main Color, Accent Color	1	22 to 26 yd/20 to 23.75 m total (22 yd/20 m Main Color, 3 to 4 yd/2.75 to 3.75 m Accent Color for optional edging)
Wing	127	Main Color Accent Color	2	140 yd/128 m Accent Color for Wings, 62 yd/56.75 m Main Color for Finishing and Assembly
Tail Ornamentation: Choose one of the following				
Spade	131	Accent Color	1	6 yd/5.5 m
Arrow	132	Accent Color	2	6 yd/5.5 m for 2 pieces
Flat Triple Spikes	132	Accent Color	1 to 3	2 yd/1.75 m per piece
5-Pointed Leaf	132	Main Color, Accent Color	2	6 yd/5.5 m Main Color, 12 yd/11 m Accent Color for 2 pieces
Crescent	135	Main or Accent Color	2	14 yd/12.75 m for 2 pieces
Ridged Fan	136	Main Color, Accent Color	2	5 yd/4.5 m Main Color, 10 yd/9 m Accent Color for 2 pieces
Heart	138	Accent Color	2	14 yd/12.75 m for 2 pieces

GALLERY

Dragon with Sitting Rear Legs, one Standing Straight Front Leg and one Begging Front Leg, Classic Belly with Ornamental Edging, Folded Ears Style 2, Back Scales in One Color, and Large Spiral Horns

Dragon with Sitting Rear Legs, Standing Straight Front Legs, Classic Belly, Folded Ears Style 2, and Back Scales in One Color

Dragon with Sitting Rear Legs, Standing Straight Front Legs, and Folded Ears Style 2

Dragon with Standing Straight Rear Legs, Standing Straight Front Legs, Back Scales in One Color, Simple Eyelids, Classic Belly with Ornamental Edging, Fin Ears, and Spiral Horns

Dragon with Sitting Rear Legs, Standing Straight Front Legs, Classic Belly, Back Scales in One Color, Folded Ears Style 1, and Head Plate

Dragon with Sitting Rear Legs, Laying Down Front Legs, Classic Belly, Back Scales in Three Colors, Long Cheek Frills, Short Cheek Frills, Curly Eyelids, Spiral Horns, and Phoenix Wings

DRAGON PARTS PATTERNS

DRAGON HEAD

NOTE: If you are using a gradient yarn, then you start with the Dragon Body first (which is formed from the tail tip to the neck of the dragon). Once the Body is complete, come back to this section and make the Head. Starting with the yarn you just finished with, measure out 20 yards of yarn (DO NOT CUT), and then begin crocheting the head and use it up to the end of the yarn. It may be a little unwieldy to start crocheting from the middle of a piece of yarn, and crochet using the "tail" up, but this method guarantees that you work your way back along the color gradient to the color that the Dragon Body ended with at the neck. The 20 yards is an approximate measure of yarn and may be affected by yarn weight, hook size, and your particular tension. You may need to adjust the length as necessary (this is why you do not cut the yarn to start).

1. SC 6 in Magic Circle, Sl St to beginning stitch, Ch 1 [6]

2. (SC, Inc) x 3, Sl St to beginning stitch, Ch 1 [9]

3. SC 4, Ch 2, SC in the 2nd Ch from hook, SC 2, Ch 2, SC in the 2nd Ch from hook, SC 3, Sl St to beginning stitch, Ch 1 [9]

> These [Ch 2, SC in the 2nd Ch from hook] instructions create nostrils. In the following row, ignore the nostrils; do not stitch into them. They are not counted in the stitch count. Keep them oriented to the outside/right side of the work.

4. (SC 2, Inc) x 3, Sl St to beginning stitch, Ch 1 [12]

5. SC 12, Sl St to beginning stitch, Ch 1 [12]

6. (SC, Inc) x 6, Sl St to beginning stitch, Ch 1 [18]

7. SC 18, Sl St to beginning stitch, Ch 1 [18]

8. (SC 5, Inc) x 3, Sl St to beginning stitch, Ch 1 [21]

9. SC 3, Inc, (SC 6, Inc) x 2, SC 3, Sl St to beginning stitch, Ch 1 [24]

10. (SC 7, Inc) x 3, Sl St to beginning stitch, Ch 1 [27]

11–13. (3 rows of) SC 27, Sl St to beginning stitch, Ch 1 [27]

14. (SC 7, Dec) x 3, Sl St to beginning stitch, Ch 1 [24]

> Insert 18 to 24 mm safety eyes between Row 9 and 10 or Row 10 and 11 with 9 full stitch spaces between the posts. The eyes should be placed in alignment with the nostrils as created in Row 3. Begin stuffing the head medium-firm with fiberfill, and continue to stuff as you work.

15. (SC 4, Dec) x 4, Sl St to beginning stitch, Ch 1 [20]

16. (SC 3, Dec) x 4, Sl St to beginning stitch, Ch 1 [16]

17. (SC 2, Dec) x 4, Sl St to beginning stitch, Ch 1 [12]

18. (SC, Dec) x 4, Sl St to beginning stitch [8]

Fasten off with 12 in/30 cm yarn tail.

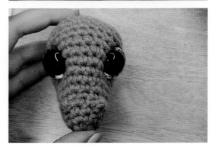

Dragon Head

1. SC 4 in Magic Circle, Sl St to beginning stitch, Ch 1 [4]

2–4. (3 rows of) SC 4, Sl St to beginning stitch, Ch 1 [4]

5. Inc, SC 3, Sl St to beginning stitch, Ch 1 [5]

6–9. (4 rows of) SC 5, Sl St to beginning stitch, Ch 1 [5]

10. Inc, SC 4, Sl St to beginning stitch, Ch 1 [6]

11–15. (5 rows of) SC 6, Sl St to beginning stitch, Ch 1 [6]

16. Inc, SC 5, Sl St to beginning stitch, Ch 1 [7]

17–22. (6 rows of) SC 7, Sl St to beginning stitch, Ch 1 [7]

23. Inc, SC 6, Sl St to beginning stitch, Ch 1 [8]

24–30. (7 rows of) SC 8, Sl St to beginning stitch, Ch 1 [8]

31. Inc, SC 7, Sl St to beginning stitch, Ch 1 [9]

32–39. (8 rows of) SC 9, Sl St to beginning stitch, Ch 1 [9]

40. Inc, SC 8, Sl St to beginning stitch, Ch 1 [10]

41–49. (9 rows of) SC 10, Sl St to beginning stitch, Ch 1 [10]

50. SC 2, Inc, SC 4, Inc, SC 2, Sl St to beginning stitch, Ch 1 [12]

51–53. (3 rows of) SC 12, Sl St to beginning stitch, Ch 1 [12]

54. (Inc, SC 5) x 2, Sl St to beginning stitch, Ch 1 [14]

55–58. (4 rows of) SC 14, Sl St to beginning stitch, Ch 1 [14]

59. SC 3, Inc, SC 6, Inc, SC 3, Sl St to beginning stitch, Ch 1 [16]

60–64. (5 rows of) SC 16, Sl St to beginning stitch, Ch 1 [16]

65. (SC 3, Inc) x 4, Sl St to beginning stitch, Ch 1 [20]

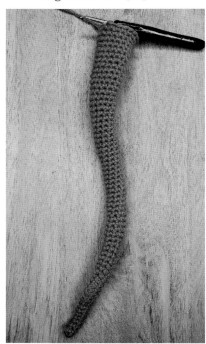

66–67. (2 rows of) SC 20, Sl St to beginning stitch, Ch 1 [20]

68. SC 2, Inc, (SC 4, Inc) x 3, SC 2, Sl St to beginning stitch, Ch 1 [24]

69–70. (2 rows of) SC 24, Sl St to beginning stitch, Ch 1 [24]

71. (SC 5, Inc) x 4, Sl St to beginning stitch, Ch 1 [28]

72. SC 3, Inc, (SC 6, Inc) x 3, SC 3, Sl St to beginning stitch, Ch 1 [32]

73. (SC 7, Inc) x 4, Sl St to beginning stitch, Ch 1 [36]

74–80. (7 rows of) SC 36, Sl St to beginning stitch, Ch 1 [36]

NOTE: Insert a wire (with the end folded over on itself and secured to itself with a strip of duct tape) to the tail tip to function as the spine of the dragon. Center the wire with the SC 15 in Row 82. Use approximately 24 in/ 61 cm of strong wire—pipe cleaners or similar will not work. You can use multiple wires if necessary and overlap them by about 6 in/15 cm and secure them to each other with thin strips of duct tape, as shown.

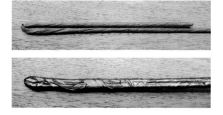

You can also choose not to use wire at all. The entire Dragon will still look the same as example photos, but you will need to be more deliberate about soft sculpting as you go, and you may want to stuff the tail lightly so that it is softer and does not stick straight out, as without wire it will not be poseable.

Begin stuffing the body. Insert stuffing to about 6 to 8 in/15 to 20.5 cm away from the tail tip; it is not necessary to stuff all the way to the tail tip. Make sure that the stuffing doesn't visibly change the shape of the tail. Continue to stuff the body as you work.

81. (SC 7, Dec) x 4, Sl St to beginning stitch, Ch 1 [32]

82. (SC 3, Dec) x 2, SC 15, Dec, SC 3, Dec, Sl St to beginning stitch, Ch 1 [28]

83. SC 28, Sl St to beginning stitch, Ch 1 [28]

84. Dec, SC 2, Dec, SC 16, Dec, SC 2, Dec, Sl St to beginning stitch, Ch 1 [24]

85–87. (3 rows of) SC 24, Sl St to beginning stitch, Ch 1 [24]

88. (SC 5, Inc) x 4, Sl St to beginning stitch, Ch 1 [28]

89. SC 3, Inc, (SC 6, Inc) x 3, SC 3, Sl St to beginning stitch, Ch 1 [32]

90. (SC 7, Inc) x 4, Sl St to beginning stitch, Ch 1 [36]

91. Dec, SC 15, Inc x 2, SC 15, Dec, Sl St to beginning stitch, Ch 1 [36]

92. SC 17, Inc x 2, SC 17, Sl St to beginning stitch, Ch 1 [38]

93. Dec, (SC 6, Inc) x 4, SC 6, Dec, Sl St to beginning stitch, Ch 1 [40]

94. Dec, SC 11, Inc, SC 12, Inc, SC 11, Dec, Sl St to beginning stitch, Ch 1 [40]

95. Dec, SC 17, Inc x 2, SC 17, Dec, Sl St to beginning stitch, Ch 1 [40]

Beginning in Row 96, the end number in the brackets for the substeps (i.e., [-46]) is the count of how many stitches you work in that substep. The end number in brackets after the final substep of that row is not the cumulative number of stitches made in the row; it is the number of available stitches once the row is complete.

Follow all substeps of each row in order (i.e., 96A, 96B, etc.). These short rows create the curves and shaping of the body. They will sometimes go beyond where the row began; follow the pattern exactly, and it will work. Each sub-row will have a stitch count for the number of stitches created in that sub-row, and there will be a final stitch count at the end of the final sub-row to indicate how many stitches are available on the edge of the work once all the sub-rows are complete.

A video tutorial for how to crochet short rows is available on the Crafty Intentions YouTube channel here: https://www.youtube.com/watch?v=sh5T-idiwm8&t=159s

Hybrid decreases like the SC/HDC Dec & HDC stitches are defined in the Glossary (page 4) and demonstrated on the Crafty Intentions YouTube channel here: https://www.youtube.com/watch?v=h4wkxMOMqXg&t=5s

From here on, crochet in spiral. Do not slip stitch, Ch 1.

96A. Dec x 2, SC 15, Inc, SC 27, Ch 1, Turn [-46]

> 96A goes 7 stitches beyond where it began. This will happen throughout; follow the pattern exactly as written.

96B. SC 6, Dec, SC 6, Ch 1, Turn [-13]

96C. SC 12, SC/HDC Dec & HDC [-14] [38]

> Both the "SC/HDC Dec" stitch and the "&" symbol are explained in the Glossary (page 4).

97A. SC 10, Inc, SC 12, HDC & HDC/SC Dec, SC 2, Dec x 3, SC 6, Ch 1, Turn [-37]

97B. SC 14, Ch 1, Turn [-14]

97C. SC 5, Dec x 2, SC 4, SC/HDC Dec & HDC [-13] [34]

98A. SC 10, Inc, SC 9, HDC & HDC/SC Dec, SC 2, Dec, SC, Dec, SC 6, Ch 1, Turn [-34]

98B. SC 14, Ch 1, Turn [-14]

98C. SC 5, Dec x 2, SC 4, SC/HDC Dec & HDC [-13] [31]

99A. SC 8, Inc, SC 8, HDC & HDC/SC Dec, SC 3, Dec x 2, SC 7, Ch 1, Turn [-32]

99B. SC 16, Ch 1, Turn [-16]

99C. SC 6, Dec x 2, SC 5, SC/HDC Dec & HDC [-15] [28]

100A. SC 6, <Dec>, SC 6, HDC & HDC/SC Dec, SC 4, Dec x 2, SC 5, Ch 1, Turn [-26]

The "<Dec>" Stitch is not a normal decrease and is defined in the Glossary (page 4).

100B. SC 12, Ch 1, Turn [-12]

100C. SC 4, Dec x 2, SC 3, SC/HDC Dec & HDC [-11] [25]

101A. SC 6, Inc, SC 6, HDC & HDC/SC Dec, SC 2, Dec x 2, SC 4, Ch 1, Turn [-24]

101B. SC 10, Ch 1, Turn [-10]

101C. SC 3, Dec x 2, SC 2, SC/HDC Dec & HDC [-9] [22]

102A. SC 6, <Dec>, SC 6, HDC & HDC/SC Dec, SC, Dec x 2, SC 4, Ch 1, Turn [-22]

102B. SC 10, Ch 1, Turn [-10]

102C. SC 3, Dec x 2, SC 2, SC/HDC Dec & HDC [-9] [19]

103. SC 9, HDC & HDC/SC Dec, SC 8 [19]

104A. SC 5, Inc, SC 13, Ch 1, Turn [-20]

104B. SC 9, Ch 1, Turn [-9]

104C. SC 2, Dec, SC, Dec, SC, SC/HDC Dec & HDC [-8] [18]

105. SC 5, Inc, SC 3, HDC & HDC/SC Dec, SC, 2 Dec in 3 SC, SC 3 [18]

The "2 Dec in 3 SC" stitch is defined in the Glossary (page 4).

106. SC, Dec, SC 5, Dec, SC 4, <Dec>, SC 4 [17]

107. SC 3, 2 Dec in 3 SC, SC 7, <Dec>, SC 4 [17]

108. SC 2, Dec x 2, SC 6, Inc, SC 4 [16]

109A. SC 7, Ch 1, Turn [-7]

109B. SC 7, Ch 1, Turn [-7]

109C. SC 6, SC/HDC Dec, SC 3, Inc, SC 3, HDC/SC Dec [-16] [15]

110A. SC 5, Ch 1, Turn [-5]

110B. SC 5, Ch 1, Turn [-5]

110C. SC 4, SC/HDC Dec, SC 4, <Dec>, SC 4, HDC & HDC/SC Dec [-16] [15]

111. 2 Dec in 3 SC, SC 6, <Dec>, SC 6 [15]

112A. Dec, SC 2, Ch 1, Turn [-3]

112B. SC 5, Ch 1, Turn [-5]

112C. SC 4, SC/HDC Dec, SC 7, HDC/SC Dec [-13] [13]

113A. SC 5, Ch 1, Turn [-5]

113B. SC 6, Ch 1, Turn [-6]

113C. SC 6, Ch 1, Turn [-6]

113D. SC 6, Ch 1, Turn [-6]

113E. SC 6 [-6]

Fasten off with 24 in/61 cm yarn tail.

Dragon Body

DRAGON FRONT LEG: STANDING/STRAIGHT

For a Standing or Sitting Dragon: Make 2

For a Sitting Dragon with one paw up as if to "shake": Make 1

1. SC 6 in Magic Circle, Sl St to beginning stitch, Ch 1 [6]

2. Inc x 6, Sl St to beginning stitch, Ch 1 [12]

3. SC 4, Bump, SC, Bump, SC, Bump, SC 3, Sl St to beginning stitch, Ch 1 [12]

A Bump Stitch is worked as follows:
YO, Insert into next stitch,
YO, pull up, YO, pull through 2 loops,
YO, insert into the same stitch,
YO, pull up, YO, pull through 2 loops,
YO twice, insert into the same stitch,
YO, pull up, YO, pull through 2 loops,
YO, pull through 2 loops,
YO, insert into the same stitch,
YO, pull up, YO, pull through 2 loops,
YO, insert into the same stitch,
YO, pull up, YO, pull through 2 loops,
YO, pull through all 6 remaining loops.

NOTE: It is optional to insert a glass gem into the foot (or alternative, like a coin or a button). The flat side of the gem should be oriented down, the curve should be oriented up. This will maintain a flat bottom to the foot and help with stability.

NOTE: It is optional at this point to insert a wire AND a glass gem (or wait until the leg is fully formed). The purpose of the wire is to stabilize the leg, strengthen the leg, and allow it to be poseable. Take a wire and bend the end into a circle the same size as the base of the foot. Bend the circle at a 90 degree angle from the wire. Insert the wire circle into the bottom of the foot. (If you want to use a glass gem, insert that now so that it sits on top of the wire circle; it may be a tight squeeze, but it should work.) Trim the wire so that it is 2 in/5 cm longer than the opening at the top of the leg, bend it, and push the end through the side of the leg that will be against the body of the dragon, about 3 rows from the top. This little bit of wire will be inserted directly into the body of the dragon and will help to stabilize and strengthen the entire leg and connection.

4. Inc, SC 4, 2 Dec in 3 SC, SC 4, Sl St to beginning stitch, Ch 1 [12]

5. SC, <Dec>, SC 2, Dec, SC, Dec, SC, Dec, SC, Sl St to beginning stitch, Ch 1 [10]

6. SC, Inc, SC 3, 2 Dec in 3 SC, SC 2, Sl St to beginning stitch, Ch 1 [10]

7. SC 2, <Dec>, SC 2, Inc, SC, Dec, SC, Inc, Sl St to beginning stitch, Ch 1 [12]

8. SC 2, Dec, SC 5, <Dec>, SC 3, Sl St to beginning stitch, Ch 1 [12]

9. SC, 2 Dec in 3 SC, SC 4, Inc, SC 3, Sl St to beginning stitch, Ch 1 [12]

10. SC 12, Sl St to beginning stitch, Ch 1 [12]

11. SC 5, HDC 6, SC, Sl St to beginning stitch, Ch 1 [12]

12. SC 9, Inc, SC 2, Sl St to beginning stitch, Ch 1 [13]

13. SC 3, <Dec>, SC 10, Sl St to beginning stitch, Ch 1 [14]

14. SC 11, Inc, SC 2, Sl St to beginning stitch, Ch 1 [15]

15. SC 4, Inc, SC 10, Sl St to beginning stitch, Ch 1 [16]

16. SC 13, <Dec>, SC 3, Sl St to beginning stitch, Ch 1 [17]

17. SC 5, Inc, SC 11, Sl St to beginning stitch, Ch 1 [18]

18. SC 6, <Dec>, SC 9, <Dec>, SC 3, Sl St to beginning stitch, Ch 1 [20]

19. SC 5, Dec x 2, SC 8, <Dec>, SC 3, Sl St to beginning stitch, Ch 1 [19]

20. SC 5, Dec, SC 8, Inc, SC 3, Sl St to beginning stitch, Ch 1 [19]

21–24. (4 rows of) SC 19, Sl St to beginning stitch, Ch 1 [19]

25. SC 5, Dec, SC 12, Sl St to beginning stitch, Ch 1 [18]

26. SC 14, 2 Dec in 3 SC, SC, Sl St to beginning stitch, Ch 1 [17]

27. SC 5, Dec, SC 7, Triple SC Dec, Sl St to beginning stitch [14]

28. Stuff the leg with dense stuffing in the foot and bottom three-quarters of the leg, almost no stuffing at the top of the leg. It is optional to fold the remaining hole in half and

Ch 1, Dec, SC 3, Dec, through both sides of the leg hole to close it [5]

Fasten off with 18 in/46 cm yarn tail.

Dragon Front Leg: Standing/ Straight

DRAGON LOWER FRONT LEG: LAYING DOWN: PART 1 (MAKE 2)

Optional

NOTE: You will also need to make the Upper Front Leg for use with this option.

1. Starting with a long enough yarn tail to weave in later, Ch 7, starting in the 3rd Ch from hook, Bump, Ch 1, SC in the next Ch stitch, Bump in the next Ch stitch, Ch 1, SC in the next Ch stitch, Bump in the last Ch stitch, Ch 1 [5]

A Bump Stitch is worked as follows:
YO, insert into next stitch, YO, pull up, YO, pull through 2 loops,
YO, insert into the same stitch, YO, pull up, YO, pull through 2 loops,
YO twice, insert into the same stitch,
YO, pull up, YO, pull through 2 loops, YO, pull through 2 loops,
YO, insert into the same stitch, YO, pull up, YO, pull through 2 loops,
YO, insert into the same stitch, YO, pull up, YO, pull through 2 loops,
YO, pull through all 6 remaining loops.

2. Reorient your work so that you are crocheting around the edge of those bump stitches: see detailed instructions below; SC 12, Sl St to beginning stitch, Ch 1 [12]

> You can force the "Bump" part of the Bump stitch to bump outward in the correct orientation by poking/pressing it with your finger.
>
> As you crochet Row 2, you will work SC 12. You will first work one SC around the side of the last Bump stitch you worked in Row 1, and then you will work 5 SC along the Original Chain stitches from Row 1, which will share chain stitches with the Bump stitches and Single Crochets from Row 1 (it will be one SC into the bottom of the 1st Bump stitch, then a SC into the bottom of the next SC between two Bumps, then a SC into the bottom of the 2nd Bump stitch, then a SC into the bottom of the next SC between two Bumps, and then a SC into the bottom of the third Bump stitch). Then you will work one SC around the side of the 1st Bump stitch you worked in Row 1; next, you will work 5 SC along the 5 stitches you worked in Row 1, and then you will Slip Stitch to the beginning stitch of this row and Chain 1. You will create a circle of stitches in this row. The start of this row is worked on what will be the bottom/underside of the foot.

Bottom

Top

3. SC 12, Sl St to beginning stitch, Ch 1 [12]

4. SC 8, Inc, SC 2, Inc, Sl St to beginning stitch, Ch 1 [14]

5. SC, Dec x 3, SC 7, Sl St to beginning stitch, Ch 1 [11]

6. SC 5, Dec, SC 2, Dec, Sl St to beginning stitch, Ch 1 [9]

7. SC 5, HDC 2, <HDC Dec>, HDC 2, Sl St to beginning stitch, Ch 1 [10]

> The <HDC Dec> Stitch is worked the same as a <Dec>, just using a HDC Decrease instead of a regular Decrease.

8. SC 6, HDC 4, Sl St to beginning stitch, Ch 1 [10]

9. SC 10, Sl St to beginning stitch, Ch 1 [10]

NOTE: At this point, you can optionally insert two standard-sized glass gems into the paw of the foot. You can also add wire if you wish to be able to pose the foot.

---

10. SC 3, Inc, SC 6, Sl St to beginning stitch, Ch 1 [11]

11. SC 9, Inc, SC, Sl St to beginning stitch, Ch 1 [12]

12. SC 4, Inc, SC 7, Sl St to beginning stitch, Ch 1 [13]

13. SC 11, Inc, SC, Sl St to beginning stitch, Ch 1 [14]

14. SC 5, Inc, SC 8, Sl St to beginning stitch, Ch 1 [15]

15. SC 13, Inc, SC, Sl St to beginning stitch, Ch 1 [16]

16–20. (5 rows of) SC 16, Sl St to beginning stitch, Ch 1 [16]

21. SC 16, Sl St to beginning stitch [16]

Fasten off with 12 in/30 cm yarn tail.

Stuff the leg firmly for the first 2 in/ 5 cm and then use light to no stuffing until the end. Attachment instructions provided in Assembly Section.

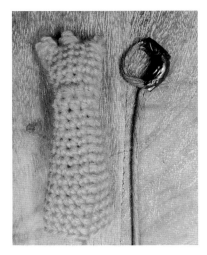

Dragon Lower Front Leg: Laying Down

DRAGON LOWER FRONT LEG: BEGGING: PART 1 (MAKE 1 OR 2)

NOTE: You will also need to make the Upper Front Leg for use with this option.

1. Starting with a long enough yarn tail to weave in later, Ch 7, Starting in the 3rd Ch from hook, Bump, Ch 1, SC in the next Ch stitch, Bump in the next Ch stitch, Ch 1, SC in the next Ch stitch, Bump in the last Ch stitch, Ch 1 [5]

A Bump Stitch is worked as follows: YO, insert into next stitch, YO, pull up, YO, pull through 2 loops, YO, insert into the same stitch, YO, pull up, YO, pull through 2 loops, YO twice, insert into the same stitch, YO, pull up, YO, pull through 2 loops, YO, pull through 2 loops, YO, insert into the same stitch, YO, pull up, YO, pull through 2 loops, YO, insert into the same stitch, YO, pull up, YO, pull through 2 loops, YO, pull through all 6 remaining loops.

2. Reorient your work so that you are crocheting around the edge of those bump stitches, SC 12, Sl St to beginning stitch, Ch 1 [12]

You can force the "Bump" part of the Bump stitch to bump outward in the correct orientation by poking/pressing it with your finger.

As you crochet Row 2, you will work SC 12. You will first work one SC around the side of the last Bump stitch you worked in Row 1, and then you will work 5 SC along the Original Chain stitches from Row 1 which will share chain stitches with the Bump stitches and Single Crochets from Row 1 (it will be one SC into the bottom of the 1st Bump stitch, then a SC into the bottom of the next SC between two Bumps, then a SC into the bottom of the 2nd Bump stitch, then a SC into the bottom of the next SC between two Bumps, and then a SC into the bottom of the third Bump stitch). Then you will work one SC around the side of the 1st Bump stitch you worked in Row 1; next, you will work 5 SC along the 5 stitches you worked in Row 1, and then you will Slip Stitch to the beginning stitch of this row and Chain 1. You will create a circle of stitches in this row. The start of this row is worked on what will be the bottom/ underside of the foot. See photos of this step on the preceding page.

3. SC 8, Inc, SC 2, Inc, Sl St to beginning stitch, Ch 1 [14]

4. SC, Dec x 3, SC 7, Sl St to beginning stitch, Ch 1[11]

5. FLO [SC, Dec, SC], HDC, DC 2, DC Inc, DC 2, HDC, Sl St to beginning stitch, Ch 1 [11]

6. Sl St 3, Dec, HDC 4, Dec, Sl St to beginning stitch, Ch 1 [9]

> When you end this row with a Slip Stitch to the beginning stitch, you can slip stitch into the same stitch you slip stitched into to start this row. You do not need to finish with a slip stitch into the slip stitch.

7. SC 9, Sl St to beginning stitch, Ch 1 [9]

> In this row, the 1st 3 SC will be made around Row 6's slip stitches and into the same row they were slip stitched into in Row 5.

8. SC 5, HDC 4, Sl St to beginning stitch, Ch 1 [9]

9. SC 2, Inc, SC 2, HDC 4, Sl St to beginning stitch, Ch 1 [10]

10. SC 7, Inc, SC 2, Sl St to beginning stitch, Ch 1 [11]

11. SC 3, Inc, SC 7, Sl St to beginning stitch, Ch 1 [12]

12. SC 10, Inc, SC, Sl St to beginning stitch, Ch 1 [13]

13. SC 4, Inc, SC 8, Sl St to beginning stitch, Ch 1 [14]

14. SC 11, Inc, SC 2, Sl St to beginning stitch, Ch 1 [15]

15. SC 5, Inc, SC 9, Sl St to beginning stitch, Ch 1 [16]

16–18. (3 rows of) SC 16, Sl St to beginning stitch, Ch 1 [16]

19. SC 16, Sl St to beginning stitch [16]

Fasten off with 18 in/46 cm yarn tail. Attachment instructions provided in Assembly Section.

OPTIONAL: Cut one piece of wire to be 6 in/15 cm longer than this piece, form a loop at the end the size of the paw. You can secure the loop of wire to itself with a small piece of duct tape wrapped around it. Insert a glass gem, round side up, into the foot of the leg, Insert the loop of the wire next under the glass gem. Stuff the leg with fiberfill about halfway up the leg around the wire evenly, leave the top half of the piece lightly or unstuffed. Once the foot is stuffed, take the end of the wire and bend it to exit the foot/leg about 3 rows from the end of the piece through the top of the leg, as shown. This wire will be inserted into the upper leg piece and help to secure the leg and make the foot poseable.

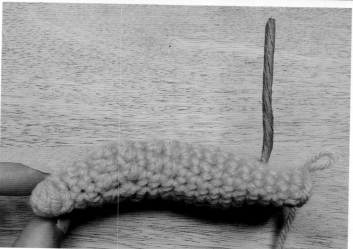

Dragon Lower Front Leg: Begging

DRAGON UPPER FRONT LEG: LAYING DOWN/ BEGGING: PART 2 (MAKE 1 OR 2)

NOTE: You will also need to make the Lower Laying Down or Begging Front Leg for use with this option.

1. Starting with a long enough yarn tail to weave in later, Ch 6, starting in the 2nd Ch from hook, Inc, SC 3, work 2 Inc stitches in the last Ch stitch, keep crocheting around to the other side of the starting chain stitches, SC in each of the next 3 Ch stitches, Inc in the last Ch stitch (same as the 1st Inc), Sl St to beginning stitch, Ch 1 [14]

2. SC 3, Inc, SC 6, Inc, SC 3, Sl St to beginning stitch, Ch 1 [16]

3. (SC 3, Inc) x 4, Sl St to beginning stitch, Ch 1 [20]

4. SC 20, Sl St to beginning stitch, Ch 1 [20]

5. (SC 9, Inc) x 2, Sl St to beginning stitch, Ch 1 [22]

6–9. (4 rows of) SC 22, Sl St to beginning stitch, Ch 1 [22]

10. (Dec, SC 9) x 2, Sl St to beginning stitch, Ch 1 [20]

11. SC 20, Sl St to beginning stitch, Ch 1 [20]

12. (SC 3, Dec) x 4, Sl St to beginning stitch, Ch 1 [16]

13–14. (2 rows of) SC 16, Sl St to beginning stitch, Ch 1 [16]

15. SC 16, Sl St to beginning stitch [16]

Fasten off with 24 in/61 cm yarn tail. For weight and stability, you can drop a small number of glass gems into the bottom of the leg piece. Stuff firmly with fiberfill in the bottom half of the piece, with very little to no stuffing in the top half of the piece. Attachment instructions provided in Assembly on page 143.

Dragon Upper Front Leg: Laying Down/Begging

DRAGON UPPER REAR LEG: SITTING, LAYING, OR BEGGING: PART 1 (MAKE 2)

NOTE: You will also need to make the Lower Rear Leg for use with this option.

This piece is crocheted in spiral; do not use Sl St, Ch 1.

1. Starting with a long enough yarn tail to weave in later, Ch 6, Inc in the 2nd Ch from hook, SC in each of the next 3 Ch stitches, work 2 Increases in the last Ch stitch, keep crocheting around to the other side of the row of Ch stitches, SC in each of the next 3 Ch stitches opposite the 1st 3 SC stitches, make an Increase in the last stitch (the same stitch as your 1st Increase) [14]

2. SC 3, Inc, SC 6, Inc, SC 3 [16]

3. (SC 3, Inc) x 4 [20]

4. SC 2, Inc, (SC 4, Inc) x 3, SC 2 [24]

5. SC 24 [24]

6. (SC 5, Inc) x 4 [28]

7. SC 28 [28]

8. SC 3, Inc, (SC 6, Inc) x 3, SC 3 [32]

9-11. (3 rows of) SC 32 [32]

12. (SC 6, Dec) x 4 [28]

13. SC 28 [28]

14. (SC 5, Dec) x 4 [24]

15. SC 24 [24]

16. (SC 4, Dec) x 4 [20]

17. (SC 3, Dec) x 4 [16]

18. (SC 2, Dec) x 4 [12]

Stuff the piece half full of stuffing. The stuffing needs to be even throughout the piece, but do not stuff it firmly. Row 19 is the "top" of the leg piece.

19. (SC, Dec) x 4, Sl St into the next stitch [8]

Fasten off with 18 in/46 cm yarn tail. Attachment instructions provided in Assembly Section.

Dragon Upper Rear Leg: Sitting, Laying, or Begging

DRAGON LOWER REAR LEG: SITTING, LAYING, OR BEGGING: PART 2 (MAKE 2)

NOTE: You will also need to make the Upper Rear Leg for use with this option.

1. Ch 7, Starting in the 3rd Ch from hook, Bump, Ch 1, SC in the next Ch stitch, Bump in the next Ch stitch, Ch 1, SC in the next Ch stitch, Bump in the last Ch stitch, Ch 1 [5]

A Bump Stitch is worked as follows: YO, insert into next stitch, YO, pull up, YO, pull through 2 loops, YO, insert into the same stitch, YO, pull up, YO, pull through 2 loops, YO twice, insert into the same stitch, YO, pull up, YO, pull through 2 loops, YO, pull through 2 loops, YO, insert into the same stitch, YO, pull up, YO, pull through 2 loops, YO, insert into the same stitch, YO, pull up, YO, pull through 2 loops, YO, pull through all 6 remaining loops.

2. Reorient your work so that you are crocheting around the edge of those bump stitches. SC 12, Sl St to beginning stitch, Ch 1 [12]

You can force the "Bump" part of the Bump stitch to bump outward in the correct orientation by poking/pressing it with your finger.

As you crochet Row 2, you will work SC 12. You will first work one SC around the side of the last Bump stitch you worked in Row 1, and then you will work 5 SC along the Original Chain stitches from Row 1, which will share chain stitches with the Bump stitches and Single Crochets from Row 1 (it will be one SC into the bottom of the 1st Bump stitch, then a SC into the bottom of the next SC between two Bumps, then a SC into the bottom of the 2nd Bump stitch, then a SC into the bottom of the next SC between two Bumps, and then a SC into the bottom of the third Bump stitch). Then you will work one SC around the side of the 1st Bump stitch you worked in Row 1; next, you will work 5 SC along the 5 stitches you worked in Row 1, and then you will Slip Stitch to the beginning stitch of this row and Chain 1. You will create a circle of stitches in this row. The start of this row is worked on what will be the bottom/underside of the foot. See photos of this step on page 101.

3–4. (2 rows of) SC 12, Sl St to beginning stitch, Ch 1 [12]

5. (SC 2, Dec) x 3, Sl St to beginning stitch, Ch 1 [9]

6–8. (3 rows of) SC 9, Sl St to beginning stitch, Ch 1 [9]

NOTE: If you are using glass gems, insert one (or two) now, or stuff with fiberfill. The flat part of the gem should be oriented down toward the side of the toes that look like they have small open holes.

------

9. Fold the hole of the work in half, SC 4 across both sides of the hole to close it [4]

Fasten off with 18 in/46 cm yarn tail. Attachment instructions provided in Assembly on page 140.

Dragon Lower Rear Leg: Sitting, Laying, or Begging

DRAGON REAR LEG: STANDING/STRAIGHT (MAKE 2)

Use the same glass gem, wire, and stuffing instructions as for the Standing Front Leg (see page 99).

1. SC 6 in Magic Circle, Sl St to beginning stitch, Ch 1 [6]

2. Inc x 6, Sl St to beginning stitch, Ch 1 [12]

3. SC 4, Bump, SC, Bump, SC, Bump, SC 3, Sl St to beginning stitch, Ch 1 [12]

A Bump Stitch is worked as follows:
YO, insert into next stitch,
YO, pull up, YO, pull through 2 loops,
YO, insert into the same stitch,
YO, pull up, YO, pull through 2 loops,
YO twice, insert into the same stitch,
YO, pull up, YO, pull through 2 loops,
YO, pull through 2 loops,
YO, insert into the same stitch,
YO, pull up, YO, pull through 2 loops,
YO, insert into the same stitch,
YO, pull up, YO, pull through 2 loops,
YO, pull through all 6 remaining loops.

4. Inc, SC 5, Dec, SC 4, Sl St to beginning stitch, Ch 1 [12]

5. SC, Inc, SC 2, Dec, 2 Dec in 3 SC, Dec, SC, Sl St to beginning stitch, Ch 1 [10]

6. SC, Inc, SC 3, 2 Dec in 3 SC, SC 2, Sl St to beginning stitch, Ch 1 [10]

7. SC 2, <Dec>, SC 4, Dec, SC 2, Sl St to beginning stitch, Ch 1 [10]

8. SC 2, Inc, SC 3, 2 Dec in 3 SC, SC, Sl St to beginning stitch, Ch 1 [10]

9. SC 3, Inc, SC 3, 2 Dec in 3, Sl St to beginning stitch, Ch 1 [10]

10. SC 4, <Dec>, SC 4, Dec, Sl St to beginning stitch, Ch 1 [10]

11. SC 4, Inc, SC 4, Inc, Sl St o beginning stitch, Ch 1 [12]

12. SC 5, Inc, SC 5, Inc, Sl St to beginning stitch, Ch 1 [14]

13. SC 6, <Dec>, SC 8, Sl St to beginning stitch, Ch 1 [15]

14. SC 5, Dec x 2, SC 5, Inc, Sl St to beginning stitch, Ch 1 [14]

15. SC 5, Dec, SC 6, Inc, Sl St to beginning stitch, Ch 1 [14]

16. Inc, SC 4, Dec, SC 4, Inc, SC 2, Sl St to beginning stitch, Ch 1 [15]

17. Inc, SC 11, Inc, SC 2, Sl St to beginning stitch, Ch 1 [17]

18. SC 16, <Dec>, SC, Sl St to beginning stitch, Ch 1 [18]

19. SC 7, Inc, SC 10, Sl St to beginning stitch, Ch 1 [19]

20. SC 19, Sl St to beginning stitch, Ch 1 [19]

21. SC 8, Inc, SC 10, Sl St to beginning stitch, Ch 1 [20]

22–25. (4 rows of) SC 20, Sl St to beginning stitch, Ch 1 [20]

26. SC 3, Dec, SC 8, Dec, SC 5, Sl St to beginning stitch, Ch 1 [18]

27. SC 3, Dec, SC 7, Dec, SC 4, Sl St to beginning stitch, Ch 1 [16]

28. SC 3, Dec, SC 6, Dec, SC 3, Sl St to beginning stitch, Ch 1 [14]

29. SC 5, Dec, SC 5, Dec, Sl St to beginning stitch [12]

Follow the glass gem, wire, and stuffing instructions as for the Standing front leg (page 99).

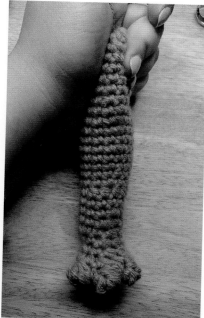

30. It is optional to fold the opening at the top of the leg in half, Ch 1, Dec, SC 2, Dec to close the leg hole [4]

Fasten off with 18 in/46 cm yarn tail. Attachment instructions provided in Assembly on page 141.

Dragon Rear Leg: Standing/Straight

DRAGON HORN: SIMPLE (MAKE 2)

Option 1

> This piece is crocheted in spiral; do not use Sl St, Ch 1.

1. SC 4 in Magic Circle [4]

NOTE: You can optionally elongate these horns by crocheting once around with no increases after each row. If you want to do this, you can SC 4 more after Row 1, SC 5 more after Row 2, SC 6 more after Row 3, and so on; this will double the amount of yarn you need for this piece.

---

2. Inc, SC 3 [5]
3. Inc, SC 4 [6]
4. Inc, SC 5 [7]
5. Inc, SC 6 [8]
6. Inc, SC 7 [9]
7. Inc, SC 8 [10]
8. Inc, SC 9 [11]
9. SC 11, Slip Stitch to the next available stitch [11]

Fasten off with 12 in/30 cm yarn tail. Stuffing is optional for this piece. Attachment instructions provided in Assembly on page 144.

Simple Horn, short version (as written)

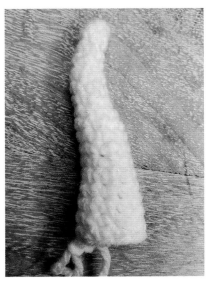

Simple Horn, elongated version (with even rows between increases)

DRAGON HORN: SPIRAL (MAKE 2)

Option 2

> This piece is crocheted in spiral; do not use Sl St, Ch 1.

1. SC 4 in Magic Circle [4]
2–3. (2 rows of) SC 4 [4]
4. Inc x 2, SC 2 [6]
5. SC 4, Dec [5]
6. Inc x 2, SC 3 [7]
7. SC 5, Dec [6]
8. Inc x 2, SC 4 [8]
9. SC 5, Dec, SC [7]
10. Inc x 2, SC 5 [9]
11. SC 6, Dec, SC [8]
12. Inc x 2, SC 6 [10]
13. SC 7, Dec, SC [9]
14. Inc x 2, SC 7 [11]
15. SC 8, Dec, SC [10]
16. Inc x 2, SC 8, Slip Stitch into the next available stitch [12]

Fasten off with 12 in/30 cm yarn tail. Stuffing is optional for this piece. Attachment instructions provided in Assembly on page 144.

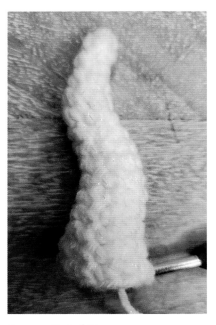

Dragon Spiral Horn

DRAGON HORN: LARGE SPIRAL WITH ACCENT COLOR (MAKE 2)

Option 3

This piece is crocheted in spiral; do not use Sl St, Ch 1.

1. SC 4 in Magic Circle [4]
2. BLO [Inc, SC 3] [5]
3. BLO [Inc, SC 4] [6]
4. BLO [Inc, SC 5] [7]
5. BLO [Inc, SC 6] [8]
6. BLO [Inc, SC 7] [9]
7. BLO [Inc, SC 8] [10]
8. BLO [SC 10] [10]
9. BLO [Inc, SC 9] [11]
10. BLO [SC 11] [11]
11. BLO [Inc, SC 10] [12]
12. BLO [SC 12] [12]
13. BLO [Inc, SC 11] [13]
14. BLO [SC, Inc, SC 5, Dec, SC 4] [13]

Fasten off with 12 in/30 cm yarn tail.

Dragon Large Spiral Horn without Accent Color

Adding the Accent Spiral Color

Starting with a long enough yarn tail to weave in later (or pull inside the top tip of the horn to hide inside the horn), attach the Accent Color at the top of the horn with a Slip Stitch to the very 1st available front loop from the very 1st row of the Main Color horn. Slip Stitch in the Front Loop Only all the way down.

Fasten off with 12 in/30 cm yarn tail. Stuff lightly with fiberfill. Attachment instructions provided in Assembly on page 144.

Dragon Large Spiral Horn with Accent Color

DRAGON FACE ORNAMENTATION: LONG CHEEK FRILL (MAKE 2)

Option 1

1. Start with a 12 in/30 cm yarn tail, Ch 17 (these 17 chain stitches are the original chains, or the "OC"), starting in the 2nd Ch from hook, Sl St 2 [2]

2. (SC, Ch 2, Sl St in 2nd Ch from hook, SC in the next available OC stitch) x 2 [4]

> The "Ch 2, Sl St in the 2nd Ch from hook" instructions are not counted in the stitch count here or anywhere, as they are picot stitches that are purely decorative.

3. (SC, Ch 3, Sl St in the 2nd Ch from hook, SC in the next Ch stitch, SC in the next available OC stitch) x 2 [6]

4. (SC, Ch 4, Sl St in the 2nd Ch from hook, SC in the next Ch stitch, HDC in next Ch stitch, SC in the next available OC stitch) x 2 [8]

5. Sl St in each of the next 2 Ch stitches [2]

Fasten off yarn with 12 in/30 cm yarn tail. Attachment instructions provided in Assembly on page 144.

Dragon Long Cheek Frill

DRAGON FACE ORNAMENTATION: SHORT CHEEK FRILL (MAKE 2)

Option 2

1. Start with a 12 in/30 cm yarn tail, Ch 10 (these 10 chain stitches are the original chains, or the "OC"), starting in the 2nd Ch from Hook, Sl St [1]

2. Inc in the next OC stitch, Ch 2, Sl St into the 2nd Ch from hook [2]

> The "Ch 2, Sl St in the 2nd Ch from hook" instructions are not counted in the stitch count here or anywhere, as they are picot stitches that are purely decorative.

3. SC in the next OC stitch [1]

4. SC & HDC in the next OC stitch, Ch 2, Sl St into the 2nd Ch from hook [2]

> Check the Glossary (page 4) for the explanation of the "&" symbol.

5. HDC in the next OC stitch [1]

6. SC & HDC in the next OC stitch, Ch 2, Sl St into the 2nd Ch from hook [2]

7. HDC in the next OC stitch [1]

8. Sl St in each of the next 2 OC Stitches [2]

Fasten off yarn with 12 in/30 cm yarn tail. Attachment instructions provided in Assembly on page 144.

Dragon Short Cheek Frill

DRAGON FACE ORNAMENTATION: HEAD PLATE (MAKE 1)

Option 3

1. Starting with a long enough yarn tail to weave in later, Ch 4 (these chain stitches are the original chains, or the "OC"), starting in the 2nd Ch from hook, SC 3, Ch 1, Turn [3]
2. SC 3, Ch 1, Turn [3]
3. SC, Inc, SC, Ch 1, Turn [4]
4. SC 4, Ch 1, Turn [4]
5. SC 2, <Dec>, SC 2, Ch 1, Turn [5]
6. SC 5, Ch 1, Turn [5]
7. SC 2, Inc, SC 2, Ch 1, Turn [6]
8. SC 6, Ch 1, Turn [6]
9. SC, Inc, SC 2, Inc, SC, Ch 1, Turn [8]
10-14. (5 rows of) SC 8, Ch 1, Turn [8]
15. Dec, SC 4, Dec, Ch 1, Turn [6]
16. Dec, SC 2, Dec, Ch 1 [4]

17. Do not turn; SC in the same stitch as where the last Dec of Row 16 ended, working up the unfinished edge of the rows back to the OC, SC about 14, working into the OC work an Inc in the 1st available stitch, work a SC in the next available OC stitch, work an Inc in the last available OC stitch, working back up the unfinished edge of the rows back to the 1st Decrease you worked in Row 16, SC about 14, SC in the same stitch that the 1st Decrease of Row 16 started into [~35]

Fasten off with 18 in/46 cm yarn tail. Attachment instructions provided in Assembly on page 144.

Dragon Head Plate

DRAGON FACE ORNAMENTATION: FANCY HEAD PLATE (MAKE 1)

Option 4

1. Starting with a long enough yarn tail to weave in later, Ch 14, Turn, starting in the 2nd Ch from hook, SC 5, HDC 5, DC 3, Ch 2, Turn [13]

Put a stitch marker in the last stitch of Row 1. The Ch 2 at the end of Row 1 is just a turning chain.

2. FLO [DC 3, HDC 5, SC 5], Ch 1, Turn [13]
3. FLO [SC 5, HDC 5, DC 3], Ch 2, Turn [13]

Put a stitch marker in the last stitch of Row 3. The Ch 2 at the end of Row 3 is just a turning chain.

4. FLO [DC 3, HDC 5, SC 5], Ch 1, Turn [13]
5. FLO [SC 5, HDC 5, DC 3], Ch 2, Turn [13]

Put a stitch marker in the last stitch of Row 5. The Ch 2 at the end of Row 5 is just a turning chain.

6. FLO [DC 3, HDC 5, SC 5], Ch 1, Turn [13]
7. FLO [SC 5, HDC 5, DC 3], Ch 1 [13]

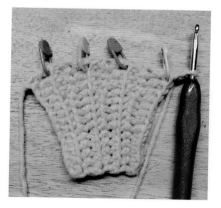

8. In the same stitch as the last DC in Row 7, DC & Half Trip & Triple Crochet [3]

9. Ch 1, SC 3 along the post of the last Triple Crochet in Row 8, Slip Stitch into the same marked stitch space as Row 8 [4]

10. Into the next available marked stitch space from Row 5, DC & Half Trip & Triple Crochet,

Ch 2, Sl St in the 2nd Ch from hook, continuing into the same marked stitch space, Triple Crochet & Half Trip & DC, Sl St in the space centered between the current marked stitch space and the next marked stitch space [7]

11. Into the next available marked stitch space from Row 3, DC & Half Trip & Triple Crochet, Ch 2, Sl St in the 2nd Ch from hook, continuing into the same marked stitch space, Triple Crochet & Half Trip & DC, Sl St in the space centered between the current marked stitch space and the next marked stitch space [7]

12. Into the next available marked stitch space from Row 1, DC & Half Trip & Triple Crochet, Ch 2, Sl St in the 2nd Ch from hook, continuing into the same marked stitch space, Triple Crochet & Half Trip & DC, Sl St in the OC of Row 1 [7]

13. Ch 3, Triple Crochet & Half Trip & DC in the same OC space, working down the opposite side of the original chain, DC 2, HDC 5, SC 5 [15]

Fasten off with 36 in/91 cm yarn tail. Attachment instructions provided in Assembly on page 144.

Dragon Fancy Head Plate

DRAGON FACE ORNAMENTATION: CURLY EYELID (MAKE 2)

Option 5

1. Starting with a long enough yarn tail to weave in later, Ch 11, Turn, starting in the 2nd Ch from hook, Sl St, SC, Inc, Sl St 7, Ch 13, Turn [11]

2. Starting in the 2nd Ch from hook, Sl St, Dec x 2, Sl St 7, Ch 1 [10]

Fasten off with 18 in/46 cm yarn tail. Attachment instructions provided in Assembly on page 144.

Dragon Curly Eyelid

DRAGON FACE ORNAMENTATION: SIMPLE EYELID (MAKE 2)

Option 6

1. Starting with a long enough yarn tail to weave in later, Ch 8, Turn, starting in the 2nd Ch from hook, Sl St, SC, HDC 3, SC, Sl St, Ch 8, Turn [7]

2. Starting in the 2nd Ch from hook, Sl St, SC, HDC 3, SC, Sl St [7]

Fasten off with 24 in/61 cm yarn tail. Attachment instructions provided in Assembly on page 144.

Dragon Simple Eyelid

DRAGON FACE ORNAMENTATION: HEART EYELID (MAKE 2)

Option 7

NOTE: You can also use this piece to ornament the tail or the back edge of the front legs.

Part 1

1. Starting with a long enough yarn tail to weave in later, Ch 8, Turn, starting in the 2nd Ch from hook, HDC & SC, SC 4, SC/HDC Dec, Ch 1, Turn [7]

2. Dec, SC 4, SC & HDC, Ch 1, Turn [7]

3. SC 5, SC/HDC Dec, Ch 1, Turn [6]

4. Dec, SC 4, Ch 1, Turn [5]

5. Dec, SC, SC/HDC Dec [3]

Fasten off with a 12 in/30 cm yarn tail.

Part 2: Edging

1. Starting with a long enough yarn tail to weave in later, reattach the same color OR accent color yarn to the OC (see note), SC around the curved edge of the half-heart. Use Increases wherever necessary around sharper curves; exact stitch count is not necessary.

You can attach the yarn to the 1st Chain in the OC (bottom part of the heart) or to the last Chain in the OC (top of the heart)—and then work SC stitches around the curved edge of the half-heart. This way you can make pieces that will look the same by having the "front" of the stitches at the front of the piece.

Fasten off with 24 in/61 cm yarn tail to use to sew to attach (or a long enough yarn tail to weave in if using a different accent color here). Attachment instructions provided in Assembly on page 144.

NOTE: You can use one piece on either side of the top of the eyelids. You can use two pieces per eyelid for a full Heart effect.

Dragon Heart Eyelid

DRAGON EAR: FOLDED, STYLE 1 (MAKE 2)

Option 1

1. Start with a 12 in/30 cm yarn tail, SC 6 in Magic Circle, Sl St to the beginning stitch, Ch 1 [6]
2. Inc x 6, Ch 1, Turn [12]
3. (SC, Inc) x 6, Ch 1, Turn [18]
4. Skip the 1st available stitch, Sl St, (SC, Ch 2, Sl St in the 2nd Ch from hook, SC) x 7, Sl St 2 [17]

The "Ch 2, Sl St in the 2nd Ch from hook" instructions are not counted in the stitch count here or anywhere, as they are picot stitches that are purely decorative.

Fasten off with 12 in/30 cm yarn tail. Fold the ear in half before attaching.

Attachment instructions provided in Assembly on page 144.

Dragon Folded Ear: Style 1

DRAGON EAR: FOLDED, STYLE 2 (MAKE 2)

Option 2

1. Start with a 12 in/30 cm yarn tail, SC 6 in Magic Circle, Sl St to the beginning stitch, Ch 1 [6]
2. Inc x 6, Ch 1, Turn [12]
3. (SC, Inc) x 6, Ch 1, Turn [18]
4. (SC 2, Inc) x 3, Ch 2, Sl St in the 2nd Ch from hook, (SC 2, Inc) x 3 [24]

The "Ch 2, Sl St in the 2nd Ch from hook" instructions are not counted in the stitch count here or anywhere, as they are picot stitches that are purely decorative.

Fasten off with 12 in/30 cm yarn tail. Attachment instructions provided in Assembly on page 144.

Dragon Folded Ear: Style 2

DRAGON EAR: FIN (MAKE 2)

Option 3

Part 1
Use an Accent Color yarn:

1. Starting with a long enough yarn tail to weave in later, Ch 8, starting in the 3rd Ch from hook, DC, HDC 2, SC 3, Ch 1, Turn [6]

Mark the Chain that you work the last SC stitch into in Row 1.

2. FLO [SC 3, HDC 2, DC], Ch 2, Turn [6]

The Ch 2 at the end of this and following rows in this section are only turning chains, they are not counted in the stitch count, and they are not crocheted into.

3. BLO [DC, HDC 2, SC 3], Ch 1, Turn [6]
4. FLO [SC 3, HDC 2, DC], Ch 2, Turn [6]
5. BLO [DC, HDC 2, SC 3], Ch 1, Turn [6]
6. FLO [SC 3, HDC 2, DC], Ch 2, Turn [6]
7. BLO [DC, HDC 2, SC 3], Ch 1, Turn [6]

8. FLO [SC 3, HDC 2, DC] [6]

Fasten off with 18 in/46 cm yarn tail.

Part 2
Use Main Body Color yarn:

1. Starting with a long enough yarn tail to weave in later, attach the yarn to the marked stitch, Sl St 6 along the edge, Ch 3, starting in the 2nd Ch from hook Sl St 2, Sl St 6 back along the same stitches you slip stitched along at the beginning of this row on the opposite side of the work, Ch 1 [14]

2. Starting in the same marked stitch space, start a Decrease stitch and complete the decrease along the edge of the ear in the side of the next stitch, just before the next FLO ridge, Ch 1 [1]

When you work the Decreases in Row 2, 4, 6, and 8, you will be working from the back side of the Fin Ear. The back side of the Fin Ear is the side without any of the leftover ridges from the FLO stitches from Part 1.

3. Working along the raised ridge of leftover FLO stitches, Sl St 6, Ch 3, starting in the 2nd Ch from hook, Sl St 2, Sl St 6 back along the same stitches you slip stitched along at the beginning of this row, Ch 1 [14]

When working the 1st Sl St 6 in this Row (also Rows 5, 7, and 9), you will keep your hook on the side of the Fin Ear closest to the starting chain. When inserting your hook under the leftover FLO to make your stitch, insert it from the side closest to the starting chain. Then, after completing the Ch 3, Sl St 2 instructions, you will work back along the other side of the same leftover FLO stitches, inserting your hook under both the leftover FLO loop and the previous Sl St. Keep your hook on the side of the Fin Ear with the final Part 1 row, inserting your hook from the side closest to the final Part 1 row.

4. Work a Decrease along the same inner edge of the ear that you completed the last Decrease in Row 2, working toward the next raised leftover ridge of FLO stitches [1]

5. Working along the next available raised ridge of leftover FLO stitches, Sl St 6, Ch 3, starting in the 2nd Ch from hook, Sl St 2, Sl St 6 back along the same stitches you slip stitched along at the beginning of this row, Ch 1 [14]

6. Work a Decrease along the same inner edge of the ear that you completed the last 2 Decreases in Rows 2 and 4, working toward the next raised leftover ridge of FLO stitches [1]

7. Working along the next available raised ridge of leftover FLO stitches, Sl St 6, Ch 3, starting in the 2nd Ch from hook, Sl St 2, Sl St 6 back along the same stitches you slip stitched along at the beginning of this row, Ch 1 [14]

8. Work a Decrease along the same inner edge of the ear that you completed the last 3 Decreases in Rows 2, 4, and 6, working toward the last edge of the ear [1]

9. Working along the last remaining FLO edge of the ear, Sl St 6, Ch 3, starting in the 2nd Ch from the hook, Sl St 2, Sl St 6 back along the same stitches that you slip stitched along at the beginning of this row [14]

Fasten off with 12 in/30 cm yarn tail. Attachment instructions provided in Assembly on page 144.

Dragon Fin Ear

DRAGON EAR: LONG DROOPY (MAKE 2)

Option 4

1. Start with a 12 in/30 cm yarn tail, SC 6 in Magic Circle, Sl St to beginning stitch, Ch 1 [6]
2. Inc x 6, Ch 1, Turn [12]
3. SC, Inc, HDC, HDC & DC, DC, Half Trip Inc, DC, DC & HDC, HDC, Inc, SC, Inc, Ch 1, Turn [18]
4. SC 8, SC & HDC & DC, Ch 2, Sl St in the 2nd Ch from hook, DC & HDC & SC, SC 8 [21]

Fasten off with 12 in/30 cm yarn tail. Attachment instructions provided in Assembly on page 144.

Dragon Long Droopy Ear

DRAGON BACK SCALES: ONE COLOR (MAKE 1)

Option 1

This piece is extremely variable in length depending on the yarn you use, the hook size, and your particular tension. The dragon you have made will require custom-length scales to reach from the forehead to the tail tip. When you create this piece, DO NOT cut the yarn until you pin the scales in place to check to make sure the length is correct.

If it is too short, rip out the stitches until you get back to Row 46 and add more rows to make it your desired length.

If it is too long, rip out the stitches until you get back to Row 41 and then purposefully rip out rows until you make it your desired length, finishing with 5 repeats of Ch 3, Sl St in the 2nd Ch from hook.

You will not know the final length of the scales until after you have slip stitched back along the scales all the way to the beginning, because the slip stitches change the length of the scale line. The slip stitches reinforce and strengthen the scales, but they also shrink the length. The following instructions should fit with all previous instructions/sizes, but adjust to the dragon that you have made, if necessary.

1. Start with 12 in/30 cm yarn tail, 3 tight Ch stitches

2. Ch 2, Sl St in the 2nd Ch from hook [1]

3. Ch 3, Sl St in the 2nd Ch from hook [1]

4–6. (3 repeats of) Ch 4, Sl St in the 2nd Ch from hook, SC in the next Ch Stitch [2]

7–23. (17 repeats of) Ch 5, Sl St in the 2nd Ch from hook, SC in the next Ch Stitch, DC in the next Ch stitch [3]

24–41. (18 repeats of) Ch 4, Sl St in the 2nd Ch from hook, SC in the next Ch stitch [2]

42–46. (5 repeats of) Ch 3, Sl St in the 2nd Ch from hook [1]

47. You can optionally fasten off here without edging the bottom of this piece in stitches. This will make for a lower-profile set of back scales.

Alternatively, you can Ch 2, Sl St in the 2nd Ch from hook. Now you have options. You can Sl St all the way back along previous rows, or you can Single Crochet along the previous rows. End with 2 Slip Stitches.

As you Slip Stitch or Single Crochet back to the beginning across the base of all the scales you've created, try to stitch once inside each scale that only has one stitch (like Rows 2 and 3 scales), stitch twice inside each scale that has two stitches (like Row 4 scales), stitch three times inside each scale that has three stitches (like Row 7 scales), and always stitch once between each scale.

Dragon Back Scales: One Color

Confirm it is the correct length by pinning in place along the center of the back of the dragon. If you need it to be shorter, you can undo some of the scales. If you want the piece to be longer, you can repeat Row 41 until you add the length you need and finish with Row 42 to Row 47.

Once the correct length is reached, fasten off with 36 in/91 cm yarn tail. Attachment instructions provided in Assembly on page 144.

DRAGON BACK SCALES: THREE COLORS (MAKE 1)

Option 2

When you create this piece, DO NOT cut the yarn when finished until you pin the scales in place, to make sure the length is correct. If it is too long or too short, figure out how many spikes of the tallest variety (Rows 6–13 of Color 1, Rows 10–18 of Color 2, Rows 9–17 of Color 3) you would need to rip out or add to make it your desired length, and go back if necessary. The final length of the scales won't be fully known until after you have crocheted all three colors. The length of scales is significantly affected by your tension and the exact weight of yarn you are using. The line of SC and Slip Stitches back reinforces and strengthens the scales. Adjust to your particular dragon length/size if necessary.

Part 1: Color 1

1. Starting with the bottom-most color of the spikes (closest to the dragon body) and a long enough yarn tail to weave in later, make 3 tight Ch stitches.
2. Ch 2, Sl St in the 2nd Ch from hook [1]
3. Ch 5, Sl St in the 2nd Ch from hook [1]
4. Ch 6, Sl St in the 2nd Ch from hook, SC in the next Ch stitch [2]
5. Ch 6, Sl St in the 2nd Ch from hook, SC in the next Ch stitch [2]
6. Ch 7, Sl St in the 2nd Ch from hook, SC in the next Ch stitch, DC in the next Ch stitch [3]
7–13. (7 rows of) Repeat Row 6 [3]
14–21. (8 rows of) Repeat Row 5 [2]

22–23. (2 rows of) Repeat Row 3 [1]
24. Ch 2, fasten off with enough yarn to weave in upon completion.

Part 2: Color 2

1. Starting with the middle color of the spikes and a long enough yarn tail to weave in later, Ch 2.
2. Slip Stitch into the 1st Ch stitch of the beginning of Part 1, SC into each of the next 2 Ch stitches [3]
3. SC in the top of the 1st spike, Ch 1, SC in the same stitch [2]
4. SC in the next Ch stitch, Slip Stitch into the next Ch stitch, SC in the next Ch stitch [3]
5. Repeat Row 3 and Row 4
6. SC into the side of the next spike, SC in the top of the spike, Ch 1, SC in the same stitch, SC 1 down the remaining side of the spike [4]
7. SC in the next Ch stitch, Slip Stitch into the next Ch stitch, SC in the next Ch stitch [3]
8. Repeat Row 6
9. SC in the next Ch stitch, Slip Stitch into next Ch stitch, SC in the next Ch stitch [3]
10. SC two times up the side of the next spike, SC in the top of the spike, Ch 1, SC in the same

stitch, SC 2 down the remaining side of the spike [6]
11. SC in the next Ch stitch, Slip Stitch into the next Ch stitch, SC in the next Ch stitch [3]
12–25. (7 total times) Repeat Row 10 and Row 11
26–41. (8 total times) Repeat Row 6 and Row 7
42–43. Repeat Row 3 and Row 4
44. Repeat Row 3
45. SC in the next Ch stitch, Sl St in the next Ch stitch, Ch 2 [2]

Fasten off with enough yarn to weave in upon completion.

Part 3: Color 3

As a rule, in this section, you will be Single Crocheting into the top of Part 2's spikes (SC, Ch 1, SC) by always using the Part 3 color to SC into the first SC of the "SC, Ch 1, SC," then you will "SC, Ch 2, Slip Stitch into the 2nd Ch from hook, SC" into the Ch 1 space, and then you will always SKIP the last SC in the Part 2 Color's "SC, Ch 1, SC."

1. Starting with a third Accent Color and a long enough yarn tail to weave in later, Ch 2

2. Slip Stitch into the first Ch stitch of the beginning of Part 2, SC in the next 5 stitches, in the Ch 1 space: (SC, Ch 2, Sl St in the 2nd Ch from hook, SC) [8]

3. Invisible Triple SC Decrease [1]

> You work an Invisible Triple SC Decrease by doing the following: Insert the hook under the FLO of the next 3 stitches, YO, pull through 3 loops, YO, pull through remaining 2 loops.

4. SC in the next stitch, in the Ch 1 space (SC, Ch 2, Sl St in the 2nd Ch from hook, SC) [3]

5. Invisible Triple SC Decrease [1]

6. SC in the next two stitches, in the Ch 1 space (SC, Ch 2, Sl St in the 2nd Ch from hook, SC), SC in the next stitch [5]

7. Invisible Triple SC Decrease [1]

8-9. Repeat Row 6 and Row 7

10. SC in the next three stitches, in the Ch 1 Space (SC, Ch 2, Sl St in the 2nd Ch from hook,

SC), SC in each of the next two stitches [7]

11. Invisible Triple SC Decrease [1]

12-25. (7 total times) Repeat Row 10 and Row 11

26-41. (8 total times) Repeat Row 6 and Row 7

42-43. Repeat Row 4 and Row 5

44. Repeat Row 4

45. SC 2, Slip Stitch in last Ch stitch available, Ch 2 [3]

Fasten off enough yarn to weave in upon completion.

Part 4

1. On either end of the bottom edge of the spikes, using the same color as Part 1 and starting with a long enough yarn tail to weave in later, Ch 2, and then attach with a SC to the 1st Ch

stitch available from Part 3. SC all the way across the flat bottom edge of the scales to the end, Ch 3, Turn

2. Starting in the 2nd Ch from hook, Sl St all the way back to the beginning

Fasten off with a 36 in/91 cm yarn tail. Attachment instructions provided in Assembly on page 144.

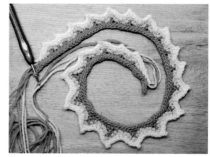

Dragon Back Scales: Three Color

DRAGON BACK SCALES: CIRCLES (MAKE 1)

Option 3

1. Ch 5, [working into the 3rd Ch from hook, make 3 DC, Ch 2, Sl St into the same Ch stitch, Ch 7] x repeat until you've created a long enough piece to stretch from the forehead of the dragon to the tail (as long as you want it to be) [4 per set]

> On your final set, end with a Ch 2 instead of a Ch 7.

Fasten off with 48 in/122 cm yarn tail. Attachment instructions provided in Assembly on page 144.

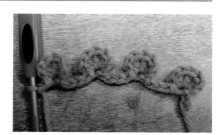

Dragon Back Scales: Circles

DRAGON BACK SCALES: TRIANGLES (MAKE 1)

Option 4

1. Chain approximately 91 stitches (see note), Turn, starting in the 2nd Ch from hook, (SC, Ch 2, Sl St in the 2nd Ch from hook, SC 2, Ch 4, Sl St in the 2nd Ch from hook, Ch 2, Skip 2 Stitches, SC) x 15 [6 per set]

You can make this piece longer or shorter by adding or subtracting chains in multiples of 6.

Fasten off with 48 in/122 cm yarn tail. Attachment instructions provided in Assembly on page 144.

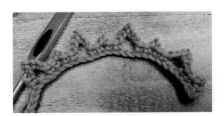

Dragon Back Scales: Triangles

DRAGON BACK SCALES: FULL HEARTS (MAKE 1)

Option 5

1. (Ch 8, working into the 3rd Ch from hook, make Half Trip & Triple Crochet & Ch 2 & HDC & Ch 2 & Triple Crochet & Half Trip & Ch 3 & Sl St), repeat these instructions until you've created a piece long enough to reach from the forehead of the dragon to the tail (or as long as you want it to be) [6 per set]

Fasten off with 48 in/122 cm yarn tail. Attachment instructions provided in Assembly on page 144.

Dragon Back Scales: Full Hearts

DRAGON BACK SCALES: CURVED (MAKE 1)

Option 6

1. Ch 5, Starting in the 2nd Ch from hook, Sl St, Dec, DC [3]
2. (Ch 6, starting in the 2nd Ch from hook, Sl St, Dec, DC) repeat these instructions until you've created a piece long enough to reach from the forehead of the dragon to the tail (or as long as you want it to be) [3 per set]

Fasten off with 48 in/122 cm yarn tail. Attachment instructions provided in Assembly on page 144.

Dragon Back Scales: Curved

DRAGON BELLY: CLASSIC (MAKE 1)

Option 1

NOTE: This piece is extremely variable in length depending on the yarn you use, the hook you use, and your particular tension. Before you fasten off, pin in place to double check it is the desirable length, aiming to end it at the base of the tail around the rear legs. Add or subtract rows as needed.

1. Ch 5, starting in the 2nd Ch from hook, SC 4, Ch 1, Turn [4]
2. SC 4, Ch 1, Turn [4]
3. BLO [SC 4], Ch 1, Turn [4]
4. SC 4, Ch 1, Turn [4]
5-8. Repeat Row 3 and Row 4 a total of two times [4]
9. BLO [SC 4], Ch 1, Turn [4]
10. SC 2, <Dec>, SC 2, Ch 1, Turn [5]
11. BLO [SC 5], Ch 1, Turn [5]
12. SC 5, Ch 1, Turn [5]
13-22. Repeat Row 11 and Row 12 a total of five times [5]
23. BLO [SC 5], Ch 1, Turn [5]
24. SC 2, Inc, SC 2, Ch 1, Turn [6]
25. BLO [SC 6], Ch 1, Turn [6]
26. SC 6, Ch 1, Turn [6]

27–36. Repeat Row 25 and Row 26 a total of five times [6]

37. BLO [SC 6], Ch 1, Turn [6]

38. SC 3, <Dec>, SC 3, Ch 1, Turn [7]

39. BLO [SC 7], Ch 1, Turn [7]

40. SC 7, Ch 1, Turn [7]

41–56. Repeat Row 39 and Row 40 a total of eight times [7]

Place a stitch marker at the end of Row 56. Leave the stitch marker in place until you have verified the length of the Belly piece.

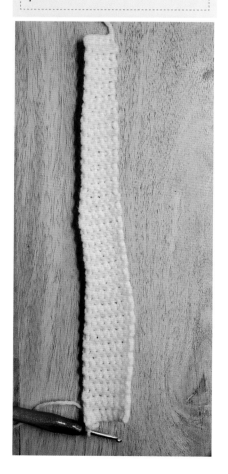

57. BLO [SC 7], Ch 1, Turn [7]

58. SC 2, 2 Dec in 3 SC, SC 2, Ch 1, Turn [6]

59. BLO [SC 6], Ch 1, Turn [6]

60. SC 6, Ch 1, Turn [6]

61–68. Repeat Row 59 and Row 60 a total of four times [6]

69. BLO [SC 2, Dec, SC 2], Ch 1, Turn [5]

70. SC 5, Ch 1, Turn [5]

71. BLO [Dec, SC, Dec] [3]

72. Continue to SC around the edge of the entire belly piece all the way back to where you began (the OC), Inc in the corner at the beginning row, SC 2, Inc in the next corner before continuing to SC down the other side of the belly piece all the way back to where this row began, slip stitch into the

1st Decrease you worked in Row 71.

Fasten off with 48 in/122 cm yarn tail. Attachment instructions provided in Assembly on page 139.

Dragon Belly: Classic

The Belly piece should be placed on the body of the dragon at the throat (not on the head at all) and stretch all the way to the base of the tail (between the back legs of the dragon). You can check the length of the belly piece against the dragon body before single crocheting around the edge to finish the piece. If it is too long, discern how many rows would need to be ripped out to make it the correct length, rip out all the rows back to the end of Row 56, where you placed a stitch marker, and then rip out the number of rows needed to correct the length and continue on to Row 57 from there. Each dragon will come out in slightly different sizes depending on your tension, hook, and the exact weight of yarn you use, and you may need to adjust this general pattern to fit your unique creation.

DRAGON BELLY: CLASSIC WITH ORNAMENTED EDGING (MAKE 1)

Option 2

1. Follow all instructions for the Classic Dragon Belly from Row 1 to Row 71, fasten off the first Accent Color yarn with a 24 in/61 cm yarn tail, and continue to Row 2 below.

2. Starting with a long enough yarn tail to weave in later, attach the second Accent Color yarn to the 1st OC from Row 1 of the Belly piece as shown, SC 3, Inc in the last OC stitch, continuing down the side of the Dragon Belly [5]

3. Work 2 SC along the side, above the 1st ridge of leftover FLO stitches, and then, just below the ridge of FLO stitches, insert your hook just below the FLO stitch ridge near the center of the Belly piece, YO, pull up a loop (make sure you pull up the loop to be even with the rest of the row) and complete a SC as shown. Repeat this technique all the way down the side of the Dragon Belly.

This type of stitch accent worked just below the FLO stitch ridges on the Belly is called a "Spike Stitch." You are accenting the ridges of the work, which is why the Spike Stitch is always worked just below the FLO stitch ridge. You will be working a Spike Stitch on either side of every ridge along the length of the Dragon Belly. You can decide how deep you want to make the Spike Stitch; I recommend only making it 2 to 3 stitches deep in toward the center of the Dragon Belly, as shown.

4. When you reach the bottom of the Dragon Belly, Row 71, work an Inc, SC, Inc, and then continue working back up the other side of the Dragon Belly

5. As you work back up the side of the Dragon Belly to where you attached the yarn at the beginning of Row 2, you will SC 2 and then work the spike stitch just under the FLO stitch ridge, When you get back to where you started this accent color, Slip Stitch to the beginning stitch and then fasten off with 48 in/122 cm yarn tail. Attachment instructions provided in Assembly on page 139.

Dragon Belly: Classic with Ornamented Edging

DRAGON BELLY: HEARTS (MAKE 1)

Option 3

> You may wish to check the length of your starting chain against the belly of your dragon. Your chain will not give you the exact length of the finished piece, but it will give you an estimate. Add or subtract chains in multiples of 6 from the 1st Ch 72 as needed.

1. Ch 72, starting in the 3rd Ch from hook, DC & Half Trip & Triple Crochet, Half Trip & DC, SC, Sl St 3, (Ch 2, starting in the next available Ch stitch of the OC, DC & Half Trip & Triple Crochet, Half Trip & DC, SC, Sl St 3) x 10, Ch 2, starting in the next available Ch stitch of the OC, DC & Half Trip & Triple Crochet, Half Trip DC, SC, Sl St, Ch 2, Turn [106]

2. Starting in the 2nd Ch from Hook, Sl St, Working along the opposite side of the Original Chain, Sl St (in the same stitch you last slip stitched into in Row 1), SC, DC & Half Trip, Triple Crochet & Half Trip & DC, Ch 2 (Sl St 3, SC, DC & Half Trip, Triple Crochet & Half Trip & DC, Ch 2) x 11, Sl St in the same stitch as the last DC you made [107]

Fasten off with 48 in/122 cm yarn tail.

Dragon Belly: Hearts

Attachment instructions provided in Assembly on page 139. When attaching, you can choose to sew along the center and tack down each side of the heart as you sew, or you can sew around the curved edges of the entire belly piece.

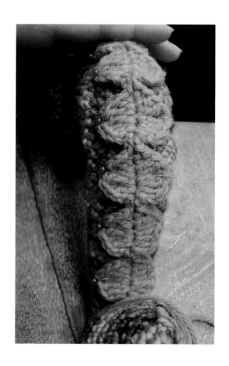

DRAGON NECK ORNAMENTATION: HEART (MAKE 2)

Part 1

> Make 4 of these frills total. Make two pieces using the Accent Color yarn and two pieces using the Main Body Color yarn.

1. Ch 26, Turn, starting in the 2nd Ch from hook, Dec, SC 22, Inc, Ch 1, Turn [25]
2. SC 23, SC/HDC Dec, Ch 1, Turn [24]
3. Dec, SC 21, Inc, Ch 1, Turn [24]
4. SC 22, SC/HDC Dec, Ch 1, Turn [23]
5. Dec, SC 20, Inc, Ch 1, Turn [23]
6. SC 21, SC/HDC Dec, Ch 1, Turn [22]
7. Dec, SC 19, Inc, Ch 1, Turn [22]
8. SC 20, SC/HDC Dec, Ch 1, Turn [21]
9. Dec, SC 19, Ch 1, Turn [20]
10. SC 18, SC/HDC Dec, Ch 1, Turn [19]
11. Dec, SC 17, Ch 1, Turn [18]
12. SC 16, SC/HDC Dec, Ch 1, Turn [17]
13. Dec, SC 15, Ch 1, Turn [16]
14. Dec, SC 12, SC/HDC Dec, Ch 1, Turn [14]
15. Dec, SC 10, SC/HDC Dec, Ch 1, Turn [12]
16. Dec, SC 8, SC/HDC Dec, Ch 1, Turn [10]
17. Dec, SC 6, SC/HDC Dec, Ch 1, Turn [8]
18. Dec, SC 4, SC/HDC Dec, Ch 1, Turn [6]
19. Dec, SC 2, SC/HDC Dec [4]

Fasten off with long enough yarn tail to weave in.

Part 2: Edging

> Hold the Accent Color Frill piece on top of the Body Color Frill piece. Attach the Body Color yarn to the OC, inserting your hook through both Frill pieces. To keep your stitches facing the same way on both sides, attach to the bottom point of the heart for one side and at the top of the heart for the second side.

1. SC around the curved edge of both pieces simultaneously (use increases around the curves anywhere you need to create a smooth curved edge). The Body Color yarn will be the back of the piece, so you want to make one set with the curved parts to the left and the Body Color piece in the back, and one set with the curved parts to the right and the

Body Color piece in the back. At this point you can fasten off with 24 in/61 cm yarn tail, or you can do any of the optional rows.

Dragon Neck Ornamentation: Heart with Row 1 of Edging

Option 1

2. Ch 1, Turn, (Sl St 2, Picot) repeat until you reach the end. Fasten off with a 24 in/61 cm yarn tail to use to sew to attach.

> If you have fewer than 2 stitches for the last repeat of this option, then Sl St to the end.

Dragon Neck Ornamentation: Heart with Option 1 Edging

Option 2

2. Ch 1, Turn, SC, (Ch 4, Sl St in the 2nd Ch from hook, Ch 2, Skip 2 stitches, SC) repeat until you reach the end. Fasten off with 24 in/61 cm yarn tail.

> If you have fewer than 3 stitches for the last repeat of this option, then SC to the end.

After sewing the head and limbs to attach in the assembly, pin the neck ornamentation to attach to the body as shown. Sew to attach using yarn tails, and weave in ends.

Dragon Neck Ornamentation: Heart with Option 2 Edging

DRAGON WING (MAKE 2)

1. Starting with a long enough yarn tail to weave in later, Ch 2, working into the 2nd Ch from hook, SC 5, Ch 1, Turn [5]

2. Inc, SC, Inc, SC, Inc, Ch 1, Turn [8]

3. SC, Inc, SC 2, Inc, SC 3, Ch 1, Turn [10]

4. Inc, SC 4, Inc, SC 3, Inc, Ch 1, Turn [13]

5. SC 3, Inc, SC 4, Inc, SC 4, Ch 1, Turn [15]

6. SC 2, Inc, SC 12, Ch 1, Turn [16]

7. Inc, SC 5, Inc, SC 9, Ch 1, Turn [18]

8. Inc, SC 17, Ch 1, Turn [19]

9. SC 5, Inc, SC 6, Inc, SC 6, Ch 1, Turn [21]

10. SC 21, Ch 1, Turn [21]

11. Inc, SC 7, Inc, SC 7, Inc, SC 4, Ch 1, Turn [24]

12. SC 24, Ch 1, Turn [24]

13. SC 7, Inc, SC 8, Inc, SC 7, Ch 1, Turn [26]

14. Inc, SC 25, Ch 1, Turn [27]

15. Inc, SC 9, Inc, SC 16, Ch 1, Turn [29]

16. SC 29, Ch 1, Turn [29]

17. Inc, SC 8, Inc, SC, Inc, SC 8, Inc, SC, Inc, SC 6, Ch 1, Turn [34]

18–19. (2 rows of) SC 34, Ch 1, Turn [34]

20. Inc, SC 8, Inc, SC 10, Inc, SC, Inc, SC 10, Inc, Ch 1, Turn [39]

21–22. (2 rows of) SC 39, Ch 1, Turn [39]

23. Inc, SC 12, Inc, SC, Inc, SC 12, Inc, SC, Inc, SC 8, Ch 1, Turn [44]

24. SC 44, Ch 1, Turn [44]

25. SC 16, <u>SC</u>, SC 16, <u>SC</u>, SC 10, Ch 1 [44]

> Put stitch markers on the two underlined stitches in this row.

26. Rotate your work to SC up along the unfinished wing edge to the Center Point/OC (OC = Original Chain), start by making a SC around the side of the last SC you made in Row 25 for a total of 25 SC, SC & HDC & SC all in the OC (the HDC here becomes the Center Point), SC (about) 25 back down along the other side of the unfinished wing edge. (The very last SC should be into the side of the very last available stitch.) [53]

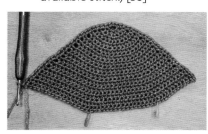

27. Ch 11, Starting in the 2nd Ch from hook, SC 10 along the Chain stitches, SC 16 along the wing edge, Sl St in the next stitch (the slip stitch should be into the stitch just before the nearest marked stitch), Ch 1, Turn [26]

> This row, and the rest in this section, do not count the Slip Stitches as stitches because you will not be crocheting into them again.

28. Skip the Slip Stitch, SC 24, Dec, Ch 1, Turn [25]

29. SC 23, Sl St, Ch 1, Turn [23]

30. Skip the Slip Stitch, SC 21, Dec, Ch 1, Turn [22]

31. SC 20, Sl St, Ch 1, Turn [20]

32. Skip the Slip Stitch, SC 18, Dec, Ch 1, Turn [19]

33. SC 17, Sl St, Ch 1, Turn [17]

34. Skip the Slip Stitch, SC 15, Dec, Ch 1, Turn [16]

35. SC 14, Sl St, Ch 1, Turn [14]

36. Skip the Slip Stitch, SC 12, Dec, Ch 1, Turn [13]

37. SC 11, Sl St, Ch 1, Turn [11]

38. Skip the Slip Stitch, SC 9, Dec, Ch 1, Turn [10]

39. SC 8, Sl St, Ch 1, Turn [8]

40. Skip the Slip Stitch, SC 6, Dec, Ch 1, Turn [7]

41. SC 5, Sl St, Ch 1, Turn [5]

42. Skip the Slip Stitch, SC 3, Dec, Ch 1, Turn [4]

43. SC 2, Sl St, Ch 1, Turn [2]

44. Skip the Slip Stitch, Dec, Ch 3, Turn [1]

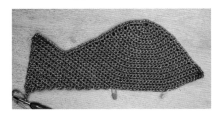

45. Proceed along unfinished wing edge: Half Trip Inc, DC, HDC, SC until three spaces before the stitch marker, HDC, DC, Half Trip Inc, Triple Crochet in the Marked Stitch (use the stitch marker to mark this stitch), Half Trip Inc, DC, HDC 2, SC 2, Sl St 4, SC 2, HDC 2, DC, Half Trip Inc, Triple Crochet in Marked Stitch (use the stitch marker to mark this stitch), Half Trip & DC, HDC 2, SC, Sl St 2, SC, HDC 2, DC & Half Trip, Triple Crochet in last possible stitch

Fasten off the wing panel, leaving a long enough yarn tail to weave in.

Finishing
Make ONE LEFT WING and ONE RIGHT WING

1. Starting with a long enough yarn tail to weave in later, attach the Main Body Color yarn to the HDC in Row 26 of the Dragon Wing, make 1 SC in that stitch.

2. Fold the Dragon Wing so that a line is visible from the OSC (OSC = Original Single Crochet, the one you just made in Row 1) to the middle Triple Crochet marked by the Stitch marker in Row 45 of the Dragon Wing.

SC with the Main Body Color yarn along that fold to the bottom edge of the wing, Ch 3, Turn, starting in the 2nd Ch from hook, Sl St, SC, and then Slip Stitch all the way back along that row of SC to the OSC.

3. Fold the Dragon Wing so that a line is visible from the OSC to the next middle Triple Crochet marked by the second stitch marker in Row 45 of the Dragon Wings. SC with the Main Body Color yarn along that fold to the bottom edge of the wing, Ch 3, Turn, starting in the 2nd Ch from hook, Sl St, SC, and then Slip Stitch all the way back along that row of SC to the OSC.

Do not fasten off. Proceed to the next applicable section for either the Assembly of the LEFT wing or the Assembly of the RIGHT wing. When you repeat the instructions above to finish a second wing, stitch on the opposite side of the wing—do not make 2 wings of the same orientation.

Assembly

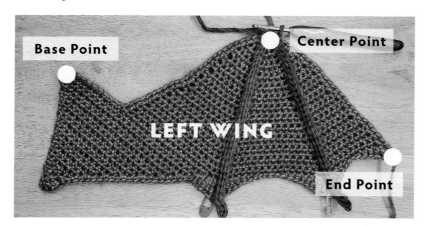

Right Wing

1. Ch 1, SC all the way to the left of where you are to the End Point of the wing. When you reach the End Point, Ch 4, Turn, starting in the 2nd Ch from hook, SC 3, SC back along the Wing Edge to the Center Point. This creates 2 rows of Body Color yarn along the Center to the End Point of the wing.

2. The Right Wing continues by single crocheting along the Wing Edge to the middle between the Center Point and the Base

Point, and then switching to HDC stitches and continuing to the Base Point. When you reach the Base Point, Ch 2, Turn, HDC back along the Wing Edge to the middle between the Base Point and the Center Point, switch to SC and continue up to the Center Point. This creates 2 rows of Body Color yarn along the Center to Base Point of the wing.

3. The Right Wing continues by crocheting from the Center Point to the End Point again. When you reach the End Point, Ch 1, Turn, and then SC back to the

Center Point. This creates a total of 4 rows of Body Color yarn along the Center to End Point of the wing.

4. The Right Wing continues by single crocheting to 2 stitches just before the middle between the Center Point to the Base Point. Switch to HDC and continue to the Base Point. When you reach the Base Point, Ch 2, Turn, and then HDC back along the previous HDC stitches, switch to SC where the HDC stitches end and SC to the Center Point. This creates a total of 4 rows of Body

Color yarn along the Center to the Base Point of the wing.

5. To continue the Right Wing, Sl St in the next stitch, Ch 1, Turn, Skip the Slip Stitch and single crochet again from the Center Point all the way to the Base Point. When you reach the Base Point, Ch 2, Turn, and then HDC back along the Wing Edge to the middle between the Base Point and the Center Point, switch to SC and continue up to the center point. This creates 6 total rows of Body Color yarn along the Center to Base Point of the wing.

6. Then SC from the Center Point to the End Point again. This creates 5 total rows of Body color Yarn along the Center to End Point of the Wing. You finish at the End point.

Fasten off with approximately 30 in/76 cm of yarn to use to sew the wing to the wing wire and secure the wing to the body of the Dragon.

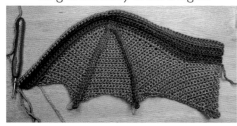

Dragon Right Wing

Left Wing

1. When you are making the Left Wing, you will be crocheting toward the Base Point of the wing. Single crochet till the middle between the Center Point and the Base Point, and then switch to HDC as you continue to the Base Point. When you reach the Base Point, Ch 2, Turn, and then HDC back along the Wing Edge to the middle point between the base Point and the Center Point, switch to SC and continue until you reach the Center Point. This creates 2 rows of Body Color yarn along the Center to Base Point of the wing.

2. To continue the Left Wing, single crochet along the wing edge from the Center Point to the End Point (capture extraneous yarn tails as you go, to avoid weaving in later). When you reach the End Point, Ch 4, Turn, SC in 2nd Ch from hook, SC in next 2 Chain stitches, SC back along the Wing Edge to the Center Point. This creates 2 rows of Body Color yarn along the Center to End Point of the wing.

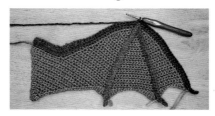

3. To continue the Left Wing, single crochet to 2 stitches before the middle between the Center Point and the Base Point. Switch to HDC and continue to the

Base Point. When you reach the Base Point, Ch 2, Turn, and then HDC back along the previous HDC stitches, switch to SC and continue to the Center Point. This creates 4 total rows of Body Color yarn along the Center to Base Point of the wing.

4. Then SC from the Center Point to the End Point again. When you reach the End Point, Ch 1, Turn, and then SC back along the Wing Edge to the Center Point. This creates 4 total rows of Body Color yarn along the Center to End Point of the wing.

5. To continue the Left Wing, single crochet from the Center Point to the Base Point. When you reach the Base Point, Ch 2, Turn, and then HDC back along the Wing Edge to the middle between the Base Point and the Center Point, switch to SC and continue up to the center Point. This creates 6 total rows of Body Color yarn along the Center to Base Point of the wing.

6. Then SC from the Center Point to the End Point again. This

creates 5 total rows of Body Color yarn along the Center to End Point of the wing. You finish at the End point.

Fasten off with approximately 36 in/91 cm of yarn tail. You will use this during assembly to sew the wing to the wing wire and secure the wing to the body of the Dragon.

Dragon Left Wing

DRAGON TAIL ORNAMENTATION: SPADE (MAKE 1)

Option 1

1. Start with long enough yarn tail to weave in later, Ch 13, Turn, starting in the 2nd Ch from hook, SC 5, Inc x 2, SC 4, Sl St, Ch 1, Turn [14]

2. Skip the Slip Stitch, SC, HDC 3, HDC & SC, Inc x 2, SC & HDC, HDC 3, SC, Sl St, Ch 1, Turn [17]

3. Skip the Slip Stitch, HDC & DC & Half Trip, Triple Crochet Increase, Triple Crochet & Half Trip, DC, HDC, HDC & SC, Inc, HDC & DC, Ch 2, Sl St in the 2nd

Ch from hook, Sl St in the top of the last DC stitch you made, DC & HDC, Inc, SC & HDC, HDC, DC, Half Trip & Triple Crochet, Triple Crochet Increase, Half Trip & DC, & HDC, Ch 1, Sl St in the 1st Chain from the OC [33]

Fasten off with 12 in/30 cm yarn tail. Attachment instructions provided in Assembly on page 145.

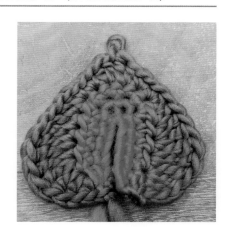

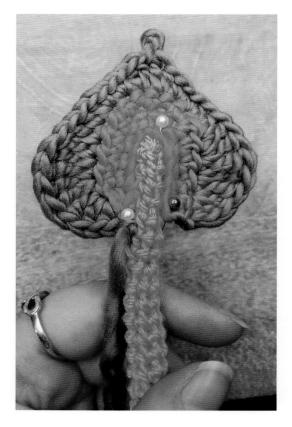

DRAGON TAIL ORNAMENTATION: ARROW (MAKE 2)

Option 2

1. Start with a long enough yarn tail to weave in later, Ch 11, Turn, starting in the 2nd Ch from hook, SC 2, HDC 2, DC 2, Half Trip x 2, Triple Crochet x 2, Ch 4, Turn [10]
2. Sl St in the 2nd Ch from hook, SC, HDC 5, SC 5, SC & HDC & DC [15]

Fasten off with 12 in/30 cm yarn tail. Attachment instructions provided in Assembly on page 145.

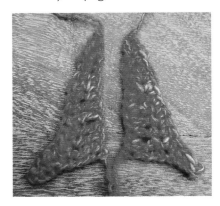

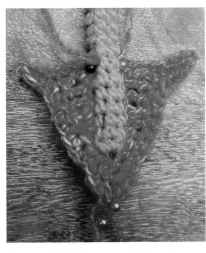

Dragon Tail Ornamentation: Arrow

DRAGON TAIL ORNAMENTATION: FLAT TRIPLE SPIKES (MAKE 1, 2, OR 3)

Option 3

1. Ch 4, Turn, starting in the 2nd Ch from hook, Sl St, SC, HDC [3]
2. Ch 6, Turn, starting in the 2nd Ch from hook, Sl St, SC, HDC 2, DC [5]
3. Ch 8, Turn, starting in the 2nd Ch from hook, Sl St, SC 2, HDC 2, DC 2 [7]

Fasten off with 12 in/30 cm yarn tail. Attachment instructions provided in Assembly on page 145.

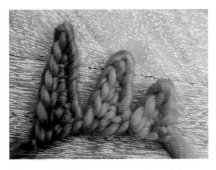

Dragon Tail Ornamentation: Flat Triple Spikes

DRAGON TAIL ORNAMENTATION: 5-POINTED LEAF (MAKE 2)

Option 4
Part 1

1. Starting with Accent Color yarn and a long enough yarn tail to weave in later, Ch 9, starting in the 2nd Ch from hook, SC 6, HDC Dec, Ch 1, Turn [7]
2. Dec, SC 5, Ch 1, Turn [6]
3. HDC & SC, SC 3, Dec, Ch 1, Turn [6]
4. Dec, SC 2, Inc, SC & DC, Ch 1, Turn [7]
5. SC 5, Dec, Ch 1, Turn [6]

Place a stitch marker into the side of the 1st SC from this row. This is one of the rows you will return to with the Accent Color to complete this piece.

6. Dec, SC 4, Ch 1, Turn [5]
7. SC 3, Dec, Ch 1, Turn [4]
8. Dec, SC 2, Ch 1, Turn [3]
9. SC, Dec, Ch 1, Turn [2]
10. Dec, Ch 2, Turn [1]

11. Starting in the 2nd Ch from hook, SC 7 down straight unfinished side, Ch 1, Turn [7]

12. SC 7, Ch 2, Pivot work [7]

Row 13 is a little bit fluid. The <DC Dec> must land on either side of where the stitch marker from Row 5 is. If you find you need fewer stitches to end up with the <DC Dec> on either side of the stitch marker, then leave out a DC before the <DC Dec>. If you need more, add a DC before the <DC Dec>. The SC & HDC at the end of Row 13 must fall at the end of the piece so that Row 14 can cover the remaining stitches along what was the original chain from Row 1. Do not remove the stitch marker.

13A. Working around the outer edge, HDC (around the side of the last SC you made) [1]

13B. SC 4 [4]
13C. HDC, DC 3 [4]
13D. <DC Dec>, DC & HDC, SC, SC 2 [6]
13E. SC & HDC, Ch 1, Pivot Work [1] [17]

14. SC 7, Inc [9]

This row is worked into the opposite side of your starting chain.

Fasten off with 6 in/15 cm yarn tail; make a second Part 1 piece.

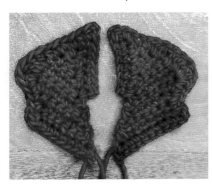

Part 2

Starting with a long enough yarn tail to weave in later, attach Main Color yarn to the last stitch you made in Row 14 on one of the two pieces you made, Ch 1.

1. SC 10, Ch 2, Turn [10]

2. Starting in the 2nd Ch from hook, Sl St 11, Ch 1, pivot piece [11]

3. Inc in OC, Ch 1, pivot piece [2]

4. SC approximately 7 along unfinished edge of the Part 1 piece until you reach the row with the stitch marked in it (the stitch marker will be in the opposite side of this row) [7]

5. Fold the piece along the line of stitches created in the row with the stitch marker, topped by the <DC Dec> from Row 13 above, SC along this folded edge to the edge of the work (approximately SC 10), Ch 2 at the end [10]

6. Starting in the 2nd Ch from hook, (approximately) Sl St 11, Ch 1, pivot piece [11]

7. SC 2 to the last straight edge of the piece, Ch 1, pivot piece [2]

8. Match the 1st stitches of Row 12 (from Part 1) on each of your tail pieces (this will create a perfectly symmetrical tail piece), SC along the straight edge to connect them (approximately SC 7), Inc (the increase should be in the last available stitch space), Ch 2, Turn [9]

9. Starting in the 2nd Ch from hook, Sl St 10 back along the same set of stitches, pivot piece [10]

10. Now repeat all steps you did on the first Part 1 piece for the second Part 1 piece, starting with the SC 2 to the last straight edge of the piece, Ch 1, pivot Piece [2]

11. Fold the piece along the line of stitches created in the row with the stitch marker, topped by the <DC Dec> from Row 13 above. SC along this folded edge to the edge (approximately SC 10), Ch 2 at the end, Turn [10]

12. Starting in the 2nd Ch from hook, (approximately) Sl St 11 [11]

13. SC 7, Inc in the OC, Ch 1, pivot piece [9]

14. SC along the OC row (approximately SC 10), Ch 2 at the end [10]

15. Starting in the 2nd Ch from hook, Sl St 11 [11]

Fasten off with 18 in/46 cm yarn tail. Attachment instructions provided in Assembly on page 145.

Dragon Tail Ornamentation: 5-Pointed Leaf

DRAGON TAIL ORNAMENTATION: CRESCENT (MAKE 2)

Option 5

1. Starting with a long enough yarn tail to weave in later, Ch 2, Turn, starting in the 2nd Ch from hook, Inc, Ch 1, Turn [2]

2. Inc, SC, Ch 1, Turn [3]

3. SC 3, Ch 1, Turn [3]

4. Inc, SC, Ch 1, Turn [3]

5. SC 3, Ch 1, Turn [3]

6. Inc, SC, SC/HDC Dec & HDC, Ch 1, Turn [5]

7. SC 5, Ch 1, Turn [5]

8. Inc, SC 2, Ch 1, Turn [4]

9. SC 4, Ch 1, Turn [4]

10. Inc, SC 2, SC/HDC Dec & HDC, SC, Ch 1, Turn [7]

11. SC 7, Ch 1, Turn [7]

12. SC 5, Ch 1, Turn [5]

13. SC 5, Ch 1, Turn [5]

14. SC 3, Ch 1, Turn [3]

15. SC 3, Ch 1, Turn [3]

16. SC, Ch 1, Turn [1]

17. SC, Ch 1, Turn [1]

18. (SC/HDC Dec & HDC) x 3, SC, Ch 1, pivot work [7]

19. SC (approximately 9) along the unfinished edge of the work to the OC [9]

20. Ch 2, Sl St in the 2nd Ch from hook, SC in the same stitch as your last SC, capture the starting yarn tail of the piece as you SC along the curved unfinished edge of the work, making an increase every 4th or 5th stitch. [21]

Fasten off with 12 in/30 cm yarn tail; make second piece. Attachment instructions provided in Assembly on page 145.

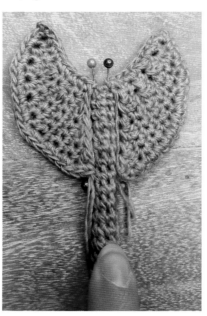

Dragon Tail Ornamentation: Crescent

DRAGON TAIL ORNAMENTATION: RIDGED FAN (MAKE 2)

Option 6

1. Starting with a long enough yarn tail to weave in later, Ch 2, Turn, starting in the 2nd Ch from hook, Inc, Ch 1, Turn [2]

2. Inc, Sc, Ch 1, Turn [3]

3. SC 3, Ch 1, Turn [3]

4. Inc, SC, Ch 1, Turn [3]

5. SC 3, Ch 1, Turn [3]

6. Inc, Ch 1, Turn [2]

7. SC 2, Ch 1, Turn [2]

8. Inc, (SC/HDC Dec & HDC) x 2, Ch 1, Turn [6]

9. SC 6, Ch 1, Turn [6]

10. Inc, SC 3, Ch 1, Turn [5]

11. SC 5, Ch 1, Turn [5]

12. Inc, SC 2, Ch 1, Turn [4]

13. SC 4, Ch 1, Turn [4]

14. Inc, SC, Ch 1, Turn [3]

15. SC 3, Ch 1, Turn [3]

16. Inc, Ch 1, Turn [2]

17. SC 2, Ch 1, Turn [2]

18. Inc, (SC/HDC Dec & HDC) x 4, SC, Ch 1, Turn [11]

19. SC 11, Ch 1, Turn [11]

20. SC 9, Ch 1, Turn [9]

21. SC 9, Ch 1, Turn [9]

22. SC 7, Ch 1, Turn [7]

23. SC 7, Ch 1, Turn [7]

24. SC 5, Ch 1, Turn [5]

25. SC 5, Ch 1, Turn [5]
26. SC 3, Ch 1, Turn [3]
27. SC 3, Ch 1, Turn [3]
28. SC, Ch 1, Turn [1]
29. SC, Ch 1, Turn [1]
30. (SC/HDC Dec & HDC) x 5, SC, Ch 1, Turn [11]
31. SC 11 [11]

Fasten off with 12 in/30 cm yarn tail; make a second piece.

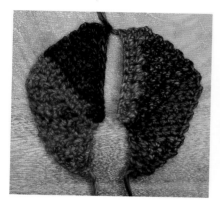

32. Identify the straight SC rows within the pieces that come after the (SC/HDC Dec & HDC) heavy rows. You will fold the piece along these rows and SC around the fold to the end, Ch 2 at the end, Turn, Sl St in the 2nd Ch from hook, and slip stitch all the way back. To start, attach the Main Color yarn with a long enough yarn tail to weave in later at the base of the 1st straight row as pictured.

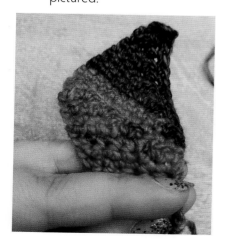

33. Make a Decrease to get to the start of the next straight row.

34. Identify the next straight row, and repeat SC along the fold on that line, Ch 2, Turn, Sl St in the 2nd Ch from hook, Sl St all the way back.

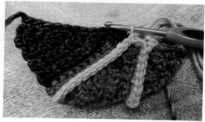

35. Make another Decrease to get to the straight edge.

36. Align the second tail piece with the 1st, SC along the straight edge of both pieces at once, Ch 2, Turn, Sl St in the 2nd Ch from hook, Sl St all the way back.

37. Make a Decrease to get to the next straight edge to mirror the last one, SC along the folded straight edge, Ch 2, Turn, Sl St in 2nd Ch from hook, Sl St all the way back.

38. Make a Decrease to get to the next straight edge to mirror the first one you made, SC along the folded straight edge, Ch 2, Turn, Sl St in the 2nd Ch from hook, Sl St all the way back.

Fasten off with 18 in/46 cm yarn tail. Attachment instructions provided in Assembly on page 145.

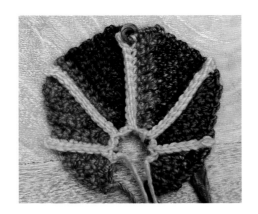

Dragon Tail Ornamentation:
Ridged Fan

DRAGON TAIL ORNAMENTATION: HEART (MAKE 2)

Option 7

1. Starting with a long enough yarn tail to weave in later, Ch 3, Turn, working into the 3rd Ch from hook, DC 4, Ch 2, Turn [4]

> The DC 4 are all worked into the same chain. The final Ch 2 is a turning chain. Do not work into it in the next row.

2. DC & HDC, HDC Inc, HDC & DC, DC 5 in the next available stitch, starting in the same stitch just worked and ending in the OC, HDC/DC Dec, Ch 1, Turn [12]

3. SC & HDC, HDC & DC, DC Inc x 4, DC & HDC, HDC, SC 3, SC & HDC & DC, Ch 1, Turn [21]

4. HDC & SC, SC 3, HDC 4, HDC & DC, DC Inc x 3, DC, DC Inc, DC, DC Inc, DC & HDC, SC 2, Sl St 2 [29]

Fasten off with 24 in/61 cm yarn tail. Attachment instructions provided in Assembly on page 145.

Dragon Tail Ornamentation: Heart

DRAGON ASSEMBLY

I. Pin the Belly in place along the front, center of the body, and sew to attach by whipstitching around the entire edge of the belly using the yarn tail. Anchor it in a few spots in the center of the belly along its length to ensure it doesn't stretch or shift. Weave in the end.

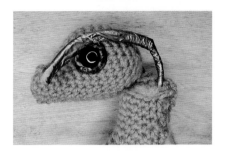

2. Compare the wire extending beyond the neck of the dragon to the head (back of the head to the nose tip). Fold the wire over on itself so that it will be a couple of centimeters shorter than the length of the head. Secure the wire to itself with a thin strip of duct tape.

Slide the head onto the spinal wire through the hole at the back of the head, aligning the wire along the top of the inside of the head, just under the surface of the yarn to the nose. Pull the neck flap up over the hole in the back of the head and the wire, and pin in place.

Sew to attach using a yarn tail; continue using the yarn tail to soft sculpt the head so that the eyes of the dragon are slightly inset. You can do this by stitching back and forth through the head around the eyes and pulling gently to pull the eyes inward into the head. Weave in ends.

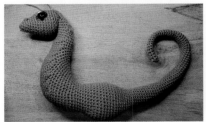

For a video demonstration of soft sculpting, go here: https://www.youtube.com/watch?v=975uCkOJNwE&t=1s

3. For a video demonstration of pinning, go here: https://www.youtube.com/watch?v=EXclcw2viO4

For a video demonstration of sewing limbs to attach, go here: https://www.youtube.com/watch?v=1MaLj7IPvU8

4. Pin to attach the back leg pieces. If you are making the **sitting**, **laying down**, or **begging dragon** position, then you will be using the upper rear leg and the lower rear foot pieces. Pin the upper rear leg part to the body first, and then pin the foot under the upper rear leg. The foot should be placed partially underneath the back leg piece, so that only part of the foot and the toes stick out from underneath the rounded upper part of the rear leg. The upper leg, once sewn on, should look seamless if you use small, neat stitches. Sew along every edge where the back foot touches the rear leg piece. Do not sew the upper rear leg to the body yet.

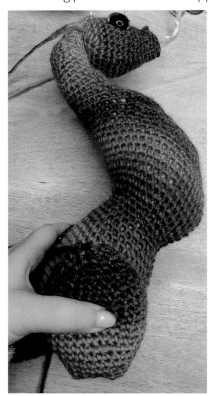

Sitting/Begging Rear Leg

Laying Down Rear Leg

If you are using the **standing rear leg** without wire, press the upper part of the leg against the body, and pin to attach (see step 3 video if you need help). If the rear legs are standing legs with wire, then hold the rear leg against the dragon body and figure out exactly where the wire that exits the inside edge of the leg should be inserted into the dragon's body. You can trim the leg wire to be short and hidden inside the dragon body. Pin both the rear and the front legs without sewing anything in order to balance the dragon before committing to the placement. In some configurations, it is easier to place the front legs first, but doing both before sewing is key.

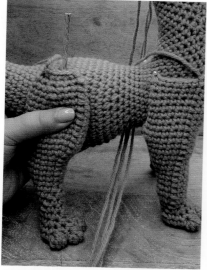

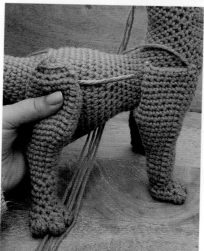

Standing Rear Leg

5. Take the front legs, pin in place. It is important to make sure that all four feet are level with each other to ensure the dragon sits or stands with stability.

If the **front legs** are **standing legs** without wire, press the upper part of the leg against the body, and pin to attach (see video if you need help). If the front legs are standing legs with wire, then hold the front leg against the dragon body and figure out exactly where the wire that exits the inside edge of the leg should be inserted into the dragon's body. You can trim the leg wire to be short and hidden inside the dragon body, or you can leave the wire long and have the wire inserted into the body and then exit the dragon body at the point where the wing will sprout from the shoulder to function as another wing support wire.

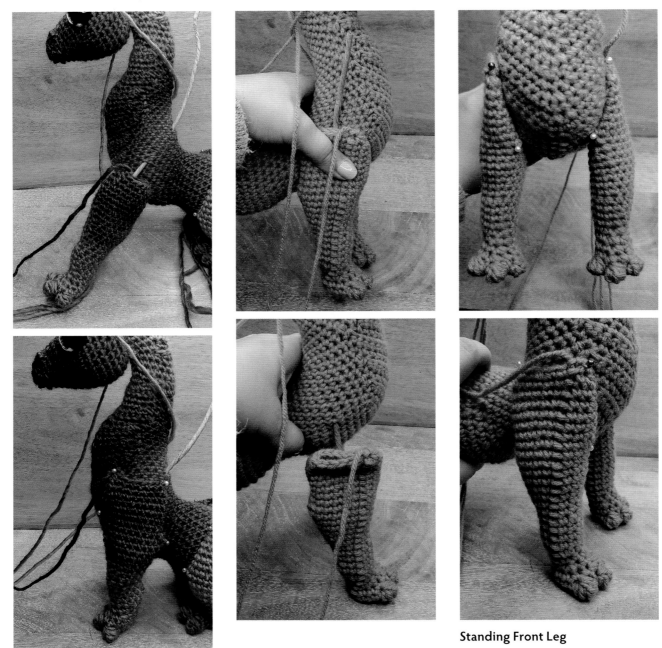

Sitting Dragon with Standing Front Leg

Standing Front Leg

If you are using the **upper front leg** with either the **laying down leg** or the **begging leg**, pin the upper part to attach first, and then pin the lower part to attach to the upper part. The lower part of the leg can and will slightly touch the body, but it should mostly be located immediately below and fully overlapping the upper part of the front leg.

Laying Down Front Legs

Standing and Begging Front Legs

Raised/Begging Front Leg

6. Once you are satisfied with the placement and balance of the Dragon, sew all limbs in place. Keep checking balance as you sew to attach. Weave in ends.

7. If you are using a head plate, pin the head plate in place and sew to attach.

Head Plate

Fancy Head Plate

8. If you are using back scales, pin the back scales in place along the spine of the dragon from the forehead to the tail and sew to attach using the yarn tail; weave in ends.

Curved Back Scales

Three-Color Back Scales

9. Pin any and all head ornamentations in place (Cheek Frills, Eyelids, etc.). Do not sew to attach until all of your Dragon head/face options are pinned in place to verify final placement.

Pin **horns** to attach. Wire is optional inside the horns to help you shape them even more dramatically if you want. You do not need wire or stuffing in the horns, but you can add them if desired.

Pin the **ears** to attach.

Spiral Horns, Three-Color Back Scales, Classic Belly, Curly Eyelids, Long Cheek Frills, and Short Cheek Frills

Simple Horns, One-Color Back Scales, Classic Belly with Ornamental Edging, Simple Eyelids, and Fin Ears

Large Spiral Horns, One-Color Back Scales, Classic Belly with Ornamental Edging, Head Plate, and Long Droopy Ears

10. Sew all face ornamentation/ horns/ears in place one at a time; weave in ends as you go, starting with the pieces that are closest to the head (like eyelids or ears).

11. Pin any tail ornamentation in place and sew to attach using yarn tails; weave in ends. If using ornamentation consisting of two pieces, pin these on either side of the tail, mirroring one another.

12. Dragon Wing Assembly:

First, bend the wire along the curvature of the wing edge. Do not be afraid to bend the wire to be slightly longer than your relaxed crocheted wing is. It is good to stretch the edges of the crocheted piece as you sew it to encase the wire; you do not want the wing to be loose on the wire. Also bend the end of the wire

at the end point of the wing over on itself to prevent it from poking out of the work once sewn; secure the wire to itself with duct tape. Compare the wire to the wing edge and mark the wire at the base of the wing so that you will know how much wire length to insert into the body of the dragon.

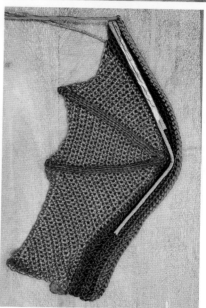

Then insert the long straight part of the wire into the shoulder of the dragon up to the mark you made. Insert the wire for the opposite wing. Using thin strips of duct tape, wrap the two wires together on either side of the dragon body.

Cut another piece of wire. It can be as long as you want (I have used as long as another full 18 in/46 cm piece, or it can be as short as 6 in/15 cm). Insert this piece of wire approximately 3 stitches away from the first insertion point of the wing wires. Tape it to secure it to the existing wing wires. This will create 2 points of entry for the wing wires and will prevent spinning or slipping. If you want to be even more proactive about support, you can insert a third wire at a third entry point.

Pin the Wing in place around the wire and along the body of the dragon. Using a darning needle, stitch in place. Use small stitches. Pull the stitches tight. Encase the wire in the crochet work fully all the way to the shoulder of the dragon.

Then anchor the rest of the wing to the body along the spine of the dragon. Sew in place.

As an alternative, you could also use the Phoenix wings (page 205) as Dragon wings, for a unique, feathered dragon!

Dragon with Phoenix Wings

Kraken

The Kraken is an enormous sea monster, similar to a giant squid or octopus, said to appear off the coasts of Norway.

SIZE:

A Kraken from this pattern is 10 in/25.5 tall from bottom of the body to the top, 20 in/ 51 cm long from top of the body to end of the regular tentacles, and 5 in/12.5 cm wide from side to side of the head.

MATERIALS

>> Yarn: See table on page 150 to choose the parts you will make for your Kraken and find the yarn amounts needed for each piece. All yarn is #4 medium/worsted weight, and all yarn amounts are approximate.

>> G (4 mm) crochet hook

>> 30 mm safety eyes

>> Fiberfill stuffing

>> Darning needle

>> Pins

>> Scissors

INSTRUCTIONS

Look at the Gallery, the chart below, and the parts patterns photos to decide the pieces you want to make for your Kraken. For the Kraken, you have the option to make a Simple Bottom or Advanced Bottom, and optional eyelids. Crochet all of the parts of your Kraken following the instructions on pages 152–159, and then proceed to Kraken Assembly on page 160 to put them all together.

PARTS TO MAKE	PAGE NO.	YARN COLOR	NUMBER TO MAKE	APPROX. AMOUNT
Kraken Head Top	152	Main Color	1	308 yd/281.75 m, plus 40 yd/36.5 m more for use with the advanced bottom
Kraken Side Fin	158	Main or Accent Color	2	26 yd/23.75 m for 2 fins
Kraken Eyelid (optional)	159	Main or Accent Color	2	5 yd/4.5 m for 2 eyelids
Kraken Head Fin	159	Main or Accent Color	1	8 yd/7.25 m
Kraken Bottom: Choose one of the following				
Simple Bottom	155	Main Color	1	15 yd/13.75 m
Advanced Bottom	155	Main Color, Accent Color	1	40 yd/36.5 m Main Color, 256 yd/234 m Accent Color

GALLERY

Kraken with Advanced Bottom

Kraken with Advanced Bottom

Kraken with Simple Bottom

Kraken with Simple Bottom

Kraken Parts Patterns

KRAKEN HEAD TOP

The head is made in spiral. Do not Sl St, Ch 1 join at the end of each row.

1. SC 8 in Magic Circle [8]
2. (SC, Inc) x 4 [12]
3. (SC 2, Inc) x 4 [16]
4. (SC 3, Inc) x 4 [20]
5. SC 20 [20]
6. (SC 3, Inc) x 5 [25]
7. (SC 2, Inc, SC 2) x 5 [30]
8. (SC 5, Inc) x 5 [35]
9. SC 35 [35]
10. SC 3, Inc, (SC 6, Inc) x 4, SC 3 [40]
11. (SC 9, Inc) x 4 [44]
12. SC 5, Inc, (SC 10, Inc) x 3, SC 5 [48]
13. SC 48 [48]
14. (SC 7, Inc) x 6 [54]
15. SC 4, Inc, (SC 8, Inc) x 5, SC 4 [60]
16. (SC 9, Inc) x 6 [66]
17–40. (24 rows of) SC 66 [66]
41. Dec, SC 62, Dec [64]
42. (SC 2, Dec) x 4, SC 32, (SC 2, Dec) x 4 [56]
43. SC 56 [56]
44. (SC 2, Dec) x 4, SC 24, (SC 2, Dec) x 4 [48]
45. SC 21, (SC, Inc, SC) x 4, SC 15 [52]
46. SC, Dec, (SC 2, Dec) x 4, SC 20, (SC 2, Dec) x 3, SC [44]
47. SC 14, (Inc, SC 4) x 4, SC 10 [48]
48. SC, Dec, (SC 2, Dec) x 4, SC 16, (SC 2, Dec) x 3, SC [40]
49. (SC 4, Inc) x 8 [48]
50. (SC 5, Inc) x 8 [56]

Front view

Side view

51. (SC 13, Inc) x 4 [60]

Insert 30 mm eyes between Row 45 and Row 46, with 13 stitch spaces between the posts.

In Row 52, you will begin to form the tentacles. Tentacle rows (Rows 52–54) are broken up into sub-rows to make them easier to read. You will work every sub-row.

52A. Sl St 4, Ch 51, Turn, starting in the 2nd Ch from the hook, SC 25, HDC 25, Skip 1 stitch on the body [54]
52B. Sl St 6, Ch 51, starting in the 2nd Ch from the hook, SC 25, HDC 25, Skip 1 stitch on the body [56]

52C. Sl St 6, Ch 51, Turn, starting in the 2nd Ch from the hook, SC 25, HDC 25, Skip 1 stitch on the body [56]

52D. Sl St 4, Ch 101, Turn, starting in the 2nd Ch from hook, SC 5, HDC 5, SC 5, Ch 1, Turn [19]

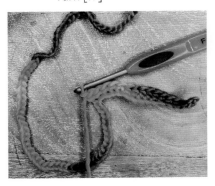

52E. SC 4, HDC 7, SC 3, Inc, continue to crochet around to the other side of the Ch stitches, Inc, SC 3, HDC 7, SC 3, Sl St, Ch 1, Turn [32]

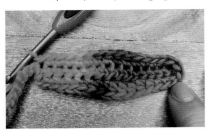

52F. Skip the Slip Stitch, SC 2, HDC 9, SC 3, Inc x 2, SC 3, HDC 9, SC 2, SC/HDC Dec & SC, SC 40, HDC 44 [118]

> Do not skip the next stitch on the body: in the next sub-row you will start into the next available body stitch.

52G. Sl St 4, Ch 51, Turn, starting in the 2nd Ch from hook, SC 25, HDC 25, Skip 1 stitch [54]

52H. Sl St 6, Ch 51, Turn, starting in the 2nd Ch from hook, SC 25, HDC 25, Skip 1 stitch [56]

52I. Sl St 4, Ch 101, Turn, starting in the 2nd Ch from hook, SC 5, HDC 5, SC 5, Ch 1, Turn [19]

52J. SC 4, HDC 7, SC 3, Inc, continue to crochet around to the other side of the Ch stitches, Inc, SC 3, HDC 7, SC 3, Sl St, Ch 1, Turn [32]

52K. Skip the Slip Stitch, SC 2, HDC 9, SC 3, Inc x 2, SC 3, HDC 9, SC 2, SC/HDC Dec & SC, SC 40, HDC 44 [118]

52L. Sl St 4, Ch 51, Turn, starting in the 2nd Ch from hook, SC 25, HDC 25, Skip 1 stitch [54]

52M. Sl St 6, Ch 51, Turn, starting in the 2nd Ch from hook, SC 25, HDC 25, Skip 1 stitch [56]

52П. Sl St 6, Ch 51, Turn, starting in the 2nd Ch from hook, SC 25, HDC 25, Skip 1 stitch, Sl St 2 [58]

> In the following rows, you will not work into the two extra-long tentacles. Only work into the eight shorter tentacles/arms.

53A. Dec, SC 2, HDC 35, SC 14, Inc x 2, SC 35, HDC 14 [105]

> When working over the top of Slip Stitches, insert your hook into the top of the stitch below (the same stitch you worked the Sl St into) and work your stitch so that it completely encases the Sl St.

53B. SC 2, Dec, SC 2, HDC 35, SC 14, Inc x 2, SC 35, HDC 14 [107]

53C. SC 2, Dec, SC 2, HDC 35, SC 14, Inc x 2, SC 35, HDC 14 [107]

53D. SC 2, Dec, Skip the next (extra-long) tentacle arm, Dec, SC 2, HDC 35, SC 14, Inc x 2, SC 35, HDC 14 [108]

> In this row, the extra-long tentacle arm will be pushed behind your work. You want it to look like the tentacle arm is coming out from more of the center of the kraken than the outer edge.

53E. SC 2, Dec, SC 2, HDC 35, SC 14, Inc x 2, SC 35, HDC 14 [107]

53F. SC 2, Dec, Skip the next (extra-long) tentacle arm, Dec, SC 2, HDC 35, SC 14, Inc x 2, SC 35, HDC 14 [108]

> In this row, the extra-long tentacle arm will be pushed behind your work. You want it to look like the tentacle arm is coming out from more of the center of the kraken than the outer edge.

53G. SC 2, Dec, SC 2, HDC 35, SC 14, Inc x 2, SC 35, HDC 14 [107]

53H. SC 2, Dec, SC 2, HDC 35, SC 14, Inc x 2, SC 35, HDC 14, SC 2, Sl St to beginning stitch of 53A, Ch 1 [109]

54A. SC, SC/HDC Dec, HDC Dec, HDC 15, SC 33, Inc x 2, SC 30, HDC 18, HDC Dec [104]

54B. HDC/SC Dec, SC, SC/HDC Dec, HDC Dec, HDC 15, SC 33, Inc x 2, SC 30, HDC 18, HDC Dec [105]

54C. HDC/SC Dec, SC, SC/HDC Dec, HDC Dec, HDC 15, SC 33, Inc x 2, SC 30, HDC 18, HDC Dec [105]

54D. HDC/SC Dec, Dec, SC/HDC Dec, HDC Dec, HDC 15, SC 33, Inc x 2, SC 30, HDC 18, HDC Dec [105]

54E. HDC/SC Dec, SC, SC/HDC Dec, HDC Dec, HDC 15, SC 33, Inc x 2, SC 30, HDC 18, HDC Dec [105]

54F. HDC/SC Dec, Dec, SC/HDC Dec, HDC Dec, HDC 15, SC 33, Inc x 2, SC 30, HDC 18, HDC Dec [105]

54G. HDC/SC Dec, SC, SC/HDC Dec, HDC Dec, HDC 15, SC 33, Inc x 2, SC 30, HDC 18, HDC Dec [105]

54H. HDC/SC Dec, SC, SC/HDC Dec, HDC Dec, HDC 15, SC 33, Inc x 2, SC 30, HDC 18, HDC Dec, HDC/SC Dec, Sl St to beginning stitch [106]

Kraken Head Top

If using the Simple Bottom, fasten off with 24 in/61 cm yarn tail. If using the Advanced Bottom, leave the yarn attached; you will use this to attach the Advanced Bottom later. Begin to stuff the body medium-firm with fiberfill; you can finish adding fiberfill before you finish attaching the bottom.

KRAKEN SIMPLE BOTTOM

NOTE: Make either the Simple Bottom or the Advanced Bottom for your Kraken.

1. SC 5 in Magic Circle, Sl St to beginning stitch, Ch 1 [5]
2. Inc x 5, Sl St to beginning stitch, Ch 1 [10]
3. (SC, Inc) x 5, Sl St to beginning stitch, Ch 1 [15]
4. (SC 2, Inc) x 5, Sl St to beginning stitch, Ch 1 [20]
5. (SC 3, Inc) x 5, Sl St to beginning stitch, Ch 1 [25]
6. SC 2, Inc, (SC 4, Inc) x 4, SC 2, Sl St to beginning stitch, Ch 1 [30]
7. (SC 5, Inc) x 5, Sl St to beginning stitch, Ch 1 [35]
8. SC 3, Inc, (SC 6, Inc) x 4, SC 3, Sl St to beginning stitch, Ch 1 [40]
9. (SC 7, Inc) x 5, Sl St to beginning stitch, Ch 1 [45]
10. SC 4, Inc, (SC 8, Inc) x 4, SC 4, Sl St to beginning stitch [50]

Fasten off with 36 in/91 cm yarn tail.

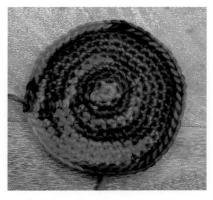

Kraken Simple Bottom

KRAKEN ADVANCED BOTTOM

NOTE: Make either the Simple Bottom or the Advanced Bottom for your Kraken Body.

1. SC 6 in Magic Circle, Sl St to beginning stitch, Ch 1 [6]
2. Inc x 6, Sl St to beginning stitch, Ch 1 [12]
3. (Bobble, Inc) x 6, Sl St to beginning stitch, Ch 1 [18]

> Your Bobble stitches may tend to pop out on the wrong side of the work. If this happens, just use the back of a crochet hook or a chopstick to push them out to the right side. A Bobble stitch is worked as follows: YO, insert into next stitch, YO, pull up, YO, pull through 2 loops, YO, insert into the same stitch, YO, pull up, YO, pull through 2 loops, YO, pull through 1 loop, YO, insert into the same stitch, YO, pull up, YO, pull through 2 loops, YO, pull through 1 loop, YO, insert into the same stitch, YO, pull up, YO, pull through 2 loops, YO, pull through all remaining loops.

4. (SC 2, Inc) x 6, Sl St to beginning stitch, Ch 1 [24]
5. (SC 2, Bobble, Inc) x 6, Sl St to beginning stitch, Ch 1 [30]

6. (Bobble, SC 3, Inc) x 6, Sl St to beginning stitch, Ch 1 [36]
7. (SC 3, Bobble, SC, Inc) x 6, Sl St to beginning stitch, Ch 1 [42]
8. (Bobble, SC 5, Inc) x 6, Sl St to beginning stitch, Ch 1 [48]
9. (SC 4, Bobble, SC 2, Inc) x 6, Sl St to beginning stitch, Ch 1 [54]
10. (SC, Bobble, SC 4, Bobble, SC, Inc) x 6, Sl St to beginning stitch, Ch 1 [60]

11. (SC 14, Inc) x 4, do not join; work in spiral for the remaining rows. [64]

> Starting in Row 12 and onward, you will follow every part of every row. Each sub-row (i.e., 12A, 12B, 12C, etc.) will have its own stitch count. This sub-row stitch count will tell you exactly how many stitches you made in the sub-row.

12A. Sl St 7, Ch 51, Turn, starting in the 2nd Ch from hook, SC 25, HDC 25, Skip 1 stitch [57]

12A creates the first tentacle. The Ch stitches are not counted in the stitch count. Turning in this and subsequent rows means working back down the chain and then continuing into the next available stitch.

12B. Sl St 7, Ch 51, Turn, starting in the 2nd Ch from hook, SC 25, HDC 25, Skip 1 stitch [57]

12B creates the second tentacle. The Ch stitches are not counted in the stitch count.

12C. Sl St 7, Ch 51, Turn, starting in the 2nd Ch from hook, SC 25, HDC 25, Skip 1 stitch [57]

12C creates the third tentacle. The Ch stitches are not counted in the stitch count.

12D. Sl St 7, Ch 51, Turn, starting in the 2nd Ch from hook, SC 25, HDC 25, Skip 1 stitch [57]

12D creates the fourth tentacle. The Ch stitches are not counted in the stitch count.

12E. Sl St 7, Ch 51, Turn, starting in the 2nd Ch from hook, SC 25, HDC 25, Skip 1 stitch [57]

12E creates the fifth tentacle. The Ch stitches are not counted in the stitch count.

12F. Sl St 7, Ch 51, Turn, starting in the 2nd Ch from hook, SC 25, HDC 25, Skip 1 stitch [57]

12F creates the sixth tentacle. The Ch stitches are not counted in the stitch count.

12G. Sl St 7, Ch 51, Turn, starting in the 2nd Ch from hook, SC 25, HDC 25, Skip 1 stitch [57]

12G creates the seventh tentacle. The Ch stitches are not counted in the stitch count.

12H. Sl St 7, Ch 51, Turn, starting in the 2nd Ch from hook, SC 25, HDC 25, Skip 1 stitch [57]

12H creates the eighth tentacle. The Ch stitches are not counted in the stitch count.

13A. Working around the Slip Stitches, Dec, SC 3, Dec, working up the first available tentacle, (HDC, Bobble, HDC) x 12, (SC, Bobble, SC) x 4, SC, Inc, continue crocheting around the edge of the tentacle, Inc, SC, (SC, Bobble, SC) x 12, (HDC, Bobble, HDC) x 4 [107]

13B. Working around the Slip Stitches, Dec, SC 3, Dec, working up the first available tentacle, (HDC, Bobble, HDC) x 12, (SC, Bobble, SC) x 4, SC, Inc, continue crocheting around the edge of the tentacle, Inc, SC, (SC, Bobble, SC) x 12, (HDC, Bobble, HDC) x 4 [107]

13C. Working around the Slip Stitches, Dec, SC 3, Dec, working up the first available tentacle, (HDC, Bobble, HDC) x 12, (SC, Bobble, SC) x 4, SC, Inc, continue crocheting around the edge of the tentacle, Inc, SC, (SC, Bobble, SC) x 12, (HDC, Bobble, HDC) x 4 [107]

13D. Working around the Slip Stitches, Dec, SC 3, Dec, working up the first available tentacle, (HDC, Bobble, HDC) x 12, (SC, Bobble, SC) x 4, SC, Inc, continue crocheting around the edge of the tentacle, Inc, SC, (SC, Bobble, SC) x 12, (HDC, Bobble, HDC) x 4 [107]

13E. Working around the Slip Stitches, Dec, SC 3, Dec, working up the first available tentacle, (HDC, Bobble, HDC) x 12, (SC, Bobble, SC) x 4, SC, Inc, continue crocheting around the edge of the tentacle, Inc, SC, (SC, Bobble, SC) x 12, (HDC, Bobble, HDC) x 4 [107]

13F. Working around the Slip Stitches, Dec, SC 3, Dec, working up the first available tentacle, (HDC, Bobble, HDC) x 12, (SC, Bobble, SC) x 4, SC, Inc, continue crocheting around the edge of the tentacle, Inc, SC, (SC, Bobble, SC) x 12, (HDC, Bobble, HDC) x 4 [107]

13G. Working around the Slip Stitches, Dec, SC 3, Dec, working up the first available tentacle, (HDC, Bobble, HDC) x 12, (SC, Bobble, SC) x 4, SC, Inc, continue crocheting around the edge of the tentacle, Inc, SC, (SC, Bobble, SC) x 12, (HDC, Bobble, HDC) x 4 [107]

13H. Working around the Slip Stitches, Dec, SC 3, Dec, working up the first available tentacle, (HDC, Bobble, HDC) x 12, (SC, Bobble, SC) x 4, SC, Inc, continue crocheting around the edge of the tentacle, Inc, SC, (SC, Bobble, SC) x 12, (HDC, Bobble, HDC) x 4 [107]

14A. HDC/SC Dec, SC, SC/HDC Dec, HDC Dec, HDC 15, SC 33, Inc x 2, SC 30, HDC 18, HDC Dec [105]

> Mark the 1st SC in Row 14A for reference on where to attach the Advanced Bottom to the Body Top.

14B. HDC/SC Dec, SC, SC/HDC Dec, HDC Dec, HDC 15, SC 33, Inc x 2, SC 30, HDC 18, HDC Dec [105]

14C. HDC/SC Dec, SC, SC/HDC Dec, HDC Dec, HDC 15, SC 33, Inc x 2, SC 30, HDC 18, HDC Dec [105]

14D. HDC/SC Dec, SC, SC/HDC Dec, HDC Dec, HDC 15, SC 33, Inc x 2, SC 30, HDC 18, HDC Dec [105]

14E. HDC/SC Dec, SC, SC/HDC Dec, HDC Dec, HDC 15, SC 33, Inc x 2, SC 30, HDC 18, HDC Dec [105]

14F. HDC/SC Dec, SC, SC/HDC Dec, HDC Dec, HDC 15, SC 33, Inc x 2, SC 30, HDC 18, HDC Dec [105]

14G. HDC/SC Dec, SC, SC/HDC Dec, HDC Dec, HDC 15, SC 33, Inc x 2, SC 30, HDC 18, HDC Dec [105]

14H. HDC/SC Dec, SC, SC/HDC Dec, HDC Dec, HDC 15, SC 33, Inc x 2, SC 30, HDC 18, HDC Dec [105]

Fasten off with 24 in/61 cm yarn tail here; when you crochet to attach, leave the yarn tail outside the work to use to secure the bottom, and soft sculpt it to be concave when complete.

Kraken Advanced Bottom

Using the Kraken Main Color yarn, continue from where you left off in the final row of the head top instructions, align the tentacle bottom with the bottom of the Kraken head so they line up. This shouldn't be difficult, because all of the tentacles (except for the extra-long tentacle arms) are the same length. Insert the hook through the right side of the Kraken head row and then insert the hook into the wrong side of the marked stitch on the Kraken tentacle bottom, Single Crochet around the entire edge. When you reach the two stitches at the tip of each tentacle, Inc in each, and then continue to SC back down the tentacle. When you reach the extra-long tentacles, work your SC so the long tentacles lie behind the SC row and look like they are emerging from farther under the body. Before you crochet around the last tentacle, finish stuffing the body (medium amount) with fiberfill; it is optional to stuff the tentacles. Sl St to beginning stitch.

NOTE: *If you want to forgo stuffing the tentacles, and you want them to be curly and spirally with the suction/tentacle bottom, then, instead of working SC around the entire edge as instructed above, work the following: SC in all stitches between tentacles. Repeat (SC, Dec) along the edge of the tentacles (to the tip). Inc in the top two stitches at the tip of each tentacle. Repeat (SC, Dec) to the base of the tentacle; follow these instructions for every tentacle.*

Fasten off with long enough yarn tail to weave in.

KRAKEN SIDE FIN (MAKE 2)

1. Starting with a long enough yarn tail to weave in later, Ch 12, Turn, starting in the 2nd Ch from hook, Sl St, Ch 1, HDC, DC 2, HDC 3, SC 4, Ch 1, Turn [11]

2. BLO [SC 4, HDC 3, DC, DC Inc], Ch 4, Turn [10]

3. Starting in the 2nd Ch from hook, Sl St, Ch 1, HDC, DC, BLO [DC 2, HDC 4, SC 4], Ch 1, Turn [13]

4. BLO [SC 4, HDC 4, DC 2, DC Inc], Ch 4, Turn [12]

5. Starting in the 2nd Ch from hook, Sl St, Ch 1, HDC, DC, BLO [DC 3, HDC 4, SC 5], Ch 1, Turn [15]

6. BLO [SC 4, HDC 4, DC 5], Ch 3, Turn [13]

7. Starting in the 2nd Ch from hook, Sl St, Ch 1, HDC, BLO [DC 4, HDC 4, SC 5], Ch 1, Turn [15]

8. BLO [SC 4, HDC 4, DC 3, DC Dec], Ch 3, Turn [12]

9. Starting in the 2nd Ch from hook, Sl St, Ch 1, BLO [HDC Dec, DC 3, HDC 4, SC 4], Ch 1, Turn [13]

10. BLO [SC 4, HDC 3, DC 2, DC Dec], Ch 3, Turn [10]

11. Starting in the 2nd Ch from hook, Sl St, Ch 1, BLO [HDC Dec, DC 2, HDC 3, SC 4] [11]

Fasten off with 18 in/46 cm yarn tail.

Kraken Side Fin

KRAKEN EYELID (MAKE 2)

Optional

1. Starting with a long enough yarn tail to weave in later, Ch 13, Turn, starting in the 2nd Ch from hook, SC, HDC, DC 8, HDC, SC, Ch 13, Turn [12]

2. Starting in the 2nd Ch from hook, SC, HDC, DC 8, HDC, SC [12]

Kraken Eyelid

Fasten off with 24 in/61 cm yarn tail.

KRAKEN HEAD FIN

1. Starting with a long enough yarn tail to weave in later, Ch 3, Turn, starting in the 2nd Ch from hook, Sl St, SC & HDC, Ch 1, Turn [3]

> This row will be front and center on the Kraken Head.

2. BLO [SC], Ch 2, Turn [1]

3. Starting in the 2nd Ch from hook, Sl St, BLO [SC & HDC], Ch 1, Turn [3]

4. BLO [SC], Ch 3, Turn [1]

> If you are having trouble with the first four rows, you can Ch 4 and start with Row 5.

5. Starting in the 2nd Ch from hook, Sl St, SC, BLO [SC & HDC], Ch 1, Turn [4]

6. BLO [SC 2], Ch 2, Turn [2]

7. Starting in the 2nd Ch from hook, Sl St, BLO [SC, SC & HDC], Ch 1, Turn [4]

8. BLO [SC 2], Ch 3, Turn [2]

9. Starting in the 2nd Ch from hook, Sl St, SC, BLO [HDC, HDC Inc], Ch 1, Turn [5]

10. BLO [SC 3], Ch 2, Turn [3]

11. Starting in the 2nd Ch from hook, Sl St BLO [SC, HDC, HDC Inc], Ch 1, Turn [5]

12. BLO [SC 3], Ch 2, Turn [3]

13. Starting in the 2nd Ch from hook, Sl St, BLO [SC, HDC, HDC Inc], Ch 1, Turn [5]

14. BLO [SC 3], Ch 3, Turn [3]

15. Starting in the 2nd Ch from hook, Sl St, SC, BLO [HDC 2, HDC Inc], Ch 1, Turn [6]

16. BLO [SC 4], Ch 2, Turn [4]

17. Starting in the 2nd Ch from Hook, Sl St, BLO [SC, HDC 2, HDC Inc], Ch 1, Turn [6]

18. BLO [SC 4], Ch 2, Turn [4]

19. Starting in the 2nd Ch from hook, Sl St, BLO [SC, HDC 2, HDC Inc], Ch 1, Turn [6]

20. BLO [SC 4], Ch 2, Turn [4]

21. Starting in the 2nd Ch from hook, Sl St, BLO [SC, HDC 2, HDC Inc], Ch 1, Turn [6]

22. BLO [SC 4], Ch 2, Turn [4]

23. Starting in the 2nd Ch from hook, Sl St, BLO [SC, HDC 3], Ch 1, Turn [5]

24. BLO [SC 3], Ch 2, Turn [3]

25. Starting in the 2nd Ch from hook, Sl St, BLO [SC, HDC, HDC Inc], Ch 1, Turn [5]

26. BLO [SC 3], Ch 2, Turn [3]

27. Starting in the 2nd Ch from hook, Sl St, BLO [SC, HDC, HDC Inc], Ch 1, Turn [5]

28. BLO [SC 3], Ch 2, Turn [3]

29. Starting in the 2nd Ch from hook, Sl St, BLO [SC, HDC 2], Ch 1, Turn [4]

30. BLO [SC 2], Ch 2, Turn [2]

31. Starting in the 2nd Ch from hook, Sl St, BLO [SC, SC & HDC], Ch 1, Turn [4]

32. BLO [SC 2], Ch 2, Turn [2]

33. Starting in the 2nd Ch from Hook, Sl St, BLO [SC, HDC], Ch 1, Turn [3]

34. BLO [SC], Ch 2, Turn [1]

35. Starting in the 2nd Ch from hook, Sl St, BLO [SC & HDC], Ch 1, Turn [3]

36. BLO [SC], Ch 2, Turn [1]

37. Starting in the 2nd Ch from hook, Sl St, BLO [SC] [2]

Fasten off with 18 in/46 cm yarn tail.

Kraken Head Fin

KRAKEN ASSEMBLY

1. FOR THE SIMPLE BOTTOM ONLY: Pin the simple circle in place on the bottom of the Kraken, sew to attach (whipstitch around the edge of the circle). Soft sculpt the bottom so that it is slightly concave, finish stuffing the Kraken body before you finish sewing; when you finish sewing, weave in ends.

2. FOR THE ADVANCED BOTTOM ONLY: Using leftover yarn tails, soft sculpt the bottom center of the Kraken to be concave. Weave in ends. Using a darning needle and your leftover yarn tail from the bottom, weave your yarn tail toward the center of the bottom and then hide the tail by pulling it in toward the center of the body, creating a concave shape.

3. Pinch together a vertical ridge along the front center length of the Kraken's head. Pin it in place. It should be about 1 in/2.5 cm deep and extend from 2 in/5 cm beyond the top center of the head to just above where the eyes are inserted.

As you sew to attach the side fins, eyelids, and head fin, use those yarn tails to stitch this shape into place by lightly sewing back and forth along the base edge of this mohawk shape. If you used an Accent Color for the fins, use a length of Main Color yarn to sew the mohawk shape in place.

4. Pin the side fins in place, and sew to attach. Position the side fins as shown in the photos, with the lowest edge slightly below the top edge of the safety eye, on either side of the head.

5. Pin the eyelids in place as shown at a significant diagonal angle; sew to attach.

6. Pin the head fin in place along the mohawk soft sculpting shape, sew to attach. Sew the mohawk soft sculpting shape in place, and weave in ends.

FEATHERED SERPENT

The Feathered Serpent—also known as Quetzalcoatl among the Aztecs, Kukulkan among the Yucatec Maya, and Q'uq'umatz and Tohil among the K'iche' Maya—is a prominent supernatural entity in many Mesoamerican religions. It has the dual nature of a deity, its feathers representing its godliness and its serpent body representing its human nature.

SIZE:

A Feathered Serpent from this pattern is 6 in/15 cm tall from the bottom of the body to the top of the head, 8 in/20.5 cm long from the neck to the tail (in the zigzag position), and 7 in/18 cm wide from side to side at its widest part.

MATERIALS

» Yarn: See table on page 164 to choose the parts you want to make for your Feathered Serpent, and find the yarn amounts needed for each piece. The number of head and tail feathers is up to you; choosing will determine your total yardage needed of each color. All yarn is #4 medium/worsted weight, and all yarn amounts are approximate. Total amounts for Feathered Serpent as pictured:
  • Main Color (dark green): 98 yd/ 89.5 m
  • Accent Color 1 (red): 16 yd/14.75 m
  • Accent Color 2 (blue): 19 yd/17.25 m
  • Accent Color 3 (yellow): 65 yd/59.5 m (includes 25 yd/22.75 m for belly)
  • Accent Color 4 (green): 51 yd/46.5 m

» US size G (4 mm) crochet hook

» Safety eyes: 18 mm safety eyes

» Fiberfill stuffing

» Darning needle

» Pins

» Scissors

» Duct Tape

» Wire strong enough to support posing. Recommend 4 pieces of 18-in/45.5-cm 18-gauge, paper-wrapped wire (found in the faux floral arrangement section of any craft store; if this exact wire cannot be found, please use 14- to 16-gauge wire—err on the side of heavier wire).

» Pliers

INSTRUCTIONS

Look at the chart and the Gallery below to choose the pieces you want to make for your Feathered Serpent. All of the Feathered Serpents shown in the photos include the maximum number of feathers, but you have the option to reduce the number of feathers for your serpent. Crochet all the parts of your Feathered Serpent following the instructions on pages 166–176, and then proceed to Feathered Serpent Assembly on page 177 to put them all together.

PARTS TO MAKE	PAGE NO.	YARN COLOR	NUMBER TO MAKE	APPROX. AMOUNT
Feathered Serpent Body	166	Main Color	1	85 yd/77.75
Feathered Serpent Head	170	Main Color	1	13 yd/12 m
Feathered Serpent Head Feathers	171	4 Accent Colors	2	6 yd/5.5 m Accent Color 1, 9 yd/8.25 m Accent Color 2, 24 yd/22 m Accent Color 3, 17 yd/15.5 m Accent Color 4 for 2 pieces
Feathered Serpent Tail Ornamentation	173	4 Accent Colors	1	3 yd/2.75 m Accent Color 1, 3 yd/2.75 m Accent Color 2, 4 yd/3.75 m Accent Color 3, 15 yd/13.75 m Accent Color 4
Feathered Serpent Belly Panel	174	Main or Any Accent Color	1	25 yd/22.75 m (shown in Accent Color 3)
Medium Feather Wing	175	4 Accent Colors	2	7 yd/6.5 m Accent Color 1, 7 yd/6.5 m Accent Color 2, 12 yd/11 m Accent Color 3, 19 yd/17.25 m Accent Color 4 for 2 wings

GALLERY

Feathered Serpent with maximum feathers

Feathered Serpent with
maximum feathers

FEATHERED SERPENT PARTS PATTERNS

FEATHERED SERPENT BODY

1. SC 5 in Magic Circle, continue in spiral [5]

2–4. (3 rows of) SC 5 [5]

5. Inc, SC 4 [6]

6–8. (3 rows of) SC 6 [6]

9. SC, Inc, SC 4 [7]

10. SC 7 [7]

11. SC 2, Inc, SC 2, Dec [7]

12. SC 7 [7]

13. SC 3, Inc, SC 3 [8]

Follow all substeps of each row in order (i.e., 14A, 14B, etc.). These short rows create the curves and shaping of the body. They will sometimes go beyond where the row began; follow the pattern exactly, and it will work. Each sub-row will have a stitch count for the number of stitches created in that sub-row, and there will be a final stitch count at the end of the final sub-row to indicate how many stitches are available on the edge of the work once all the sub-rows are complete.

A video tutorial for how to crochet short rows is available on the Crafty Intentions YouTube channel here: https://www.youtube.com/watch?v=sh5T-idiwm8&t=159s

Hybrid decreases like the SC/HDC Dec & HDC stitches are defined in the Glossary (page 4) and demonstrated on the Crafty Intentions YouTube channel here: https://www.youtube.com/watch?v=h4wkxMOMqXg&t=5s

---

14A. SC 3, Ch 1, Turn [3]

14B. SC 6, Ch 1, Turn [6]

14C. SC 5, SC/HDC Dec & HDC, HDC & HDC/SC Dec [9 stitches are worked in this row in total; however, since the final stitch overlaps with the 1st stitch of the row, 8 will be available to work into in the next row]

15A. SC 5, Ch 1, Turn [5]
15B. SC 6, Ch 1, Turn [6]
15C. SC 5, SC/HDC Dec & HDC, <HDC Dec>, HDC & HDC/SC Dec [10 stitches are worked in this row in total, and it overlaps with the 1st stitch of the row; 9 stitches remain to be worked into in the following row]
16A. SC 5, Ch 1, Turn [5]
16B. SC 6, Ch 1, Turn [6]
16C. SC 5, SC/HDC Dec & HDC, SC, HDC & HDC/SC Dec [10 stitches are worked in this row in total, and it overlaps with the 1st stitch of the

row; 9 stitches remain to be worked into in the following row]
17A. SC 4, Ch 1, Turn [4]
17B. SC 3, Ch 1, Turn [3]
17C. SC 2, SC/HDC Dec & HDC, SC, Ch 1, Turn [5]
17D. SC 4, SC/HDC Dec & HDC, SC, Ch 1, Turn [7]
17E. SC 6, SC/HDC Dec & HDC, <Dec>, HDC & HDC/SC Dec [11 stitches are worked in this row in total, and it overlaps with the 1st stitch of the row; 10 stitches remain to be worked into in the following row]

18A. SC 6, Ch 1, Turn [6]
18B. SC 4, Ch 1, Turn [4]
18C. SC 3, SC/HDC Dec & HDC, SC, Ch 1, Turn [6]
18D. SC 5, SC/HDC Dec & HDC, SC, Ch 1, Turn [8]
18E. SC 7, SC/HDC Dec & HDC, HDC & HDC/SC Dec [11 stitches are worked in this row in total, and it overlaps with the 1st stitch of the row; 10 stitches remain to be worked into in the following row]
19–22. (4 Rows of) SC 10 [10]

NOTE: Stuff the body medium firmly as you go. The shape of the serpent is entirely created through the crochet work, so wire is not necessary, but if you would like your serpent to be poseable, you can add one 18-in/45.5-cm 18-gauge, paper-wrapped stem wire (or similar substitute that is strong, yet moldable—pipe cleaners are not strong enough). Fold the wire over on itself and tape the end to itself so that you are inserting the folded end of the wire into the tip of the serpent's tail (this is so that the end of the wire is dull and won't poke through the work). Have the wire follow the curve of the body as you continue to crochet. If necessary, you can add another length of wire to the first by overlapping the two wires by at least 4 in/10 cm and securing together by wrapping it in thin strips of duct tape. You want the wire to extend beyond the neck of the serpent, and you can bend the wire back on itself so that it will extend no farther than the inside of the nose of the head. Then, when you assemble the Feathered Serpent, you will slide the head onto the extended wire, giving you the option of custom posing. Wire is OPTIONAL but recommended.

23A. SC 10, Ch 1, Turn [10]
23B. SC 3, Ch 1, Turn [3]
23C. SC 2, SC/HDC Dec & HDC, SC, Ch 1, Turn [5]
23D. SC 4, SC/HDC Dec & HDC, SC, Ch 1, Turn [7]
23E. SC 6, SC/HDC Dec & HDC, Inc, HDC & HDC/SC Dec [12 stitches are worked in this row in total, and it overlaps with the 1st stitch of the row;

11 stitches remain to be worked into in the following row]
24A. SC 4, Ch 1, Turn [4]
24B. SC 2, Ch 1, Turn [2]
24C. SC, SC/HDC Dec & HDC, SC, Ch 1, Turn [4]
24D. SC 3, SC/HDC Dec & HDC, SC, Ch 1, Turn [6]
24E. SC 5, SC/HDC Dec & HDC, SC, Ch 1, Turn [8]

24F. SC 7, SC/HDC Dec & HDC, SC, Ch 1, Turn [10]
24G. SC 9, SC/HDC Dec & HDC & HDC/SC Dec [12 stitches are worked in this row in total, and it overlaps with the 1st stitch of the row; 11 stitches remain to be worked into in the following row]
25A. SC 5, Ch 1, Turn [5]

25B. SC 2, Ch 1, Turn [2]

25C. SC, SC/HDC Dec & HDC, SC, Ch 1, Turn [4]

25D. SC 3, SC/HDC Dec & HDC, SC, Ch 1, Turn [6]

25E. SC 5, SC/HDC Dec & HDC, SC, Ch 1, Turn [8]

25F. SC 7, SC/HDC Dec & HDC, SC, Ch 1, Turn [10]

25G. SC 9, SC/HDC Dec & HDC & HDC/SC Dec [12 stitches are worked in this row in total, and it overlaps with the 1st stitch of the row; 11 stitches remain to be worked into in the following row]

26A. SC 5, Ch 1, Turn [5]

26B. SC 2, Ch 1, Turn [2]

26C. SC, SC/HDC Dec & HDC, SC, Ch 1, Turn [4]

26D. SC 3, SC/HDC Dec & HDC, SC, Ch 1, Turn [6]

26E. SC 5, SC/HDC Dec & HDC, SC, Ch 1, Turn [8]

26F. SC 7, SC/HDC Dec & HDC, SC, Ch 1, Turn [10]

26G. SC 9, SC/HDC Dec & HDC & HDC/SC Dec [12 stitches are worked in this row in total, and it overlaps with the 1st stitch of the row; 11 stitches remain to be worked into in the following row]

27. SC 9, Inc, SC [12]

28–37. (10 Rows of) SC 12 [12]

38A. SC, Ch 1, Turn [1]

38B. SC 2, Ch 1, Turn [2]

38C. SC, SC/HDC Dec & HDC, SC, Ch 1, Turn [4]

38D. SC 3, SC/HDC Dec & HDC, SC, Ch 1, Turn [6]

38E. SC 5, SC/HDC Dec & HDC, SC, Ch 1, Turn [8]

38F. SC 7, SC/HDC Dec & HDC, SC, Ch 1, Turn [10]

38G. SC 9, SC/HDC Dec & HDC, HDC & HDC/SC Dec [13 stitches are worked in this row in total, and it overlaps with the 1st stitch of the row; 12 stitches remain to be worked into in the following row]

39A. SC 5, Ch 1, Turn [5]

39B. SC 2, Ch 1, Turn [2]

39C. SC, SC/HDC Dec & HDC, SC, Ch 1, Turn [4]

39D. SC 3, SC/HDC Dec & HDC, SC, Ch 1, Turn [6]

39E. SC 5, SC/HDC Dec & HDC, SC, Ch 1, Turn [8]

39F. SC 7, SC/HDC Dec & HDC, SC, Ch 1, Turn [10]

39G. SC 9, SC/HDC Dec & HDC, HDC & HDC/SC Dec [13 stitches are worked in this row in total, and it overlaps with the 1st stitch of the row; 12 stitches remain to be worked into in the following row]

40A. SC 5, Ch 1, Turn [5]

40B. SC 2, Ch 1, Turn [2]

40C. SC, SC/HDC Dec & HDC, SC, Ch 1, Turn [4]

40D. SC 3, SC/HDC Dec & HDC, SC, Ch 1, Turn [6]

40E. SC 5, SC/HDC Dec & HDC, SC, Ch 1, Turn [8]

40F. SC 7, SC/HDC Dec & HDC, SC, Ch 1, Turn [10]

40G. SC 9, SC/HDC Dec & HDC, HDC & HDC/SC Dec [13 stitches are worked in this row in total, and it overlaps with the 1st stitch of the row; 12 stitches remain to be worked into in the following row]

41A. SC 5, Ch 1, Turn [5]

41B. SC 2, Ch 1, Turn [2]

41C. SC, SC/HDC Dec & HDC, SC, Ch 1, Turn [4]

41D. SC 3, SC/HDC Dec & HDC, SC, Ch 1, Turn [6]

41E. SC 5, SC/HDC Dec & HDC, SC, Ch 1, Turn [8]

41F. SC 7, SC/HDC Dec & HDC, SC, Ch 1, Turn [10]

41G. SC 9, SC/HDC Dec & HDC, HDC & HDC/SC Dec [13 stitches are worked in this row in total, and it overlaps with the 1st stitch of the row; 12 stitches remain to be worked into in the following row]

42–57. (16 rows of) SC 12 [12]

58A. SC 4, Ch 1, Turn [4]

58B. SC 2, Ch 1, Turn [2]

58C. SC, SC/HDC Dec & HDC, SC, Ch 1, Turn [4]

58D. SC 3, SC/HDC Dec & HDC, SC, Ch 1, Turn [6]

58E. SC 5, SC/HDC Dec & HDC, SC, CH 1, Turn [8]

58F. SC 7, SC/HDC Dec & HDC, SC, Ch 1, Turn [10]

58G. SC 9, SC/HDC Dec & HDC, HDC & HDC/SC Dec [13 stitches are worked in this row in total, and it overlaps with the 1st stitch of the row; 12 stitches remain to be worked into in the following row]

59A. SC 5, Ch 1, Turn [5]

59B. SC 2, Ch 1, Turn [2]

59C. SC, SC/HDC Dec & HDC, SC, Ch 1, Turn [4]

59D. SC 3, SC/HDC Dec & HDC, SC, Ch 1, Turn [6]

59E. SC 5, SC/HDC Dec & HDC, SC, Ch 1, Turn [8]

59F. SC 7, SC/HDC Dec & HDC, SC, Ch 1, Turn [10]

59G. SC 9, SC/HDC Dec & HDC, HDC & HDC/SC Dec [13 stitches are worked in this row in total, and it overlaps with the 1st stitch of the row; 12 stitches remain to be worked into in the following row]

60A. SC 5, Ch 1, Turn [5]

60B. SC 2, Ch 1, Turn [2]

60C. SC, SC/HDC Dec & HDC, SC, Ch 1, Turn [4]

60D. SC 3, SC/HDC Dec & HDC, SC, Ch 1, Turn [6]

60E. SC 5, SC/HDC Dec & HDC, SC, Ch 1, Turn [8]

60F. SC 7, SC/HDC Dec & HDC, SC, Ch 1, Turn [10]

60G. SC 9, SC/HDC Dec & HDC, HDC & HDC/SC Dec [13 stitches are worked in this row in total, and it overlaps with the 1st stitch of the row; 12 stitches remain

to be worked into in the following row]

61A. SC 5, Ch 1, Turn [5]

61B. SC 2, Ch 1, Turn [2]

61C. SC, SC/HDC Dec & HDC, SC, Ch 1, Turn [4]

61D. SC 3, SC/HDC Dec & HDC, SC, Ch 1, Turn [6]

61E. SC 5, SC/HDC Dec & HDC, SC, Ch 1, Turn [8]

61F. SC 7, SC/HDC Dec & HDC, SC, Ch 1, Turn [10]

61G. SC 9, SC/HDC Dec & HDC, HDC/SC Dec [12 stitches are worked in this row in total, and it overlaps with the 1st stitch of the row; 11 stitches remain to be worked into in the following row]

62–65. (4 rows of) SC 11 [11]

66A. SC, Ch 1, Turn [1]

66B. SC 4, Ch 1, Turn [4]

66C. SC 3, SC/HDC Dec & HDC, SC, Ch 1, Turn [6]

66D. SC 5, SC/HDC Dec & HDC, SC, Ch 1, Turn [8]

66E. SC 7, SC/HDC Dec & HDC, SC, HDC/SC Dec [11 stitches are worked in

total, and it overlaps with the 1st stitch of the row; 10 stitches remain to be worked into in the following row]

67A. SC 4, Ch 1, Turn [4]

67B. SC 2, Ch 1, Turn [2]

67C. SC, SC/HDC Dec & HDC, SC, Ch 1, Turn [4]

67D. SC 3, SC/HDC Dec & HDC, SC, Ch 1, Turn [6]

67E. SC 5, SC/HDC Dec & HDC, SC 2, HDC & HDC/SC Dec [11 stitches are worked in this row in total, and it overlaps with the 1st stitch of the row; 10 stitches remain to be worked into in the following row]

68–74. (7 rows of) SC 10 [10]

75. Dec x 2, SC 3, <Dec>, SC 3 [9]

76. SC 9 [9]

77. Dec, SC 3, Inc, SC 3 [9]

78. SC 9 [9]

79. Dec, SC 7 [8]

80–84. (5 rows of) SC 8 [8]

85A. SC 8, Ch 1, Turn [8]

85B. SC 5, Ch 1, Turn [5]

85C. SC 5, Ch 1, Turn [5]

85D. SC 5, Ch 1, Turn [5]

85E. SC 5 [5]

Fasten off with 18 in/46 cm yarn tail.

Feathered Serpent Body

FEATHERED SERPENT HEAD

1. Start with a long enough yarn tail to weave in, Ch 7, Turn, starting in the 2nd Ch from hook, SC 5, Inc, continue to crochet around to the other side of the starting Chain, SC 4, SC in the same Ch as the 1st SC you worked in this row, continue in spiral [12]

2. SC, Inc, (SC 2, Inc) x 3, SC [16]

3–4. (2 rows of) SC 16 [16]

5. SC 9, Inc, SC 5, Inc [18]

6. SC 18 [18]

7. SC 10, Inc, SC 6, Inc [20]

8. SC 20 [20]

9. (SC 2, Inc, SC 2) x 4 [24]

10. SC 24 [24]

11. (SC 4, Dec) x 4 [20]

Insert 18 mm safety eyes between Row 7 and Row 8, with 6 stitch spaces between the posts. Stuff medium-firm with fiberfill, and continue to stuff as you crochet.

12. (SC 3, Dec) x 4 [16]

13. (SC 2, Dec) x 4 [12]

14. (SC, Dec) x 4 [8]

15. (SC, Dec, SC) x 2 [6]

Fasten off with 18 in/46 cm yarn tail.

Feathered Serpent Head

FEATHERED SERPENT HEAD FEATHERS: PART 1 (MAKE 2)

Optional

NOTE: All Head Feathers are marked optional, as you are not required to make all 4 parts if you want a simpler look. To create a Feathered Serpent that looks the same as the ones in the photos, you need to make all 4 parts.

With Accent Color 1:

1. Start with a long enough yarn tail to weave in later, Ch 3, starting in the 2nd Ch from hook, HDC, SC, Ch 1, Turn [2]
2. BLO [SC], Ch 3, Turn [1]
3. Starting in the 2nd Ch from hook, HDC, SC, BLO [SC], Ch 1, Turn [3]
4. BLO [SC 2], Ch 3, Turn [2]
5. Starting in the 2nd Ch from hook, HDC 2, BLO [SC 2], Ch 1, Turn [4]
6. BLO [SC 2], Ch 2, Turn [2]
7. Starting in the 2nd Ch from hook, HDC, BLO [SC 2], Ch 1, Turn [3]
8. BLO [SC], Ch 2, Turn [1]
9. Starting in the 2nd Ch from hook, HDC, BLO [SC] [2]

Fasten off with 18 in/46 cm yarn tail.

Feathered Serpent Head Feathers: Part 1

FEATHERED SERPENT HEAD FEATHERS: PART 2 (MAKE 2)

Optional

With Accent Color 2:

1. Start with a long enough yarn tail to weave in later, Ch 3, starting in the 2nd Ch from hook, HDC, SC, Ch 1, Turn [2]
2. BLO [SC], Ch 4, Turn [1]
3. Starting in the 2nd Ch from hook, HDC 2, SC, BLO [SC], Ch 1, Turn [4]
4. BLO [SC 3], Ch 4, Turn [3]
5. Starting in the 2nd Ch from hook, HDC 3, BLO [SC 3], Ch 1, Turn [6]
6. BLO [SC 4], Ch 4, Turn [4]
7. Starting in the 2nd Ch from hook, HDC 3, BLO [SC 4], Ch 1, Turn [7]
8. BLO [SC 4], Ch 3, Turn [4]
9. Starting in the 2nd Ch from hook, HDC 2, BLO [HDC, SC 3], Ch 1, Turn [6]
10. BLO [SC 3], Ch 2, Turn [3]
11. Starting in the 2nd Ch from hook, HDC, BLO [HDC, SC 2], Ch 1, Turn [4]
12. BLO [SC], Ch 2, Turn [1]
13. Starting in the 2nd Ch from hook, HDC, BLO [SC] [2]

Fasten off with 18 in/46 cm yarn tail.

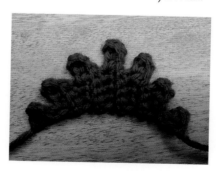

Feathered Serpent Head Feathers: Part 2

FEATHERED SERPENT HEAD FEATHERS: PART 3 (MAKE 2)

Optional

With Accent Color 3:

1. Start with a long enough yarn tail to weave in later, Ch 6, starting in the 2nd Ch from hook, HDC 3, SC 2, Ch 1, Turn [5]
2. BLO [SC, HDC 2], Ch 4, Turn [3]
3. Starting in the 2nd Ch from hook, HDC 3, BLO [SC 3], Ch 1, Turn [6]
4. BLO [SC 2, HDC 2], Ch 4, Turn [4]
5. Starting in the 2nd Ch from hook, HDC 3, BLO [HDC, SC 3], Ch 1, Turn [7]
6. BLO [SC 2, HDC 3], Ch 4, Turn [5]
7. Starting in the 2nd Ch from hook, HDC 3, BLO [HDC 2, SC 3], Ch 1, Turn [8]
8. BLO [SC 3, HDC 3], Ch 4, Turn [6]
9. Starting in the 2nd Ch from hook, HDC 3, BLO [HDC 2, SC 4], Ch 1, Turn [9]
10. BLO [SC 3, HDC 4], Ch 3, Turn [7]
11. Starting in the 2nd Ch from hook, HDC 2, BLO [HDC 4, SC 3], Ch 1, Turn [9]
12. BLO [SC 3, HDC 4], Ch 2, Turn [7]
13. Starting in the 2nd Ch from hook, HDC, BLO [HDC 4, SC 3], Ch 1, Turn [8]
14. BLO [SC 3, HDC 3], Ch 2, Turn [6]
15. Starting in the 2nd Ch from hook, HDC, BLO [HDC 3, SC 3], Ch 1, Turn [7]
16. BLO [SC 2, HDC 3], Ch 2, Turn [5]
17. Starting in the 2nd Ch from hook, HDC, BLO [HDC 2, SC 3], Ch 1, Turn [6]
18. BLO [SC 2, HDC 2], Ch 2, Turn [4]
19. Starting in the 2nd Ch from hook, HDC, BLO [HDC 2, SC 2], Ch 1, Turn [5]
20. BLO [SC, HDC 2], Ch 2, Turn [3]
21. Starting in the 2nd Ch from hook, HDC, BLO [HDC, SC 2], Ch 1, Turn [4]
22. BLO [SC, HDC], Ch 2, Turn [2]
23. Starting in the 2nd Ch from hook, HDC, BLO [HDC, SC], Ch 1, Turn [3]
24. BLO [SC], Ch 2, Turn [1]
25. Starting in the 2nd Ch from hook, HDC, BLO [SC] [2]

Fasten off with 18 in/46 cm yarn tail.

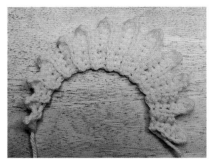

Feathered Serpent Head Feathers: Part 3

FEATHERED SERPENT HEAD FEATHERS: PART 4 (MAKE 1)

Optional

With Accent Color 4:

1. Start with a long enough yarn tail to weave in later, Ch 9, starting in the 2nd Ch from hook, HDC 4, SC 4, Ch 1, Turn [8]
2. BLO [SC 3, HDC 3], Ch 5, Turn [6]
3. Starting in the 2nd Ch from hook, HDC 4, BLO [HDC 2, SC 4], Ch 1, Turn [10]
4. BLO [SC 3, HDC 4], Ch 5, Turn [7]
5. Starting in the 2nd Ch from hook, HDC 4, BLO [HDC 2, SC 5], Ch 1, Turn [11]
6. BLO [SC 4, HDC 4], Ch 5, Turn [8]
7. Starting in the 2nd Ch from hook, HDC 4, BLO [HDC 3, SC 5], Ch 1, Turn [12]
8. BLO [SC 4, HDC 5], Ch 5, Turn [9]
9. Starting in the 2nd Ch from hook, HDC 4, BLO [HDC 3, SC 6], Ch 1, Turn [13]
10. BLO [SC 5, HDC 5], Ch 4, Turn [10]
11. Starting in the 2nd Ch from hook, HDC 3, BLO [HDC 6, SC 4], Ch 1, Turn [13]
12. BLO [SC 5, HDC 5], Ch 3, Turn [10]
13. Starting in the 2nd Ch from hook, HDC 2, BLO [HDC 5, SC 5], Ch 1, Turn [12]

14. BLO [SC 4, HDC 5], Ch 3, Turn [9]

15. Starting in the 2nd Ch from hook, HDC 2, BLO [HDC 4, SC 5], Ch 1, Turn [11]

16. BLO [SC 4, HDC 4], Ch 3, Turn [8]

17. Starting in the 2nd Ch from hook, HDC 2, BLO [HDC 3, SC 5], Ch 1, Turn [10]

18. BLO [SC 3, HDC 4], Ch 3, Turn [7]

19. Starting in the 2nd Ch from hook, HDC 2, BLO [HDC 3, SC 4], Ch 1, Turn [9]

20. BLO [SC 3, HDC 3], Ch 3, Turn [6]

21. Starting in the 2nd Ch from hook, HDC 2, BLO [HDC 3, SC 3], Ch 1, Turn [8]

22. BLO [SC 2, HDC 3], Ch 3, Turn [5]

23. Starting in the 2nd Ch from hook, HDC 2, BLO [HDC 2, SC 3], Ch 1, Turn [7]

24. BLO [SC 2, HDC 2], Ch 3, Turn [4]

25. Starting in the 2nd Ch from hook, HDC 2, BLO [HDC 2, SC 2] [6]

Fasten off with an 18 in/46 cm yarn tail.

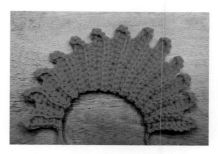

Feathered Serpent Head Feathers: Part 4

FEATHERED SERPENT TAIL ORNAMENTATION (MAKE 1)

Optional

Use the same colors that you used for Parts 1 through 4 of the Head Feathers (Accent Colors 1–4).

Part 1

1. Starting with Accent Color 2 yarn and a long enough yarn tail to weave in later, Ch 12, Sl St to the beginning stitch without twisting the chain to make a perfect circle of Ch stitches, Ch 1 [12]

2. Working into the Chain stitches, SC 12, Sl St to beginning stitch, Ch 1 [12]

> Mark the BLO of the 1st stitch of this row for reference in Row 4.

3. FLO [(SC, Ch 2, Sl St in the 2nd Ch from hook, SC) x 6], Sl St to beginning stitch, fasten off with a long enough yarn tail to weave in later [12]

4. Attach Accent Color 1 yarn to the marked leftover BLO stitch from Row 2 starting with a long enough yarn tail to weave in later, continuing into all of the leftover BLO stitches from Row 2, HDC 12, Sl St to beginning stitch, Ch 1 [12]

> Mark the BLO of the 1st stitch of this row for reference in Row 6.

5. FLO [(HDC 2, HDC Inc) x 4], Sl St to beginning stitch, fasten off with a long enough yarn tail to weave in later [16]

6. Attach Accent Color 3 to the marked leftover BLO from Row 4. Starting with a long enough yarn tail to weave in later, continuing into all of the leftover BLO stitches from Row 5, Ch 2, (DC 3, DC Inc) x 3, Sl St to beginning DC stitch, Ch 1 [15]

7. (HDC, HDC Inc, HDC) x 5, Sl St to beginning stitch [20]

Fasten off with 18 in/46 cm yarn tail.

Feathered Serpent Tail Ornamentation: Part 1

Part 2

1. Starting with Accent Color 4 and a long enough yarn tail to weave in later, Ch 13, Starting in the 2nd Ch from hook, HDC 6, SC 6, Ch 1, Turn [12]

2. BLO [SC 6], Ch 7, Turn [6]

3. Starting in the 2nd Ch from hook, HDC 6, BLO [HDC 3, SC 3], Ch 1, Turn [12]

4. BLO [SC 6], Ch 7, Turn [6]

5. Starting in the 2nd Ch from hook, HDC 6, BLO [SC 6], Ch 1, Turn [12]

6. BLO [SC 6], Ch 7, Turn [6]

7. Starting in the 2nd Ch from hook, HDC 6, BLO [HDC 3, SC 3], Ch 1, Turn [12]

8. BLO [SC 6], Ch 7, Turn [6]

9. Starting in the 2nd Ch from hook, HDC 6, BLO [SC 6], Ch 1, Turn [12]

10. BLO [SC 6], Ch 7, Turn [6]

11. Starting in the 2nd Ch from hook, HDC 6, BLO [HDC 3, SC 3], Ch 1, Turn [12]

12. BLO [SC 6], Ch 7, Turn [6]

13. Starting in the 2nd Ch from hook, HDC 6, BLO [SC 6], Ch 1, Turn [12]

14. BLO [SC 6], Ch 7, Turn [6]

15. Starting in the 2nd Ch from hook, HDC 6, BLO [HDC 3, SC 3], Ch 1, Turn [12]

16. BLO [SC 6], Ch 7, Turn [6]

17. Starting in the 2nd Ch from hook, HDC 6, BLO [SC 6], Ch 1, Turn [12]

18. BLO [SC 6], Ch 7, Turn [6]

19. Starting in the 2nd Ch from hook, HDC 6, BLO [HDC 3, SC 3] [12]

Fasten off with 18 in/46 cm yarn tail.

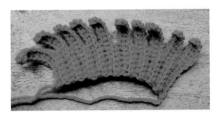

Feathered Serpent Tail Ornamentation: Part 2

FEATHERED SERPENT BELLY (MAKE 1)

Optional

1. Starting with a long enough yarn tail to weave in later, Ch 3, Turn, starting in the 2nd Ch from hook, SC 2, Ch 1, Turn [2]

2–15. (14 rows of) BLO [SC 2], Ch 1, Turn [2]

16. BLO [SC, <Dec>, SC], Ch 1, Turn [3]

17–94. (78 Rows of) BLO [SC 3], Ch 1, Turn [3]

95. BLO [2 Dec in 3 SC], Ch 1, Turn [2]

96–110. (15 rows of) BLO [SC 2], Ch 1, Turn [2]

Before fastening off, compare this piece to your body. Row 1 should align with the top of the neck, just under the head, and the belly piece should extend down to the underside of the body and be pinned in place along all of the curves of the body to the tail tip. If your belly piece is too long, you can undo some of the rows before fastening off. If your belly piece is too short, you can repeat the final row until it is long enough before fastening off.

Fasten off with a 48 in/122 cm yarn tail.

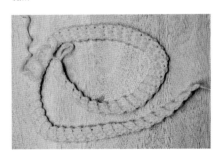

Feathered Serpent Belly

MEDIUM FEATHER WING (MAKE 2)

Part 1

NOTE: *For the Feathered Serpent, start with Accent Color 4. For the Owl Griffin, start with Accent Color 1.*

1. Starting with a 12 in/30 cm yarn tail, Ch 9, starting in the 2nd Ch from hook, HDC 8, Ch 1, Turn [8]
2. BLO [SC 7], Ch 2, Turn [7]
3. Starting in the 2nd Ch from hook, HDC, BLO [HDC 3, SC 2], Ch 1, Turn [6]
4. BLO [SC 5], Ch 3, Turn [5]
5. Starting in the 2nd Ch from hook, HDC 2, BLO [HDC 2, SC 2, SC/HDC Dec & HDC, SC], Ch 1, Turn [9]
6. BLO [SC 8], Ch 3, Turn [8]
7. Starting in the 2nd Ch from hook, HDC 2, BLO [HDC 2, SC 2], Ch 1, Turn [6]
8. BLO [SC 5], Ch 3, Turn [5]
9. Starting in the 2nd Ch from hook, HDC 2, BLO [HDC 2, SC 2, SC/HDC Dec & HDC, SC], Ch 1, Turn [9]
10. BLO [SC 8], Ch 3, Turn [8]
11. Starting in the 2nd Ch from hook, HDC 2, BLO [HDC 2, SC 4], Ch 1, Turn [8]
12. BLO [SC 7], Ch 3, Turn [7]
13. Starting in the 2nd Ch from hook, HDC 2, BLO [HDC 2, SC 3], Ch 1, Turn [7]
14. BLO [SC 6], Ch 3, Turn [6]
15. Starting in the 2nd Ch from hook, HDC 2, BLO [HDC 2, SC 2], Ch 1, Turn [6]
16. BLO [SC 5], Ch 3, Turn [5]

17. Starting in the 2nd Ch from hook, HDC 2, BLO [HDC 3, SC, (SC/HDC Dec & HDC) x 4, SC] [15]
18. Working along the unfinished edge of the wing back toward the OC, SC about 4 [4]

Fasten off with 18 in/46 cm yarn tail.

Medium Feather Wings: Part 1

Part 2

NOTE: *For the Feathered Serpent, use Accent Color 3. For the Owl Griffin, use Accent Color 2.*

1. Starting with a 12 in/30 cm yarn tail, Ch 5, starting in the 2nd Ch from hook, HDC 4, Ch 1, Turn [4]
2. BLO [SC 3], Ch 2, Turn [3]
3. Starting in the 2nd Ch from hook, HDC, BLO [SC], Ch 1, Turn [2]
4. BLO [SC], Ch 3, Turn [1]
5. Starting in the 2nd Ch from hook, HDC 2, BLO [SC/HDC Dec & HDC, SC], Ch 1, Turn [5]
6. BLO [SC 4], Ch 3, Turn [4]
7. Starting in the 2nd Ch from hook, HDC 2, BLO [SC], Ch 1, Turn [3]
8. BLO [SC 2], Ch 3, Turn [2]

9. Starting in the 2nd Ch from hook, HDC 2, BLO [SC, SC/HDC Dec & HDC, SC], Ch 1, Turn [6]
10. BLO [SC 5], Ch 3, Turn [5]
11. Starting in the 2nd Ch from hook, HDC 2, BLO [HDC, SC 2], Ch 1, Turn [5]
12. BLO [SC 4], Ch 3, Turn [4]
13. Starting in the 2nd Ch from hook, HDC 2, BLO [SC 2], Ch 1, Turn [4]
14. BLO [SC 3], Ch 3, Turn [3]
15. Starting in the 2nd Ch from hook, HDC, SC, BLO [SC 2, (SC/HDC Dec & HDC) x 3] [10]
16. Working along the unfinished edge of the wing back toward the OC, SC about 4 [4]

Row 16 should have the same number of stitches as Row 18 of Part 1.

Fasten off with 18 in/46 cm yarn tail.

Medium Feather Wings: Part 2

Part 3

NOTE: For the Feathered Serpent, use Accent Color 2. For the Owl Griffin, use the Main Color.

1. Starting with a 12 in/30 cm yarn tail, Ch 3, starting in the 2nd Ch from hook, HDC 2, Ch 1, Turn [2]
2. BLO [SC], Ch 2, Turn [1]
3. Starting in the 2nd Ch from hook, HDC, BLO [HDC], Ch 1, Turn [2]
4. BLO [SC], Ch 3, Turn [1]
5. Starting in the 2nd Ch from hook, HDC, SC, Ch 1, Turn [2]

> To help keep track of stitches and prevent the piece from twisting and becoming confusing, you can put stitch markers in all unused stitches from Rows 5 and 7. These unused stitches are located on the side of the wing with the ends of feathers.

6. BLO [SC], Ch 4, Turn [1]
7. Starting in the 2nd Ch from hook, HDC, SC, Ch 1, Turn [2]
8. BLO [SC], Ch 4, Turn [1]
9. Starting in the 2nd Ch from hook, HDC 3, BLO [(SC/HDC Dec & HDC) x 2] [7]
10. Working along the unfinished edge of the wing back toward the OC, SC about 4 [4]

Fasten off with 18 in/46 cm yarn tail.

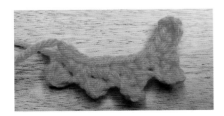

Medium Feather Wings: Part 3

Part 4

NOTE: For the Feathered Serpent, use Accent Color 1. For the Owl Griffin, use Accent Color 1.

1. Starting with a 12 in/30 cm yarn tail, layer parts 1 through 3 on top of each other with the bottom edges (starting chains on all pieces) aligned to create a Left Wing and a Right Wing. Use the Part 4 yarn color to attach them together, starting by working through all 3 panels at once through the OC (and continue toward the tip of the wing feathers until you run out of stitches on Part 3, and continue working into Part 1 and Part 2 at the same time until you run out of stitches on Part 2, and then continue working into Part 1), SC 17, Ch 3, Turn [17]

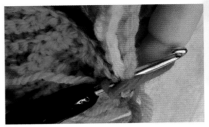

2. Starting in the 2nd Ch from hook, HDC 3, SC 2, Sl St 6, Ch 2, starting in the 2nd Ch from hook, HDC, working into the same stitch as your last Slip Stitch, HDC, continuing into the next available stitch, SC, Sl St 6 [20]

Fasten off with 18 in/46 cm yarn tail.

Medium Feather Wings: Part 4

FEATHERED SERPENT ASSEMBLY

1. Pin the Belly panel in place along the Body, starting with the OC at the neck as shown, sew to attach by whipstitching around the entire edge of the belly piece, and weave in ends.

2. Compare the head to the wire (if you used wire in the body) extending from the neck, bend the wire over on itself, optionally secure the wire to itself with a small strip of duct tape, and then slide the head onto the wire; pull the neck flap over the back of the head and pin in place. Sew the head to attach using yarn tails, and weave in ends.

3. Pin the head feathers in place as shown. It is optional to use all of the head feathers; you can choose to use only some or none of the head feathers. Sew to attach using yarn tails, and weave in ends. The starting yarn tail for each feather piece should be at the head end. The best way to sew to attach is to pin all the feathers in place and then unpin all but the center-most feathers, sew that to attach, and weave in ends. Repin. Repeat the process.

4. Slide the OC end of Part 1 of the tail ornamentation onto the end of the body's tail. Wrap Part 2 of the tail around the end of the body's tail as shown. Pin in place on the end of the tail. Slide Part 1 of the tail up to meet Part 2, and pin in place so that it covers the base of Part 2. Sew to attach using yarn tails, and weave in ends.

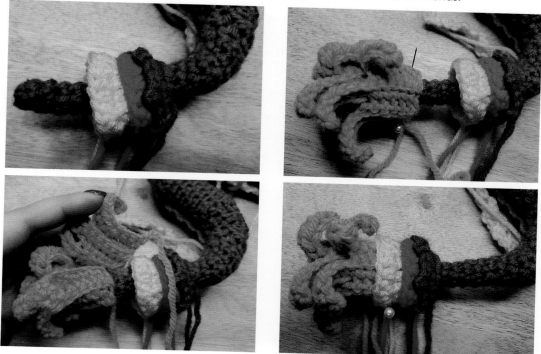

5. Determine where you want to place the wings. You can place them along the neck part of the body, you can place them along the body, you can even make multiple pairs of wings to place along the length of the body. Take a wire, bend the tip of it over on itself by about 1 to 2 in/2.5 to 5 cm, and secure it to itself with duct tape.

Insert the straight end of the wire into the body where you want the wings to go. Hold one set of wings up against the secured side of the wire; push the wire through the body until the secured side reaches just to the end of the first wing (bend the wire to fit the wing shape as necessary). Hold the other wing against the opposite end of the wire; trim this end so that it extends 1 to 2 in/2.5 to 5 cm beyond the end of the wing. Fold down this end of the wire by 1 to 2 in/2.5 to 5 cm and secure in place. With only one single wire, the wing wire will be fairly stable, particularly after you use the yarn tails to sew the wing in place.

6. If you want an even more stable wing, insert a slightly shorter second wire 1 to 2 stitches below the first wire into or through the body parallel to the first wire. The second wire will stabilize the wing and prevent spinning. Both wires will be hidden between the wing layers.

7. Using thin strips of duct tape, wrap the end of the folded wire to secure it to itself and then secure the second wire to the first wire.

8. Pin the open wings in place with the wire sandwiched between the two largest wing panels.

Sew to attach where the wing touches along the body and sew the two wing panels to each other. Use very small stitches to do so, and try to minimize the impact of the stitches showing texture or showing yarn color. Again, make sure you sew along the base edge of the wing that touches the body to attach the wing to the body (this will increase stability).

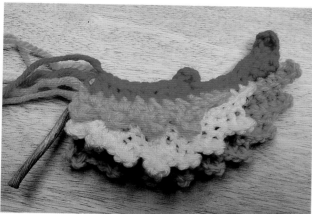

OWL GRIFFIN

The Owl Griffin is similar to the Griffin in having a lion-like body, but it has an owl-like head and wings.

SIZE:

An Owl Griffin from this pattern is about 7 in/18 cm tall from the bottom of the body to the top of the ears on the head, about 9 in/ 23 cm long from the neck to the curved tail tip, 4 in/10 cm wide from side to side at its widest part of the body, and 9 in/23 cm wide from wing tip to wing tip.

MATERIALS

» Yarn: See table on page 184 to see the parts you will make for your Owl Griffin, and find the yarn amounts needed for each piece. All yarn is #4 medium/worsted weight, and all yarn amounts are approximate. Total amounts:
  • Main Color (white): 104 yd/ 95 m
  • Accent Color 1 (light mottled brown): 57 yd/52 m
  • Accent Color 2 (dark brown): 14 yd/12.75 m

» US size G (4 mm) hook

» Safety eyes: 12 mm or 15 mm

» Fiberfill stuffing

» Darning needle

» Pins

» Scissors

» Duct tape

» Wire strong enough to support posing. Recommend 3 pieces of 18-in/46-cm, 18-gauge, paper-wrapped wire (found in the faux floral arrangement section of any craft store; if this exact wire cannot be found, please use 14- to 16-gauge wire—err on the side of heavier wire)

» Pliers

» Optional: Glass gems for weighted feet

INSTRUCTIONS

Look at the chart below to see the pieces you need to make for your Owl Griffin. The Medium Feather Wings are the same as those for the Feathered Serpent (page 175). Crochet all of the parts of your Owl Griffin following the instructions on pages 186–192, and then proceed to Owl Griffin Assembly on page 193 to put them all together.

PARTS TO MAKE	PAGE NO.	NUMBER TO MAKE	YARN COLOR	APPROX. YARN NEEDED
Owl Griffin Face Plate	186	1	Main Color, Accent Color 1	8 yd/7.25 m Main Color, 2 yd/1.75 m Accent Color 1
Owl Griffin Body	187	1	Main Color	25 yd/22.75 m
Owl Griffin Beak	188	1	Accent Color 2	2 yd/1.75 m
Owl Griffin Body Accent Color	189	1	Accent Color 1	23 yd/21 m
Owl Griffin Rear Leg	189	2	Main Color	35 yd/32 m for 2 legs
Owl Griffin Front Leg	190	2	Main Color	25 yd/22.75 m for 2 legs
Owl Griffin Tail	191	1	Main Color	16 yd/14.75 m
Owl Griffin Ear	192	2	Main Color, Accent Color 1	4 yd/3.75 m Main Color, 6 yd/5.5 m Accent Color 1 for 2 ears
Medium Feather Wing	175	2	Main Color, Accent Colors 1 and 2	7 yd/6.5 m Main Color, 26 yd/23.75 m Accent Color 1, 12 yd/11 m Accent Color 2 for 2 wings

GALLERY

Owl Griffin in natural colors

Owl Griffin in fantasy colors

Owl Griffin in fantasy colors

OWL GRiFFin PARTS PATTERNS

OWL GRIFFIN FACE PLATE

For a realistic owl, I recommend white (main color) for Parts 1, 2, and 3 and cream/brown/gradient mottled color or heathered for the Accent Color in Part 4.

Part 1
Using the Main Body Color yarn (white):

1. Starting with a long enough yarn tail to weave in later, Ch 6, Turn, starting in the 2nd Ch from hook, (HDC Inc, HDC) x 2, HDC Inc [8]

> Mark the 5th stitch on this piece for reference on where to attach the Accent color in Part 4.

Fasten off with 12 in/30 cm yarn tail.

Part 2
Using the Main Body Color yarn (white):

1. Starting with a long enough yarn tail to weave in later, Ch 4, Sl St to beginning Ch stitch, Ch 1, HDC 8 around the Ch stitch circle, Sl St to beginning stitch, Ch 2 [8]

2. HDC Inc, HDC & SC, Inc x 4, Sl St [13]

> On your Part 2 piece, mark the 4th stitch in Row 2.

Fasten off with a 12 in/30 cm yarn tail.

Part 3
Using the Main Body Color yarn (white):

1. Starting with a long enough yarn tail to weave in later, Ch 4, Sl St to beginning Ch Stitch, Ch 1, HDC 8 around the Ch stitch circle, Sl St to beginning stitch, Ch 2, Turn [8]

2. HDC Inc, HDC & SC, Inc x 4, Sl St [13]

> Mark the front-most loop of the 12th stitch in Row 2. When you join Parts 1–4 below, the "wrong side" of Part 3 Row 2 will face out.

Fasten off with a 12 in/30 cm yarn tail.

Part 4
Using the Accent Feather color yarn:

1A. Starting with a long enough yarn tail to weave in later, attach the accent color yarn to the BLO of the marked stitch from Part 1, BLO Sl St a total of 4 to the end of Part 1 [Sl St 4]

1B. Continuing into the BLO of the marked stitch on Part 3, BLO [Sl St 9]

IC. Continuing into the BLO of the marked stitch on Part 2, BLO [Sl St 9]

ID. Continuing into the BLO of the 1st stitch on Part 1, BLO [Sl St 4], BLO [Sl St] into the same stitch you 1st slip stitched into in this row [Sl St 5]

Fasten off with 18 in/46 cm yarn tail.

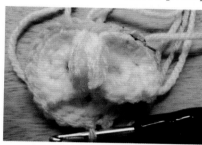

OWL GRIFFIN BODY

1. SC 6 in Magic Circle, Sl St to beginning stitch, Ch 1 [6]

2. Inc x 6, Sl St to beginning stitch, Ch 1 [12]

3. (SC, Inc) x 6, Sl St to beginning stitch, Ch 1 [18]

4–8. (5 rows of) SC 18, Sl St to beginning stitch, Ch 1 [18]

Follow all substeps of each row in order (i.e., 9A, 9B, etc.). These short rows create the curves and shaping of the body. They will sometimes go beyond where the row began; follow the pattern exactly, and it will work. Each sub-row will have a stitch count for the number of stitches created in that sub-row, and there will be a final stitch count at the end of the final sub-row to indicate how many stitches are available on the edge of the work once all the sub-rows are complete.

A video tutorial for how to crochet short rows is available on the Crafty Intentions YouTube channel here: https://www.youtube.com/watch?v=sh5T-idiwm8&t=159s

Hybrid decreases like the SC/HDC Dec & HDC stitches are defined in the Glossary (page 4) and demonstrated on the Crafty Intentions YouTube channel here: https://www.youtube.com/watch?v=h4wkxMOMqXg&t=5s

9A. SC 6, Inc, SC 3, Ch 1, Turn [11]

9B. SC 8, Ch 1, Turn [8]

9C. SC 7, SC/HDC Dec & HDC, SC 4, Inc, SC 2, Sl St to beginning stitch, Ch 1 [17 stitches are worked in this sub-row in total; 20 stitches are available to be worked into in the following row]

10. SC 2, HDC & HDC/SC Dec, SC 16, Sl St to beginning stitch, Ch 1 [20]

11. SC, Inc, SC 9, Inc, SC 8, Sl St to beginning stitch, Ch 1 [22]

12A. SC 14, Ch 1, Turn [14]

12B. SC 11, Ch 1, Turn [11]

12C. SC 10, SC/HDC Dec & HDC, SC 7, Sl St to beginning stitch, Ch 1 [19 stitches are worked in this sub-row in total; 22 stitches are available to be worked into in the following row]

13. SC 2, HDC & HDC/SC Dec, SC 18, Sl St to beginning stitch, Ch 1 [22]

14A. SC 15, Ch 1, Turn [15]

14B. SC 13, Ch 1, Turn [13]

14C. SC 12, SC/HDC Dec, SC 6, Sl St to beginning stitch, Ch 1 [19 stitches are worked in this sub-row in total; 21 stitches are available to be worked into in the following row]

15. SC, HDC/SC Dec, SC 18, Sl St to beginning stitch, Ch 1 [20]

16–19. (4 rows of) SC 20, Sl St to beginning stitch, Ch 1 [20]

20. (SC, Dec, SC) x 5, Sl St to beginning stitch, Ch 1 [15]

21. (SC, Dec) x 5, Sl St to beginning stitch, Ch 1 [10]

Insert 12 mm or 15 mm black safety eyes THROUGH the face plate eye holes, between Row 18 and Row 19 on the body with 3 stitch spaces between the posts, fasten securely. Stuff the body medium-firm with fiberfill, and continue to stuff as you finish the work. If you are having issues fastening the safety eyes through multiple layers of crochet work, you can insert them solely through the face plate, and then you'll have to sew the face place to attach to the head securely.

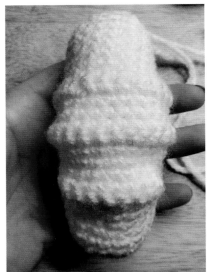

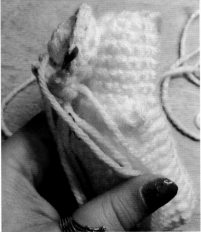

Owl Griffin Body with Face Plate

22. Dec x 5 [5]

Fasten off with 18 in/46 cm yarn tail.

OWL GRIFFIN BEAK

1. Starting with a long enough yarn tail to weave in later, Ch 5, starting in the 2nd Ch from hook, Sl St 3, SC [4]

Fasten off with 12 in/30 cm yarn tail.

Owl Griffin Beak

OWL GRIFFIN BODY ACCENT COLOR

Work in an Accent Color, such as a mottled or heathered brown.

1. SC 6 in Magic Circle, Sl St to beginning stitch, Ch 1 [6]
2. Inc x 6, Sl St to beginning stitch, Ch 1 [12]
3. (SC, Inc) x 6, Sl St to beginning stitch, Ch 1 [18]
4. (SC 5, Inc) x 3, Sl St to beginning stitch, Ch 1 [21]
5. SC 21, Sl St to beginning stitch, Ch 1 [21]
6-9. (4 rows of) SC 18, Ch 1, Turn [18]

> The rest of this piece will be worked back and forth in rows.

10. Inc, SC 16, Inc, Ch 1, Turn [20]
11-13. (3 rows of) SC 20, Ch 1, Turn [20]
14. SC, Dec, SC 14, Dec, SC, Ch 1, Turn [18]
15. SC 18, Ch 1, Turn [18]
16. SC, Dec, SC 12, Dec, SC, Ch 1, Turn [16]
17. SC 16, Ch 1, Turn [16]
18. SC, Dec, SC 10, Dec, SC, Ch 1, Turn [14]
19. SC 14, Ch 1, Turn [14]
20. SC, Dec, SC 8, Dec, SC, Ch 1, Turn [12]
21. SC 12, Ch 1, Turn [12]
22. SC, Dec, SC 6, Dec, SC, Ch 1, Turn [10]
23. SC 10, Ch 1, Turn [10]
24. SC, Dec, SC 4, Dec, SC, Ch 1, Turn [8]
25. SC 8, Ch 1, Turn [8]
26. Dec, SC 4, Dec, Ch 1, Turn [6]
27. Dec, SC 2, Dec [4]

Fasten off with 24 in/61 cm yarn tail.

Owl Griffin Body Accent Color

OWL GRIFFIN REAR LEG (MAKE 2)

Part 1
Make 1 Knee piece:

1. SC 6 in Magic Circle, Sl St to beginning stitch, Ch 1 [6]
2. Inc x 6, Sl St to beginning stitch, Ch 1 [12]
3. (SC, Inc, SC) x 4, Sl St to beginning stitch, Ch 1 [16]
4. SC 4, HDC 8, SC 4, Sl St to beginning stitch, Ch 1 [16]
5. SC 3, Inc, SC 8, Inc, SC 3, Sl St to beginning stitch, Ch 1 [18]

Fasten off with a long enough yarn tail to weave in.

Part 2
Start the Foot; you will use the Part 1: Knee piece in Row 8:

1. HDC, SC, HDC 5 in Magic Circle, Sl St to beginning stitch, Ch 1 [7]
2. SC, Inc, SC, Inc, SC 2, Inc, Sl St to beginning stitch, Ch 1 [10]
3-5. (3 rows of) SC 10, Sl St to beginning stitch, Ch 1 [10]
6. SC 2, Dec x 2, SC 4, Sl St to beginning stitch, Ch 1 [8]
7. SC 8, Sl St to beginning stitch, Ch 1 [8]
8. SC 2, Inc, starting in the 1st stitch of Row 5 on the Knee, SC 18 around the knee, Starting into the next available stitch on the foot, Inc, SC 4, Sl St to beginning stitch, Ch 1 [28]

> When working into the Knee, insert your hook from the outside to the inside of the work, just as you normally would. Work around the entire outside edge of the Knee, and then complete your row by working the last stitches on the Foot.

9. SC 28, Sl St to beginning stitch, Ch 1 [28]

10. SC 3, Dec, SC 16, Dec, SC 5, Sl St to beginning stitch, Ch 1 [26]

> Mark the 7th stitch in this row to reference in attaching the yarn in Part 3 of the Rear Leg.

11. SC 5, Start a Decrease in the next available stitch, skip 13 stitches and complete the decrease into the next available stitch, SC 6, Sl St to beginning stitch, Ch 1 [12]

> Stuff medium-firm with fiberfill in Part 1. Stuff lightly in Part 2. Part 3 should have little to no stuffing in it.

12. (SC, Dec) x 4, Sl St to beginning stitch, Ch 1 [8]

> Row 12 will be worked only into the stitches from Row 11 and not into any of the skipped stitches from Row 10.

13. SC 2, Dec x 2, SC 2, Sl St to beginning stitch [6]

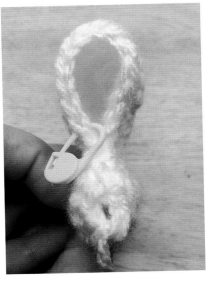

Fasten off with 12 in/30 cm yarn tail to use to sew hole shut.

Part 3

Starting with a long enough yarn tail to weave in later, attach the yarn to the marked stitch from Row 10 of Part 2.

1. SC 12, Inc, SC in the same stitch that you worked the 1st SC into, Sl St to beginning stitch, Ch 1 [15]

2–3. (2 rows of) SC 15, Sl St to beginning stitch, Ch 1 [15]

> You do not need to Ch 1 on the final repeat of this row.

Fasten off with 18 in/46 cm yarn tail.

Owl Griffin Rear Leg

OWL GRIFFIN FRONT LEG (MAKE 2)

1. SC 8 in Magic Circle, Sl St to beginning stitch, Ch 1 [8]

2. Inc x 2, HDC Inc x 4, Inc x 2, Sl St to beginning stitch, Ch 1 [16]

3. SC 5, Dec, SC 2, Dec, SC 5, Sl St to beginning stitch, Ch 1 [14]

4. SC 4, HDC Dec, HDC 2, HDC Dec, SC 4, Sl St to beginning stitch, Ch 1 [12]

5. SC 4, Dec x 2, SC 4, Sl St to beginning stitch, Ch 1 [10]

6. SC 2, Dec, SC 2, Dec, SC 2, Sl St to beginning stitch, Ch 1 [8]

7–8. (2 rows of) SC 8, Sl St to beginning stitch, Ch 1 [8]

9. SC 4, Inc, SC 3, Sl St to beginning stitch, Ch 1 [9]

10. SC 9, Sl St to beginning stitch, Ch 1 [9]

11. Dec, SC 5, Dec, Sl St to beginning stitch, Ch 1 [7]

12. SC 7, Sl St to beginning stitch, Ch 1 [7]

13. Inc, SC 5, Inc, Sl St to beginning stitch, Ch 1 [9]

14. (SC 2, Inc) x 3, Sl St to beginning stitch, Ch 1 [12]

15–19. (5 rows of) SC 12, Sl St to beginning stitch, Ch 1 [12]

20. (SC, Dec, SC) x 3, Sl St to beginning stitch [9]

NOTE: Before stuffing, you can optionally insert a glass gem into the foot of the front leg. This will help keep the bottom of the paw flat (the flat side of the gem should be down) and prevent you from rounding it out with stuffing as you stuff the leg. Then stuff the leg; the foot to middle should be medium-firm, but the upper part of the leg should have little to no stuffing.

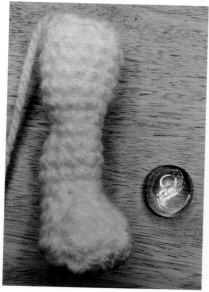

Fasten off with 18 in/46 cm yarn tail.

Owl Griffin Front Leg

OWL GRIFFIN TAIL

1. SC 8 in Magic Circle, Sl St to beginning stitch, Ch 1 [8]
2. (SC 3, Inc) x 2, Sl St to beginning stitch, Ch 1 [10]
3-12. (10 rows of) SC 10, Sl St to beginning stitch, Ch 1 [10]

> The tail will use a wire inside to stabilize your Owl Griffin, so it is not necessary to stuff it with fiberfill. If you do not want to use wire, you can stuff it lightly with fiberfill as you go.

13. SC 4, Dec, SC 4, Sl St to beginning stitch, Ch 1 [9]
14-18. (5 Rows of) SC 9, Sl St to beginning stitch, Ch 1 [9]
19. SC 3, 2 Dec in 3 SC, SC 3, Sl St to beginning stitch, Ch 1 [8]

20-23. (4 rows of) SC 8, Sl St to beginning stitch, Ch 1 [8]
24. SC 3, Dec, SC 3, Sl St to beginning stitch, Ch 1 [7]
25-27. (3 rows of) SC 7, Sl St to beginning stitch, Ch 1 [7]
28. SC 2, 2 Dec in 3 SC, SC 2, Sl St to beginning stitch, Ch 1 [6]
29-30. (2 Rows of) SC 6, Sl St to beginning stitch, Ch 1 [6]

> You do not need to Ch 1 on the final repeat of this row.

Fasten off with 12 in/30 cm yarn tail.

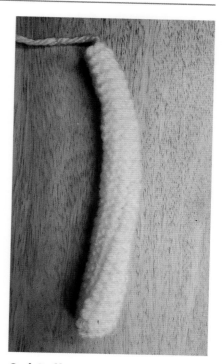

Owl Griffin Tail

OWL GRIFFIN EAR (MAKE 2)

Part 1
Using the Body Color yarn (white):

1. Starting with a long enough yarn tail to weave in later, Ch 2, working into the 2nd Ch from hook, SC 4, Ch 1 [4]
2. SC, HDC Inc x 2, SC [6]

Fasten off with 12 in/30 cm yarn tail.

Part 2
Using the Accent Color yarn:

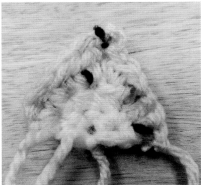

1. Starting with a long enough yarn tail to weave in later, Ch 2, working into the 2nd Ch from hook, SC 4, Ch 1, Turn [4]
2. SC, HDC Inc x 2, SC, Ch 1, Turn [6]
3. Hold this Part 2 piece against the Part 1 piece, and working through both pieces at the same time, Inc, SC & HDC, HDC & DC, Ch 2, Sl St in the 2nd Ch from Hook, DC & HDC, HDC & SC, Inc [12]

Fasten off with 12 in/30 cm yarn tail.

Owl Griffin Ear

OWL GRIFFIN ASSEMBLY

1. Sew the hole shut in the top of the head, and weave in that yarn tail.

2. Pin the rear legs and the front legs in place, and make sure that the feet/legs are positioned such that the body sits evenly and securely on a flat surface. The bottom of the body should not sit directly on the surface but should be held up by the rear legs. The entire body should be at an angle, with the face farther forward than the rear. The tops of the front legs should rest just below the bottom of the face plate and wrap slightly around the sides of the body. Using yarn tails, use small whipstitches to sew ONLY the rear legs in place. Sew shut the small holes on the back joint of the rear legs and, using the same yarn tail, sew shut the small gap in the front bend of the rear legs as well.

3. Unpin the front legs.

4. Place and pin to attach the Owl Griffin Body Accent Color, layering it over the back legs. Smooth it down over the back of the body, and, after finalizing placement, use a yarn tail to sew it to attach and weave in ends. It should adhere to the curves of the rear legs.

5. Repin to attach the front legs, verify placement, and ensure that your Owl Griffin can sit securely on a flat surface. Once placement is finalized, use yarn tails to sew the front legs to attach, and weave in ends.

6. Before you sew anything to attach as far as the center of the face/beak goes, using the face yarn tails, sew just inside the outer edge of the face to attach it to the body. Leave the edge of the face slightly standing apart from the body as you do this. Shape the top edge of the face to be slightly indented, like the top of a heart. See photos for clarity. Weave in ends as you go.

7. Pin the beak in place just inside the nose area of the face so that it peeks out below the nose area. Sew to attach using its yarn tails, and weave in ends.

8. Using the remaining face yarn tails, sew the nose feathers over the beak, reinforce the eye area to secure the face plate to the body just inside the outer edge of the face plate as you sew to attach (leave the outer edge of the face plate slightly outstanding from the body), and weave in all face yarn tails.

9. Fold the ears in half and pin to attach. Once placement is finalized, use yarn tails to sew to attach, and weave in ends.

10. Wire for the tail is optional, but without wire the tail will not be poseable. Take one wire, fold the end of the wire over on itself, secure it to itself with a thin strip of duct tape, and insert the folded end of the wire into the tail piece for the owl griffin. Stuff the rest of the tail lightly if desired; trim the wire that extends out of the tail to only be 2 to 3 in/5 to 7.5 cm long. Insert the wire that extends beyond the base of the tail into the body of the owl griffin where you want the tail to be placed (recommended just under the body accent color, between the rear legs). Once placement is finalized, use yarn tails to sew to attach, and weave in ends.

11. Take 2 18-in/46-cm, 18-gauge, paper-wrapped stem wires or a suitable alternative that is strong yet moldable (pipe cleaners are not strong enough), and insert the first wire through the body at the point where you want the

upper edge of the wing to sit on either side of the body.

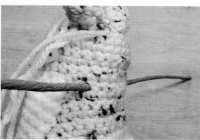

12. Compare each side of the wire to the corresponding wing. Fold the wire over on itself so that it does not extend beyond the shorter/front panel of the wing. The wire will be sandwiched between the largest two wing panels. Bend the wire to match the inner edge of where the two wing panels meet.

13. Insert a second, slightly shorter wire into the body 1 to 2 stitches below the first wire. The second wire will stabilize the wing and prevent spinning.

Both wires will be hidden between the wing layers.

14. Using thin strips of duct tape, wrap the end of the folded wire to secure it to itself and then secure the second wire to the first wire.

15. Pin the wings in place with the wire sandwiched between the two largest wing panels. Sew to attach where the wing touches along the body and sew the two wing panels to each other. Use very small stitches to do so, and try to minimize the impact of the stitches showing texture or showing yarn color.

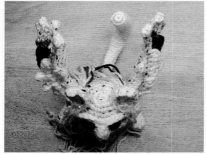

PHOENIX

The magnificent Phoenix has long, shining wings and tail feathers and is glorious and regal in bearing. It is a very rare sight, as it comes to the human realm only once every thousand years to die and be reborn.

SIZE:

A Phoenix from this pattern is 6 in/15 cm tall standing from toes to the top of the head, it is 7 in/18 cm long from the butt to the beak, and the wingspan is 16 in/40.5 cm.

MATERIALS

- Yarn: See table on page 198 to find the parts you will make for your Phoenix and the yarn amounts needed for each piece. All yarn is #4 medium/worsted weight, and all yarn amounts are approximate. Total amounts:
  - Main Color: 235 to 350 yd/ 215 m to 320 m (depending on number of tail feathers)
  - Beak Color: 6 yd/5.5 m
  - Foot Color: 28 yd/25.5 m

- US size G (4 mm) crochet hook
- US size D (3.25 mm) crochet hook
- US size C (2.75 mm) crochet hook
- 12 mm safety eyes
- Fiberfill stuffing
- Darning needle
- Pins
- Scissors
- Duct tape
- Wire strong enough to support posing. I recommend 6 pieces of 18-in/46-cm, 18-gauge, paper-wrapped wire (found in the faux floral arrangement section of any craft store; if this exact wire cannot be found, please use 14- to 16-gauge wire—err on the side of heavier wire).
- Pliers

INSTRUCTIONS

Look at the chart and the Gallery below to choose the pieces you want to make for your Phoenix. For the Phoenix, you have options on how many head and tail feathers you want and whether you want a tail fan and where to position it. Crochet all of the parts of your Phoenix following the instructions on pages 200–213, and then proceed to Phoenix Assembly on page 214 to put them all together.

PARTS TO MAKE	PAGE NO.	NUMBER TO MAKE	YARN COLOR	APPROX. YARN NEEDED
Phoenix Tail Fan	200	1	Main Color	25 yd/22.75 m
Phoenix Body	200	1	Main Color	35 yd/32 m
Phoenix Head	202	1	Main Color, Beak Color	7 yd/6.5 m Main Color, 3 yd/2.75 m Beak Color
Phoenix Beak	202	1	Beak Color	3 yd/2.75 m
Phoenix Head Ornament (3 Feathers)	203	1	Main Color	2 yd/1.75 m
Phoenix Head Ornament (7 Feathers)	203	1	Main Color	4 yd/3.75 m
Phoenix Foot	203	2	Foot Color	18 yd/16.5 m for 2 feet
Phoenix Leg	204	2	Main Color, Foot Color	8 yd/7.25 m Main Color, 10 yd/9 m Foot Color for 2 legs
Phoenix Wing	205	2	Main Color	108 yd/98.75 m for 2 wings
Phoenix Long Tail Feather	208	1	Main Color	30 yd/27.5 m per feather
Phoenix Short Tail Feather	212	1	Main Color	16 yd/14.75 m per feather

GALLERY

Phoenix with 1 long tail feather,
2 short tail feathers, plus
tail fan on top of all feathers
(both head feather options)

Phoenix with 1 long tail feather, 2 short tail feathers, plus tail fan placed between the 2 short tail feathers and the long tail feather (both head feather options)

Phoenix with tail fan, plus 3-feather head ornament

PHOENIX PARTS PATTERNS

PHOENIX TAIL FAN (MAKE 1)

Optional

> The reason to make this piece first is for continuity if you are using a gradient/color-changing yarn. By making this first, you can lead straight into the body and it will be cohesive when you sew them together.

With US size G (4 mm) crochet hook:

1. Ch 26, Turn, starting in the 2nd Ch from hook, Sl St, SC, HDC, DC 16, HDC Dec x 3, Ch 1, Turn [22]

2. BLO [SC 15], Ch 17, Turn [15]

3. Starting in the 2nd Ch from hook, Sl St, SC, BLO [HDC, DC 20, HDC Dec x 3, Dec], Ch 1, Turn [27]

4. BLO [SC 18], Ch 17, Turn [18]

5. Starting in the 2nd Ch from hook, Sl St, SC, BLO [HDC, DC 23, HDC Dec x 3, Dec], Ch 1, Turn [30]

6. BLO [SC 21], Ch 17, Turn [21]

7. Starting in the 2nd Ch from hook, Sl St, SC, BLO [HDC, DC 26, HDC 6, SC 2], Ch 1, Turn [37]

8. BLO [SC 21], Ch 10, Turn [21]

9. Starting in the 2nd Ch from hook, Sl St, SC, BLO [HDC, DC 23, HDC Inc x 3, Inc], Ch 1, Turn [34]

10. BLO [SC 18], Ch 9, Turn [18]

11. Starting in the 2nd Ch from hook, Sl St, SC, BLO [HDC, DC 20, HDC Inc x 3], Ch 1, Turn [29]

12. BLO [SC 15], Ch 8, Turn [15]

13. Starting in the 2nd Ch from hook, Sl St, SC, BLO [HDC, DC 16, HDC Inc x 3] [25]

Fasten off with 18 in/46 cm yarn tail.

Phoenix Tail Fan

PHOENIX BODY

With US size G (4 mm) crochet hook:

1. Ch 4, Turn, starting in the 2nd Ch from hook, Inc, SC, Inc x 2 in the last available Ch stitch, Keep crocheting around to the other side of the row of Ch stitches, SC, Inc into the same stitch as the 1st Inc in this row, Sl St to beginning stitch, Ch 1 [10]

2. SC 10, Sl St to beginning stitch, Ch 1 [10]

3. (Inc, SC 4) x 2, Sl St to beginning stitch, Ch 1 [12]

4. SC 12, Sl St to beginning stitch, Ch 1 [12]

5. (SC 3, Inc) x 3, Sl St to beginning stitch, Ch 1 [15]

6. SC 2, Inc, (SC 4, Inc) x 2, SC 2, Sl St to beginning stitch, Ch 1 [18]

7. (SC 5, Inc) x 3, Sl St to beginning stitch, Ch 1 [21]

8. SC 3, Inc, (SC 6, Inc) x 2, SC 3, Sl St to beginning stitch, Ch 1 [24]

9. SC 24, Sl St to beginning stitch, Ch 1 [24]

10. SC 24, Sl St to beginning stitch, Ch 1 [24]

11. SC 24, Sl St to beginning stitch, Ch 1 [24]

Beginning in Row 12, the stitch count is the topmost stitch count once the row is complete, not the cumulative number of stitches made in the row instructions. You will sometimes go beyond where the row began or where the previous row ended. Always work into stitches as normal; do not work into the side of stitches. Follow the instructions exactly as written. For a video demonstration on short rows, go here: https://www.youtube.com/watch?v=sh5T-idiwm8

Begin to stuff the body medium-firm with fiberfill. Continue to stuff as you work.

12A. SC 16, Ch 1, Turn [16]
12B. SC 16, Ch 1, Turn [16]
12C. SC 24 [24]
13A. SC 17, Ch 1, Turn [17]
13B. SC 16, Ch 1, Turn [16]
13C. SC 24 [24]
14. SC 24 [24]
15. (SC 10, Dec) x 2, Sl St to beginning stitch, Ch 1 [22]
16. SC 22, Sl St to beginning stitch, Ch 1 [22]
17. SC 6, Inc x 3, SC 13, Sl St to beginning stitch, Ch 1 [25]
18. SC 25, Sl St to beginning stitch, Ch 1 [25]
19–21. (3 rows of) SC 25, Sl St to beginning stitch, Ch 1 [25]
22. SC, (SC 4, Dec) x 3, SC 6, Sl St to beginning stitch, Ch 1 [22]

23A. SC 18, Ch 1, Turn [18]
23B. SC 6, Dec x 2, SC 6, Ch 1, Turn [14]
23C. SC 20 [20]
24A. (SC 3, Dec) x 3, Ch 1, Turn [12]
24B. SC 12, Ch 1, Turn [12]
24C. SC 14, Inc, SC 2 [18]
25. SC 4, Dec x 2, SC 7, <Dec>, SC 3, Sl St to beginning stitch, Ch 1 [17]
26. SC 3, Dec x 2, SC 6, Inc, SC 3, Sl St to beginning stitch, Ch 1 [16]
27. SC 2, Dec x 2, SC 10, Sl St to beginning stitch, Ch 1 [14]
28. SC, Dec x 2, SC 9, Sl St to beginning stitch, Ch 1 [12]
29. SC 12, Sl St to beginning stitch, Ch 1 [12]

30A. SC 13, Ch 1, Turn [13]

This row goes one stitch beyond where it starts.

30B. SC 8, Ch 1, Turn [8]
30C. SC 7 [7] [12]

Row 30C has a stitch count of 7. Row 30 overall has a stitch count of 12 after all stitches are completed; 12 is the number of stitches available for the next row to work into.

31. SC 12, Sl St to beginning stitch, Ch 1 [12]
32A. SC 13, Ch 1, Turn [13]

This row goes one stitch beyond where it starts.

32B. SC 8, Ch 1, Turn [8]
32C. SC 8 [8]

Fasten off with 18 in/46 cm yarn tail.

Phoenix Body

PHOENIX HEAD

With US size G (4 mm) crochet hook:

1. Start with Beak color yarn, SC 6 in Magic Circle, Sl St to beginning stitch, Ch 1 [6]

2. SC 6, Sl St to beginning stitch, Ch 1 [6]

3. SC 6, Sl St to beginning stitch, Ch 1 [6]

Fasten off Beak Color yarn. Attach Body Color yarn to the BLO on the 3rd stitch of Row 3.

4. BLO [Inc x 6], Sl St to beginning stitch, Ch 1 [12]

5. (SC 2, Inc) x 4, Sl St to beginning stitch, Ch 1 [16]

6. (SC 3, Inc) x 4, Sl St to beginning stitch, Ch 1 [20]

7. SC 20, Sl St to beginning stitch, Ch 1 [20]

8. SC 20, Sl St to beginning stitch, Ch 1 [20]

9. (SC 2, Dec) x 5, Sl St to beginning stitch, Ch 1 [15]

Insert 12 mm safety eyes between Row 6 and Row 7, with 8 stitch spaces between the posts. If possible, use pliers to trim the posts short. Begin to stuff the head medium-firm with fiberfill. Continue to stuff as you work.

10. (SC, Dec) x 5, Sl St to beginning stitch [10]

Fasten off with 18 in/46 cm yarn tail.

PHOENIX BEAK

With US size C (2.75 mm) crochet hook:

1. Starting with a long enough yarn tail to weave in later, Ch 5, Turn, starting in the 2nd Ch from hook, SC, HDC, DC, Half Trip, Ch 1, Turn [4]

2. HDC Inc, HDC, SC 2, Ch 2, Sl St in the 2nd Ch from hook, SC in the same space as the last SC you made; working along the other side of the starting Ch, SC, HDC 3 [11]

Fasten off with 12 in/30 cm yarn tail.

Phoenix Head with Beak

PHOENIX HEAD ORNAMENT: THREE FEATHERS (MAKE 1)

Option 1

With US size D (3.25 mm) crochet hook:

1. Starting with a long enough yarn tail to weave in later, Ch 7, Turn, starting in the 2nd Ch from hook, HDC, DC, HDC, SC 2, Sl St [6]

2. Ch 9, Turn, starting in the 2nd Ch from hook, HDC, DC, HDC 2, SC 3, Sl St [8]

3. Ch 7, Turn, starting in the 2nd Ch from hook, HDC, DC, HDC, SC 2, Sl St [6]

Fasten off with 12 in/30 cm yarn tail.

Phoenix Head Ornament: Three Feathers

PHOENIX HEAD ORNAMENT: SEVEN FEATHERS (MAKE 1)

Option 2

With US size D (3.25 mm) crochet hook:

1. Starting with a long enough yarn tail to weave in later, Ch 5, Turn, starting in the 2nd Ch from hook, Sl St, SC, Dec, Ch 1, Turn [3]

2. BLO [SC], Ch 6, Turn [1]

3. Starting in the 2nd Ch from hook, Sl St, BLO [SC 3, Dec], Ch 1, Turn [5]

4. BLO [SC 2], Ch 7, Turn [2]

5. Starting in the 2nd Ch from hook, Sl St, BLO [SC 5, Dec], Ch 1, Turn [7]

6. BLO [SC 3], Ch 8, Turn [3]

7. Starting in the 2nd Ch from hook, Sl St, BLO [SC, HDC 2, SC 6], Ch 1, Turn [10]

8. BLO [SC 3], Ch 5, Turn [3]

9. Starting in the 2nd Ch from hook, Sl St, BLO [SC 5, Inc], Ch 1, Turn [8]

10. BLO [SC 2], Ch 4, Turn [2]

11. Starting in the 2nd Ch from hook, Sl St, BLO [SC 3, Inc], Ch 1, Turn [6]

12. BLO [SC], Ch 3, Turn [1]

13. Starting in the 2nd Ch from hook, Sl St, BLO [SC, Inc] [4]

Fasten off with 18 in/46 cm yarn tail.

Phoenix Head Ornament: Seven Feathers

PHOENIX FOOT (MAKE 2)

With US size C (2.75 mm) crochet hook:

1. Starting with a long enough yarn tail to weave in later, Ch 6, Turn, starting in the 2nd Ch from hook, SC 5 [5]

2. Ch 6, Turn, starting in the 2nd Ch from hook, SC 5, Sl St in the side of the last SC in Row 1 [5]

3. Ch 6, Turn, starting in the 2nd Ch from hook, SC 5, Sl St in the side of the last SC in Row 1 [5]

4. Ch 6, Turn, starting in the 2nd Ch from hook, SC 5, Sl St in the side of the last SC in Row 1 [5]

5. Ch 1, Inc in every available stitch along the entire edge of the existing Rows 1–4, Sl St to beginning stitch, Ch 1 [80]

Rows 5 and 6 are worked along the outside edge of the "toes" you have made; in Row 5, you will place your increases along the tops of the stitches and along the unused loops from the chains made in Rows 1–4.

6. Dec along the entire foot edge, Sl St to beginning stitch [40]

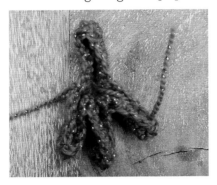

Fasten off with 36 in/91 cm yarn tail to use to sew the foot shut around the wire and weave in.

Bend the wire to match the foot as shown.

Sew foot shut around the wire.

Phoenix Foot

PHOENIX LEG (MAKE 2)

With US size D (3.25 mm) crochet hook:

1. Start with Bird Foot color yarn with 18 in/46 cm yarn tail to use to sew the Leg to the Phoenix

Foot, Ch 8, Sl St to the 1st chain, Ch 1 [1]

2. SC 9 around the Chain Circle, Sl St to the beginning stitch, Ch 1 [9]

> Make these Single Crochet stitches around the line of Ch stitches and not into the Ch stitches.

3. (SC, Dec) x 3, Sl St to beginning stitch, Ch 1 [6]

4–6. (3 rows of) SC 6, Sl St to beginning stitch, Ch 1 [6]

7. SC 5, Inc, Sl St to beginning stitch, Ch 1 [7]

8. SC 6, Inc, Sl St to beginning stitch, Ch 1 [8]

9. (SC 3, Inc) x 2, Sl St to beginning stitch [10]

Fasten off Bird Foot Color yarn; attach the Body Color yarn to the FLO of the same stitch you slip stitched into before fastening off.

10. FLO [SC 10], Sl St to beginning stitch, Ch 1 [10]

11. SC 10, Sl St to beginning stitch, Ch 1 [10]

12. SC 2, Inc, SC 3, 2 Dec in 3 SC, SC, Sl St to beginning stitch, Ch 1 [10]

13. SC, Inc, SC 2, Inc, SC 2, Dec, SC, Sl St to beginning stitch [11]

Fasten off Body Color yarn with 18 in/46 cm yarn tail.

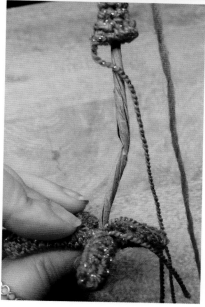

Phoenix Leg

PHOENIX WING (MAKE 2)

With US size D (3.25 mm) crochet hook:

1. Starting with a 24 in/61 cm yarn tail, Ch 15, Turn, starting in the 2nd Ch from hook, Sl St, SC, HDC 12, Ch 1, Turn [14]

2. BLO [SC 10], Ch 7, Turn [10]

3. Starting in the 2nd Ch from hook, Sl St, SC, HDC 4, BLO [HDC 6, SC 2, Dec], Ch 1, Turn [15]

4. BLO [SC 10], Ch 7, Turn [10]

5. Starting in the 2nd Ch from hook, Sl St, SC, HDC 4, BLO [HDC 6, SC 2, Dec], Ch 1, Turn [15]

6. BLO [SC 10], Ch 7, Turn [10]

7. Starting in the 2nd Ch from hook, Sl St, SC, HDC 4, BLO [HDC 6, SC 2, Dec], Ch 1, Turn [15]

8. BLO [SC 10], Ch 7, Turn [10]

9. Starting in the 2nd Ch from hook, Sl St, SC, HDC 4, BLO [HDC 6, SC 2, Dec], Ch 1, Turn [15]

10. BLO [SC 10], Ch 7, Turn [10]

11. Starting in the 2nd Ch from hook, Sl St, SC, HDC 4, BLO [HDC 6, SC 2, Dec], Ch 1, Turn [15]

12. BLO [Inc, SC 9], Ch 7, Turn [11]

13. Starting in the 2nd Ch from hook, Sl St, SC, HDC 4, BLO [HDC 6, SC 5], Ch 1, Turn [17]

14. BLO [SC 13], Ch 6, Turn [13]

15. Starting in the 2nd Ch from hook, Sl St, SC, HDC 3, BLO [HDC 7, SC 6], Ch 1, Turn [18]

16. BLO [SC 13], Ch 7, Turn [13]

17. Starting in the 2nd Ch from hook, Sl St, SC, HDC 4, BLO [HDC 6, SC 7], Ch 1, Turn [19]

18. BLO [SC 13], Ch 7, Turn [13]

19. Starting in the 2nd Ch from hook, Sl St, SC, HDC 4, BLO [HDC 6, SC 7], Ch 1, Turn [19]

20. BLO [Inc, SC 13], Ch 8, Turn [15]

21. Starting in the 2nd Ch from hook, Sl St, SC, HDC 5, BLO [HDC 15], Ch 1, Turn [22]

22. BLO [SC 16], Ch 8, Turn [16]

23. Starting in the 2nd Ch from hook, Sl St, SC, HDC 5, BLO [HDC 5, SC 5], Ch 1, Turn [17]

Leave the last 6 stitches unworked.

24. BLO [SC 10], Ch 9, Turn [10]

25. Starting in the 2nd Ch from hook, Sl St, SC, HDC 6, BLO [HDC 6, SC 3, SC/HDC Dec, SC 5], Ch 1, Turn [23]

The SC/HDC Dec is worked into the last available stitch from Row 24 and the 1st available unworked stitch from Row 22.

26. BLO [SC 17], Ch 8, Turn [17]

27. Starting in the 2nd Ch from hook, Sl St, SC, HDC 5, BLO [HDC 5, SC 5], Ch 1, Turn [17]

Seven stitches remain unworked.

28. BLO [SC 11], Ch 8, Turn [11]

29. Starting in the 2nd Ch from hook, Sl St, SC, HDC 5, BLO [HDC 7, SC 3, SC/HDC Dec, SC 6], Ch 1, Turn [24]

The SC/HDC Dec is worked into the last available stitch from Row 28 and the 1st available unworked stitch from Row 26.

30. BLO [Dec, SC 16], Ch 8, Turn [17]

31. Starting in the 2nd Ch from hook, Sl St, SC, HDC 5, BLO [HDC 5, SC 5], Ch 1, Turn [17]

Leave the last 7 stitches unworked.

32. BLO [SC 12], Ch 8, Turn [12]

33. Starting in the 2nd Ch from hook, Sl St, SC, HDC 5, BLO [HDC 5, SC 6, SC/HDC Dec, SC 3], Ch 1, Turn [22]

The SC/HDC Dec is worked into the last available stitch from Row 32 and the 1st available unworked stitch from Row 30; leave the last 3 stitches unworked.

34. BLO [SC 12], Ch 7, Turn [12]

35. Starting in the 2nd Ch from hook, Sl St, SC, HDC 4, BLO [HDC 6, SC 5, SC/HDC Dec, SC 2], Ch 1, Reorient [20]

The SC/HDC Dec is worked into the last available stitch from Row 34 and the 1st available unworked stitch from Row 32.

36. SC in the same stitch you last stitched into, SC along the wing edge back to where you started, for a total of about 27 Single Crochet stitches [~27]

37. Ch 10, Turn, starting in the 2nd Ch from hook, Sl St, SC, HDC 7, Ch 1, Turn [9]

38. BLO [SC 6], Ch 5, Turn [6]

39. Starting in the 2nd Ch from hook, Sl St, SC, HDC 2, BLO [HDC 2, SC 2, Dec], Ch 1, Turn [9]

40. BLO [SC 6], Ch 5, Turn [6]

41. Starting in the 2nd Ch from Hook, Sl St, SC, HDC 2, BLO [HDC 2, SC 2, Dec], Ch 1, Turn [9]

42. BLO [SC 6], Ch 5, Turn [6]

43. Starting in the 2nd Ch from hook, Sl St, SC, HDC 2, BLO [HDC 2, SC 2, Dec], Ch 1, Turn [9]

44. BLO [SC 6], Ch 5, Turn [6]

45. Starting in the 2nd Ch from hook, Sl St, SC, HDC 2, BLO [HDC 2, SC 2, Dec], Ch 1, Turn [9]

46. BLO [SC 6], Ch 5, Turn [6]

47. Starting in the 2nd Ch from hook, Sl St, SC, HDC 2, BLO [HDC 2, SC 2, Dec], Ch 1, Turn [9]

48. BLO [Inc, SC 5], Ch 5, Turn [7]

49. Starting in the 2nd Ch from hook, Sl St, SC, HDC 2, BLO [HDC 3, SC 4], Ch 1, Turn [11]

50. BLO [SC 8], Ch 5, Turn [8]

51. Starting in the 2nd Ch from hook, Sl St, SC, HDC 2, BLO [HDC 4, SC 4], Ch 1, Turn [12]

52. BLO [SC 9], Ch 5, Turn [9]

53. Starting in the 2nd Ch from hook, Sl St, SC, HDC 2, BLO [HDC 5, SC 4], Ch 1, Turn [13]

54. BLO [SC 10], Ch 5, Turn [10]

55. Starting in the 2nd Ch from hook, Sl St, SC, HDC 2, BLO [HDC 5, SC 5], Ch 1, Turn [14]

56. BLO [Inc, SC 10], Ch 6, Turn [12]

57. Starting in the 2nd Ch from hook, Sl St, SC, HDC 3, BLO [HDC 12], Ch 1, Turn [17]

58. BLO [SC 12], Ch 6, Turn [12]

59. Starting in the 2nd Ch from hook, Sl St, SC, HDC 3, BLO [HDC 4, SC 3], Ch 1, Turn [12]

Leave the last 5 stitches unworked.

60. BLO [SC 7], Ch 6, Turn [7]

61. Starting in the 2nd Ch from hook, Sl St, SC, HDC 3, BLO [HDC 3, SC 3, SC/HDC Dec, SC 4], Ch 1, Turn [16]

The SC/HDC Dec is worked into the last available stitch from Row 60 and the 1st available unworked stitch from Row 58.

62. BLO [SC 13], Ch 6, Turn [13]

63. Starting in the 2nd Ch from hook, Sl St, SC, HDC 3, BLO [HDC 4, SC 4], Ch 1, Turn [13]

Leave the last 5 stitches unworked.

64. BLO [SC 8], Ch 6, Turn [8]

65. Starting in the 2nd Ch from hook, Sl St, SC, HDC 3, BLO [HDC 4, SC 3, SC/HDC Dec, SC 4], Ch 1, Turn [17]

The SC/HDC Dec is worked into the last available stitch of Row 64 and the 1st available unworked stitch of Row 62.

66. BLO [Dec, SC 11], Ch 6, Turn [12]

67. Starting in the 2nd Ch from hook, Sl St, SC, HDC 3, BLO [HDC 4, SC 4], Ch 1, Turn [13]

> Leave the last 4 stitches unworked.

68. BLO [SC 9], Ch 6, Turn [9]

69. Starting in the 2nd Ch from hook, Sl St, SC, HDC 3, BLO [HDC 4, SC 4, SC/HDC Dec, SC 3], Ch 1, Reorient [17]

> Work the SC/HDC Dec into the last available stitch from Row 68 and the 1st available unworked stitch from Row 66.

70. SC down the unfinished wing edge to the base of where this wing panel started in Row 37, Ch 1, Turn

71. Sl St along the top edge of both wing pieces (Row 36 and Row 70) to attach them together. When you reach the end of the top edge (Row 36 and Row 70), reorient so that you are working along the tops of Row

69 and Row 35 (the sides of the "feathers"); SC along the edge toward the feather tips, until you get to the last 3 HDC of Row 69. Leave these HDC and the remaining stitches in Row 69 and Row 35 unworked.

Fasten off with 30 in/76 cm yarn tail.

Repeat all of the instructions. Make one wing oriented to the left and one wing oriented to the right. The second wing needs to be the mirror image of the first, so make sure you slip stitch the smaller part of the wing to the other side of the larger part so that you have a right wing and a left wing. The edges of the feathers will curl in one direction, and so when you create a left and a right wing, the edges of the feathers will look like they slightly curl in different directions; that is okay and expected. If the curling is particularly pronounced, you can block your wing by pinning it down on a piece of foam matting and steaming or wetting the piece and allowing it to dry. The wings you see in the example photos in the book have not been blocked and the curling is not noticeable.

Phoenix Wings

PHOENIX LONG TAIL FEATHER

Make as many as you want (typically between 1 and 3)

With US size D (3.25 mm) crochet hook:

1. Starting with a long enough yarn tail to weave in later, Ch 6, Turn, starting in the 2nd Ch from hook, Sl St, SC 2, Dec, Ch 1, Turn [4]

2. BLO [SC 3], Ch 3, Turn [3]

3. Starting in the 2nd Ch from hook, Sl St, SC, BLO [SC, Dec], Ch 1, Turn [4]

4. BLO [SC 3], Ch 3, Turn [3]

5. Starting in the 2nd Ch from hook, Sl St, SC, BLO [SC, Dec], Ch 1, Turn [4]

6. BLO [SC 3], Ch 3, Turn [3]

7. Starting in the 2nd Ch from hook, Sl St, SC, BLO [SC, Dec], Ch 1, Turn [4]

8. BLO [SC 3], Ch 4, Turn [3]

9. Starting in the 2nd Ch from hook, Sl St, SC 2, BLO [SC, Dec], Ch 1, Turn [5]

10. BLO [SC 4], Ch 4, Turn [4]

11. Starting in the 2nd Ch from hook, Sl St, SC 2, BLO [SC 2, Dec], Ch 1, Turn [6]

12. BLO [SC 4], Ch 4, Turn [4]

13. Starting in the 2nd Ch from hook, Sl St, SC 2, BLO [SC 2, Dec], Ch 1, Turn [6]

14. BLO [SC 4], Ch 4, Turn [4]

15. Starting in the 2nd Ch from hook, Sl St, SC 2, BLO [SC 2, Dec], Ch 1, Turn [6]

16. BLO [SC 4], Ch 4, Turn [4]

17. Starting in the 2nd Ch from hook, Sl St, SC 2, BLO [SC 2, Dec], Ch 1, Turn [6]

18. BLO [SC 5], Ch 4, Turn [5]

19. Starting in the 2nd Ch from hook, Sl St, SC 2, BLO [SC 3, Dec], Ch 1, Turn [7]

20. BLO [SC 5], Ch 4, Turn [5]

21. Starting in the 2nd Ch from hook, Sl St, SC 2, BLO [SC 3, Dec], Ch 1, Turn [7]

22. BLO [SC 5], Ch 4, Turn [5]

23. Starting in the 2nd Ch from hook, Sl St, SC 2, BLO [SC 3, Dec], Ch 1, Turn [7]

24. BLO [SC 5], Ch 4, Turn [5]

25. Starting in the 2nd Ch from hook, Sl St, SC 2, BLO [SC 3, Dec], Ch 1, Turn [7]

26. BLO [SC 5], Ch 4, Turn [5]

27. Starting in the 2nd Ch from hook, Sl St, SC 2, BLO [SC 3, Dec], Ch 1, Turn [7]

28. BLO [SC 6], Ch 4, Turn [6]

29. Starting in the 2nd Ch from hook, Sl St, SC 2, BLO [SC 4, Dec], Ch 1, Turn [8]

30. BLO [SC 6], Ch 4, Turn [6]

31. Starting in the 2nd Ch from hook, Sl St, SC 2, BLO [SC 4, Dec], Ch 1, Turn [8]

32. BLO [SC 6], Ch 4, Turn [6]

33. Starting in the 2nd Ch from hook, Sl St, SC 2, BLO [SC 4, Dec], Ch 1, Turn [8]

34. BLO [SC 6], Ch 4, Turn [6]

35. Starting in the 2nd Ch from hook, Sl St, SC 2, BLO [SC 4, Dec], Ch 1, Turn [8]

36. BLO [SC 6], Ch 4, Turn [6]

37. Starting in the 2nd Ch from hook, Sl St, SC 2, BLO [SC 4, Dec], Ch 1, Turn [8]

38. BLO [SC 6], Ch 4, Turn [6]

39. Starting in the 2nd Ch from hook, Sl St, SC 2, BLO [SC 4, Dec], Ch 1, Turn [8]

40. Sl St 4, Turn [4]

41. Working in the 1st stitch of Row 40, Triple Crochet three times, Ch 1, Turn [3]

42. Inc x 3, Sl St in the next available stitch in Feather, Ch 3, Turn [6]

43A. Starting in the 2nd Ch from hook, Sl St, SC, Sl St in each of the next 2 SC [4]

43B. Ch 4, Turn, starting in the 2nd Ch from hook, Sl St, SC 2, Sl St in each of the next 2 SC [6]

43C. Ch 3, Turn, starting in the 2nd Ch from hook, Sl St, SC, Sl St in each of the next 2 SC, Ch 4, Turn [4]

43D. Starting in the 2nd Ch from hook, Sl St, SC 2, SC inside of the side of the available SC stitch, SC around the top of the Triple Crochet, SC 2 more around Triple Crochet post, Ch 1, Turn [7]

44. BLO [SC 6], Ch 3, Turn [6]

45. Starting in the 2nd Ch from hook, Sl St, SC, BLO [SC 5, Inc], Ch 1, Turn [9]

46. BLO [SC 6], Ch 3, Turn [6]

47. Starting in the 2nd Ch from hook, Sl St, SC, BLO [SC 5, Inc], Ch 1, Turn [9]

48. BLO [SC 6], Ch 3, Turn [6]

49. Starting in the 2nd Ch from hook, Sl St, SC, BLO [SC 5, Inc], Ch 1, Turn [9]

50. BLO [SC 6], Ch 3, Turn [6]

51. Starting in the 2nd Ch from hook, Sl St, SC, BLO [SC 5, Inc], Ch 1, Turn [9]

52. BLO [SC 6], Ch 3, Turn [6]

53. Starting in the 2nd Ch from hook, Sl St, SC, BLO [SC 5, Inc], Ch 1, Turn [9]

54. BLO [SC 5], Ch 3, Turn [5]

55. Starting in the 2nd Ch from hook, Sl St, SC, BLO [SC 4, Inc], Ch 1, Turn [8]

56. BLO [SC 5], Ch 3, Turn [5]

57. Starting in the 2nd Ch from hook, Sl St, SC, BLO [SC 4, Inc], Ch 1, Turn [8]

58. BLO [SC 5], Ch 3, Turn [5]

59. Starting in the 2nd Ch from hook, Sl St, SC, BLO [SC 4, Inc], Ch 1, Turn [8]

60. BLO [SC 5], Ch 3, Turn [5]

61. Starting in the 2nd Ch from hook, Sl St, SC, BLO [SC 4, Inc], Ch 1, Turn [8]

62. BLO [SC 5], Ch 3, Turn [5]

63. Starting in the 2nd Ch from hook, Sl St, SC, BLO [SC 4, Inc], Ch 1, Turn [8]

64. BLO [SC 4], Ch 3, Turn [4]

65. Starting in the 2nd Ch from hook, Sl St, SC, BLO [SC 3, Inc], Ch 1, Turn [7]

66. BLO [SC 4], Ch 3, Turn [4]

67. Starting in the 2nd Ch from hook, Sl St, SC, BLO [SC 3, Inc], Ch 1, Turn [7]

68. BLO [SC 4], Ch 3, Turn [4]

69. Starting in the 2nd Ch from hook, Sl St, SC, BLO [SC 3, Inc], Ch 1, Turn [7]

70. BLO [SC 4], Ch 3, Turn [4]

71. Starting in the 2nd Ch from hook, Sl St, SC, BLO [SC 3, Inc], Ch 1, Turn [7]

72. BLO [SC 3], Ch 3, Turn [3]

73. Starting in the 2nd Ch from hook, Sl St, SC, BLO [SC 2, Inc], Ch 1, Turn [6]

74. BLO [SC 3], Ch 3, Turn [3]

75. Starting in the 2nd Ch from hook, Sl St, SC, BLO [SC 2, Inc], Ch 1, Turn [6]

76. BLO [SC 3], Ch 3, Turn [3]

77. Starting in the 2nd Ch from hook, Sl St, SC, BLO [SC 2, Inc], Ch 1, Turn [6]

78. BLO [SC 3], Ch 3, Turn [3]

79. Starting in the 2nd Ch from hook, Sl St, SC, BLO [SC 2, Inc], Ch 1, Turn [6]

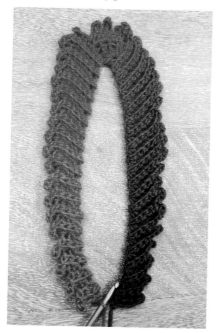

80. Fold the Feather in half as shown.

Single Crochet along the straight edge of the two sides of the Feather together at once, Ch 1, Turn

81. *To continue without wire:* Slip Stitch back along the row of Single Crochet stitches you just made. Fasten off with 12 in/30 cm yarn tail to use to sew to attach.

To continue with wire: Hold a wire in place along the spine of Single Crochet stitches you just made, and Single Crochet into that row around the wire for the length of the feather.

Fasten off with 12 in/30 cm yarn tail.

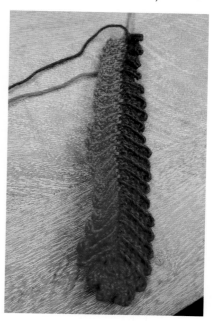

Phoenix Long Tail Feather

PHOENIX SHORT TAIL FEATHER

Make as many as you want (typically between 1 and 3)

With US size D (3.25 mm) crochet hook:

1. Starting with a long enough yarn tail to weave in later, Ch 4, Turn, starting in the 2nd Ch from hook, Sl St, Dec, Ch 1, Turn [2]

2. BLO [SC], Ch 3, Turn [1]

3. Starting in the 2nd Ch from hook, Sl St, BLO [Dec], Ch 1, Turn [2]

4. BLO [SC], Ch 3, Turn [1]

5. Starting in the 2nd Ch from hook, Sl St, BLO [Dec], Ch 1, Turn [2]

6. BLO [SC], Ch 4, Turn [1]

7. Starting in the 2nd Ch from hook, Sl St, SC, BLO [Dec], Ch 1, Turn [3]

8. BLO [SC 2], Ch 3, Turn [2]

9. Starting in the 2nd Ch from hook, Sl St, SC, BLO [Dec], Ch 1, Turn [3]

10. BLO [SC 2], Ch 3, Turn [2]

11. Starting in the 2nd Ch from hook, Sl St, SC, BLO [Dec], Ch 1, Turn [3]

12. BLO [SC 2], Ch 3, Turn [2]

13. Starting in the 2nd Ch from hook, Sl St, SC, BLO [Dec], Ch 1, Turn [3]

14. BLO [SC 2], Ch 4, Turn [2]

15. Starting in the 2nd Ch from hook, Sl St, SC 2, BLO [Dec], Ch 1, Turn [3]

16. BLO [SC 3], Ch 3, Turn [3]

17. Starting in the 2nd Ch from hook, Sl St, SC, BLO [SC, Dec], Ch 1, Turn [4]

18. BLO [SC 3], Ch 3, Turn [3]

19. Starting in the 2nd Ch from hook, Sl St, SC, BLO [SC, Dec], Ch 1, Turn [4]

20. BLO [SC 3], Ch 3, Turn [3]

21. Starting in the 2nd Ch from hook, Sl St, SC, BLO [SC, Dec], Ch 1, Turn [4]

22. BLO [SC 3], Ch 3, Turn [3]

23. Starting in the 2nd Ch from hook, Sl St, SC, BLO [SC, Dec], Ch 1, Turn [4]

24. BLO [SC 3], Ch 4, Turn [3]

25. Starting in the 2nd Ch from hook, Sl St, SC 2, BLO [SC, Dec], Ch 1, Turn [5]

26. BLO [SC 4], Ch 3, Turn [4]

27. Starting in the 2nd Ch from hook, Sl St, SC, BLO [SC 2, Dec], Ch 1, Turn [5]

28. BLO [SC 4], Ch 3, Turn [4]

29. Starting in the 2nd Ch from hook, Sl St, SC, BLO [SC 2, Dec], Ch 1, Turn [5]

30. BLO [SC 4], Ch 3, Turn [4]

31. Starting in the 2nd Ch from hook, Sl St, SC, BLO [SC 2, Dec], Ch 1, Turn [5]

32. Sl St 3, Turn [3]

33. DC 3 in the 1st stitch from Row 32, Ch 1, Turn [3]

34. Inc x 3, Sl St in the next available stitch in Feather, Ch 1, Turn [6]

35A. Sl St, Ch 3, Turn, starting in the 2nd Ch from hook, Sl St, SC, Sl St in the next 2 stitches [5]

35B. Ch 4, Turn, starting in the 2nd Ch from hook, Sl St, SC 2, Sl St in the next 2 stitches [5]

35C. Ch 3, Turn, starting in the 2nd Ch from hook, Sl St, SC, Sl St in the next stitch [3]

35D. Ch 2, Turn, starting in the 2nd Ch from hook, Sl St, SC into the side of the next available SC stitch, SC 4 around DC post, Ch 1, Turn [6]

36. BLO [SC 4], Ch 2, Turn [4]
37. Starting in the 2nd Ch from hook, Sl St, BLO [SC 3, Inc], Ch 1, Turn [6]
38. BLO [SC 4], Ch 2, Turn [4]
39. Starting in the 2nd Ch from hook, Sl St, BLO [SC 3, Inc], Ch 1, Turn [6]
40. BLO [SC 4], Ch 2, Turn [4]
41. Starting in the 2nd Ch from hook, Sl St, BLO [SC 3, Inc], Ch 1, Turn [6]
42. BLO [SC 3], Ch 2, Turn [3]
43. Starting in the 2nd Ch from hook, Sl St, BLO [SC 2, Inc], Ch 1, Turn [5]
44. BLO [SC 3], Ch 2, Turn [3]
45. Starting in the 2nd Ch from hook, Sl St, BLO [SC 2, Inc], Ch 1, Turn [5]
46. BLO [SC 3], Ch 2, Turn [3]
47. Starting in the 2nd Ch from hook, Sl St, BLO [SC 2, Inc], Ch 1, Turn [5]
48. BLO [SC 3], Ch 2, Turn [3]
49. Starting in the 2nd Ch from hook, Sl St, BLO [SC 2, Inc], Ch 1, Turn [5]
50. BLO [SC 3], Ch 2, Turn [3]
51. Starting in the 2nd Ch from hook, Sl St, BLO [SC 2, Inc], Ch 1, Turn [5]
52. BLO [SC 2], Ch 2, Turn [2]
53. Starting in the 2nd Ch from hook, Sl St, BLO [SC, Inc], Ch 1, Turn [4]
54. BLO [SC 2], Ch 2, Turn [2]
55. Starting in the 2nd Ch from hook, Sl St, BLO [SC, Inc], Ch 1, Turn [4]
56. BLO [SC 2], Ch 2, Turn [2]
57. Starting in the 2nd Ch from hook, Sl St, BLO [SC, Inc], Ch 1, Turn [4]
58. BLO [SC 2], Ch 2, Turn [2]

59. Starting in the 2nd Ch from hook, Sl St, BLO [SC, Inc], Ch 1, Turn [4]
60. BLO [SC], Ch 2, Turn [1]
61. Starting in the 2nd Ch from hook, Sl St, BLO [Inc], Ch 1, Turn [3]
62. BLO [SC], Ch 2, Turn [1]
63. Starting in the 2nd Ch from hook, Sl St, BLO [Inc], Ch 1, Turn [3]
64. BLO [SC], Ch 2, Turn [1]
65. Starting in the 2nd Ch from hook, Sl St, BLO [Inc], Ch 1, Turn [3]

66. Fold the Feather in half.

Single Crochet along the straight edge of the two sides of the Feather together at once.

For photos of this technique, see Row 80 and Row 81 in the Long Phoenix Tail Feather instructions (page 211).

To continue without wire: Slip Stitch back along the row of Single Crochet stitches you just made, fasten off with 12 in/30 cm yarn tail.

To continue with wire: Hold a wire in place along the spine of Single Crochet stitches you just made, and Single Crochet into that row around the wire for the length of the feather. Fasten off with 12 in/30 cm yarn tail.

PHOENIX ASSEMBLY

1. Slide the Phoenix Leg onto the wire sticking out of the Phoenix Foot.

2. Sew the foot to the leg, ensuring that the back of the leg is oriented as shown in step 1, and weave in ends.

3. Stuff the Phoenix Body medium-firm with fiberfill.

4. Take the Phoenix Body and one completed Leg, align the leg as shown, and insert the leg wire into the body and force the wire to exit the body where the wing will be positioned on the shoulder of the body as shown.

5. Do the same with the other Leg.

6. Sew the legs to the body.

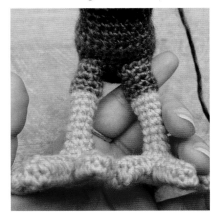

7. Optional: Insert a wire in the spine of the Phoenix.

The bird does not require a spinal wire, but it does help with stability and gives the option of posing the bird's head in different ways. If you are not using a long feather with wire, you can insert the wire into the neck hole of the bird along where the spine is to the end of the body. You will trim the wire in later instructions.

If you are using at least one long feather with wire, you can utilize that as your spinal wire for the phoenix. Insert the wire into the butt end of the phoenix where the tail feather will be attached. Keep the wire aligned with where the spine would be and push it all the way up through the neck hole as shown.

8. Trim the spinal wire in relation to the size of the bird head. You can first fold the wire over on itself so that the end you insert into the head is not sharp, but the bird head is small, so try it out first to ensure it will fit before committing. If it is too small for the folded over wire to work, trim as shown. Make sure the wire extends to the end of the beak/head inside the head.

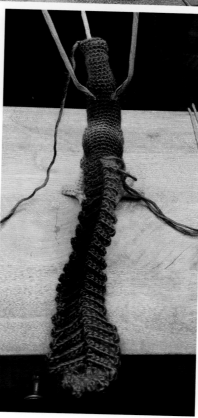

9. Insert the head onto the wire; the wire should be aligned along the top of the bird's head to the nose. Stretch the back of the neck on the body of the Phoenix up over the top of the back of the head. Pin in place.

10. Sew the head in place, and weave in ends.

11. Pin the beak in place, sew the beak in place, and weave in ends.

12. If you are using any of the head ornament feathers, pin in place and sew to attach; weave in ends.

13. Insert, pin, and sew in place any additional long or short tail feathers.

14. Compare the wings to the wing wires. If the wires are long enough to extend all the way along the edge of the wings, then continue to the next assembly instruction. If the wires are not long enough, add some more wire length, using duct tape wrapped around the wire to secure it.

15. Insert the wing onto the wing wire. Bend the wire to fit the wing's bends.

16. Sew the wing in place, and weave in ends. Using the long yarn tail from the end of the wings, sew a single line down the wing with tiny stitches to secure the wire against the edge of the wing, and then secure both panels of the wing to the body of the Phoenix (along the yellow line in the photo).

NOTE: If you use a color transitioning yarn, you can sew through the inside loops of the wing pieces so that your stitches do not show on the outside.

17. If you want to include a tail fan, pin to attach and sew to attach. You can position it above tail feathers, below tail feathers, or use it by itself without any additional tail feathers. Weave in ends.

Unicorn

Unicorns are often portrayed as white wild horses with one spiral horn possessing magical abilities. Only the pure of heart could get near them, and the unicorns would fall asleep in their laps.

SIZE:

A Unicorn from this pattern is 12 in/30 cm tall from head to hoof (14 in/35.5 cm tall including the horn), 8 in/20.5 cm long from nose to rump, 3 in/7.5 cm wide from shoulder to shoulder.

MATERIALS

>> Yarn: See table on page 220 to choose the options you will make for your Unicorn and find the yarn amounts needed for each piece. All yarn is #4 medium/worsted weight except for the Advanced Spiral Horn, which is doubled lace or sock (#0 or #1) yarn, and all yarn amounts are approximate.
  * Main Color: 179 yd/163.75 m
  * Hoof Color: 8 yd/7.25 m
  * Horn Color: 4 yd/3.75 m for Simple Horn, 13 yd/12 m for Advanced Spiral Horn
  * Accent Color: 226 to 255 yd/206.75 to 233.25 m (depending on mane and tale options)

>> US size G (4 mm) crochet hook

>> US size C (2.75 mm) crochet hook (for Advanced Spiral Horn only)

>> 18 mm safety eyes

>> Optional: Glass gems for weighted feet

>> Fiberfill stuffing

>> Darning needle

>> Pins

>> Scissors

>> Duct tape

>> Wire strong enough to support posing. Recommend 5 pieces of 18-in/46-cm, 18-gauge, paper-wrapped wire (found in the faux floral arrangement section of any craft store; if this exact wire cannot be found, please use 14- to 16-gauge wire—err on the side of heavier wire)

>> Pliers

INSTRUCTIONS

Look at the Gallery on the next page and the chart below to determine the pieces you want to make for your Unicorn. You have two options each for the mane, tail, and horn. The Unicorn is assembled as you go.

Use US size G (4 mm) hook for all parts except the Advanced Spiral Horn.

PARTS TO MAKE	PAGE NO.	NUMBER TO MAKE	YARN COLOR	APPROX. AMOUNT
Unicorn Front Leg	223	2	Main Color, Hoof Color	32 yd/29.25 Main Color, 4 yd/3.75 m Hoof Color for 2 legs
Unicorn Rear Leg	224	2	Main Color, Hoof Color	46 yd/42 m Main Color, 4 yd/3.75 m Hoof Color for 2 legs
Unicorn Body	225	1	Main Color	51 yd/46.5 m
Unicorn Neck	228	1	Main Color	35 yd/32 m
Unicorn Head	229	1	Main Color	15 yd/13.75 m
Mane: Choose 1 of the following				
Unicorn Puffy Cloud Mane	231	1	Accent Color	135 yd/123.5 m
Unicorn Ruffle Wavy Mane	232	1	Accent Color	110 yd/100.5 m
Tail: Choose 1 of the following				
Unicorn Puffy Cloud Tail	231	1	Accent Color	116 yd/106 m
Unicorn Ruffle Wavy Tail	233	1	Accent Color	120 yd/109.75
Horn: Choose 1 of the following				
Unicorn Simple Horn	233	1	Horn Color	4 yd/3.75 m
Unicorn Advanced Spiral Horn	234	1	Horn Color in doubled lace or sock yarn	13 yd/12 m

GALLERY

Unicorn with Ruffle Wavy Mane and Tail, Advanced Spiral Horn

Unicorn with Ruffle Wavy Mane and Tail, Advanced Spiral Horn

Unicorn with Puffy Cloud Mane and Tail, Advanced Spiral Horn

Unicorn with simplified
Ruffle Wavy Mane and Tail,
Simple Horn, and Phoenix Wings
(see page 205)

UПICORП PARTS PATTERПS

UNICORN FRONT LEG (MAKE 2)

Optional: You can make the hooves in an accent color yarn (approximately 4 yd/3.75 m).

Optional: 2 pieces of 18-in/46-cm, 18-gauge, paper-wrapped stem wire, or alternative that is strong yet moldable

With US size G (4 mm) crochet hook:

1. Optionally start with the Hoof Color yarn, SC 6 in Magic Circle, Sl St to beginning stitch, Ch 1 [6]
2. Inc x 6, Sl St to beginning stitch, Ch 1 [12]
3. BLO [SC 6, HDC 6], Sl St to beginning stitch, Ch 1 [12]
4. SC 6, HDC 6, Sl St to beginning stitch, Ch 1 [12]

> If you started with the Hoof Color yarn, switch to the Main Body Color yarn here.

5. SC 2, Dec, SC 8, Sl St to beginning stitch, Ch 1 [11]
6. SC, 2 Dec in 3 SC, SC 7, Sl St to beginning stitch, Ch 1 [10]
7. SC, Dec, SC 7, Sl St to beginning stitch, Ch 1 [9]

NOTE: At this point, you can take one wire and bend the end of it into a circle the size of the diameter of the inside of the bottom of the hoof. Then bend the circle to be perpendicular to the rest of the wire, and insert the wire circle into the bottom of the hoof. This wire will support the weight of the Unicorn and be poseable. It is optional. You can also wait to insert this wire until the leg is complete, but it will be a small challenge to fit it through the leg to the hoof. Pipe cleaners are not strong enough to function as the wire for this soft sculpture. If you want the support of wire, it needs to be robust. Begin to stuff the leg medium-firm with fiberfill; continue to stuff as you work.

NOTE: Optionally, you can add a glass gem to the base of the hoof by itself or you can add it on top of the wire loop at the base of the hoof or you can skip the glass gems all together.

8. SC, <Dec>, SC, <Dec>, SC 7, Sl St to beginning stitch, Ch 1 [11]
9. SC 11, Sl St to beginning stitch, Ch 1 [11]
10. SC 2, 2 Dec in 3 SC, SC 6, Sl St to beginning stitch, Ch 1 [10]
11. SC 2, Dec, SC 6, Sl St to beginning stitch, Ch 1 [9]
12. SC 2, Dec, SC 2, 2 Dec in 3 SC, Sl St to beginning stitch, Ch 1 [7]
13–17. (5 rows of) SC 7, Sl St to beginning stitch, Ch 1 [7]
18. SC 2, Inc, SC 4, Sl St to beginning stitch, Ch 1 [8]

19. (SC, Inc) x 4, Sl St to beginning stitch, Ch 1 [12]
20. SC 12, Sl St to beginning stitch, Ch 1 [12]
21. (SC, Dec) x 4, Sl St to beginning stitch, Ch 1 [8]
22. SC 8, Sl St to beginning stitch, Ch 1 [8]
23. SC 3, Inc, SC 4, Sl St to beginning stitch, Ch 1 [9]
24. SC 9, Sl St to beginning stitch, Ch 1 [9]
25. SC 8, Inc, Sl St to beginning stitch, Ch 1 [10]
26. SC 10, Sl St to beginning stitch, Ch 1 [10]
27. SC 5, <Dec>, SC 5, Sl St to beginning stitch, Ch 1 [11]
28. SC 10, Inc, Sl St to beginning stitch, Ch 1 [12]
29. SC 12, Sl St to beginning stitch, Ch 1 [12]

Fasten off with short yarn tail; tuck this yarn tail inside the leg.

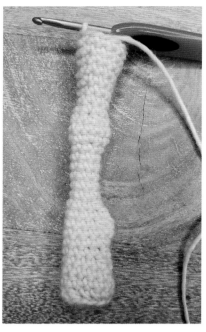

Unicorn Front Leg

Your two front legs will be numbered as #2 and #3. Mark the following stitches accordingly; this is for assembly when you create the body.

Leg #2: Mark the 6th stitch

Leg #3: Mark the 12th stitch

UNICORN REAR LEG (MAKE 2)

Optional: Hoof color yarn (approximately 4 yds/3.75 m)

Optional: 2 pieces of 18-in/46-cm, 18-gauge, paper-wrapped stem wire, or alternative that is strong yet moldable

With US size G (4 mm) crochet hook:

1. Optionally start with the Hoof color yarn, SC 6 in Magic Circle, Sl St to beginning stitch, Ch 1 [6]

2. Inc x 6, Sl St to beginning stitch, Ch 1 [12]

3. BLO [SC 6, HDC 6], Sl St to beginning stitch, Ch 1 [12]

4. SC 6, HDC 6, Sl St to beginning stitch, Ch 1 [12]

> If you started with the Hoof Color yarn, switch to the Main Body Color yarn here.

5. SC 8, Dec, SC 2, Sl St to beginning stitch, Ch 1 [11]

6. SC, 2 Dec in 3 SC, SC 7, Sl St to beginning stitch, Ch 1 [10]

7. SC, Dec, SC 7, Sl St to beginning stitch, Ch 1 [9]

NOTE: At this point, you can take one wire and bend the end of it into a circle the size of the diameter of the inside of the bottom of the hoof. Then bend the circle to be perpendicular to the rest of the wire, and insert the wire circle into the bottom of the hoof. This wire will support the weight of the Unicorn and be poseable. It is optional. You can also wait to insert this wire until the leg is complete, but it will be a small challenge to fit it through the leg to the hoof. Pipe cleaners are not strong enough to function as the wire for this soft sculpture. If you want the support of wire, it needs to be robust. Begin to stuff the leg medium-firm with fiberfill; continue to stuff as you work.

NOTE: Optionally, you can add a glass gem to the base of the hoof by itself or you can add it on top of the wire loop at the base of the hoof or you can skip the glass gems all together.

---

8. SC, <Dec>, SC, <Dec>, SC 7, Sl St to beginning stitch, Ch 1 [11]

9. SC 11, Sl St to beginning stitch, Ch 1 [11]

10. SC, 2 Dec in 3 SC, SC 7, Sl St to beginning stitch, Ch 1 [10]

11. SC 6, 2 Dec in 3 SC, SC, Sl St to beginning stitch, Ch 1 [9]

12. SC, 2 Dec in 3 SC, SC 2, Dec, SC, Sl St to beginning stitch, Ch 1 [7]

13–14. (2 rows of) SC 7, Sl St to beginning stitch, Ch 1 [7]

15. SC 2, <Dec>, SC 2, 2 Dec in 3 SC, Sl St to beginning stitch, Ch 1 [7]

16–18. (3 rows of) SC 7, Sl St to beginning stitch, Ch 1 [7]

19. SC 2, Inc, SC 4, Sl St to beginning stitch, Ch 1 [8]

20. SC, Inc x 4, SC 3, Sl St to beginning stitch, Ch 1 [12]

21. SC 12, Sl St to beginning stitch, Ch 1 [12]

22. SC, Dec, HDC 4, Dec, SC 3, Sl St to beginning stitch, Ch 1 [10]

23. SC 3, HDC 5, SC 2, Sl St to beginning stitch, Ch 1 [10]

24. SC, <Dec>, SC 4, Dec, SC 3, Sl St to beginning stitch, Ch 1 [10]

25. SC 7, <Dec>, SC 3, Sl St to beginning stitch, Ch 1 [11]

26. HDC, <HDC Dec>, HDC 2, SC 7, HDC, Sl St to beginning stitch, Ch 1 [12]

27. SC 12, Sl St to beginning stitch, Ch 1 [12]

28. HDC 2, <HDC Dec>, HDC 3, SC 3, <Dec>, SC 3, HDC, Sl St to beginning stitch, Ch 1 [14]

29. SC 8, Inc, SC 2, Inc, SC 2, Sl St to beginning stitch, Ch 1 [16]

30. SC 13, Inc, SC 2, Sl St to beginning stitch, Ch 1 [17]

31. SC 4, <Dec>, SC 13, Sl St to beginning stitch, Ch 1 [18]

32. SC 18, Sl St to beginning stitch, Ch 1 [18]

33. (SC 5, Inc) x 3, Sl St to beginning stitch, Ch 1 [21]

34. SC 21, Sl St to beginning stitch, Ch 1 [21]

35. SC 3, Inc, (SC 6, Inc) x 2, SC 3, Sl St to beginning stitch, Ch 1 [24]

Fasten off with short yarn tail; tuck this yarn tail inside the leg.

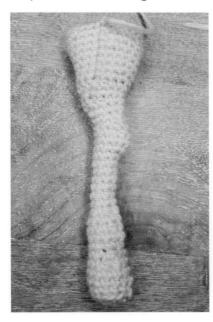

Unicorn Rear Leg

Your two back legs will be numbered as #1 and #4. Mark the following stitches accordingly; this is for assembly when you create the body.

Leg #1: Mark the 16th stitch

Leg #4: Mark the 5th stitch

UNICORN BODY

With US size G (4 mm) crochet hook:

1. Ch 24, starting in the 2nd Ch from hook, Inc, SC 21, Inc x 2 in the same stitch, continue to crochet around to the opposite side of the starting chain, SC 21, Inc, Sl St to beginning stitch, Ch 1 [50]

2. Inc x 2, SC 21, Inc x 4, SC 21, Inc x 2, Sl St to beginning stitch, Ch 1 [58]

3A. Inc into the first available stitch on the current work (aka the body)

3B. SC into Leg #1's marked stitch AND the next available stitch on the body at the same time

Whenever you insert your hook into any Leg and the Body in this row, you will be inserting your hook from the inside/wrong side of the stitch on the Leg to the outside/right side of the Leg and then into the outside/right side to the inside/wrong side of the stitch on the Body.

3C. Working into both Leg #1 and the Body at the same time, SC 3

3D. SC in the next available stitch on Leg #1 and the SAME body stitch that you last crocheted into

3E. Working into both Leg #1 and the Body at the same time, SC 3

3F. SC 16 in the Body only

3G. SC into Leg #2's marked stitch AND the next available stitch on the Body at the same time

3H. Working into both Leg #2 and the Body at the same time, SC 3

3I. Inc x 2 into only the body

3J. SC into Leg #3's marked stitch AND the next available stitch on the Body at the same time

3K. Working into both Leg #3 and the Body at the same time, SC 3

3L. SC 16 in the Body only

3M. SC into Leg #4's marked stitch AND the next available stitch on the Body at the same time

3N. Working into both Leg #4 and the Body at the same time, SC 2

3O. SC in the next available stitch on Leg #4 & the same Body stitch you last crocheted into

3P. Working into both Leg #4 and the Body at the same time, SC 4

3Q. Inc in the Body only, Sl St to beginning stitch, Ch 1 [64]

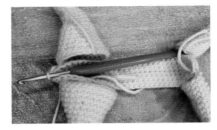

4. SC, Dec (Into the Body & Connect), SC 15, Triple SC Decrease (Leg & Connect & Body), SC 15, Dec (Connect & Leg), SC 7, Dec (Connect & Body), SC 2, Dec (Body & Connect), SC 7, Dec (Leg & Connect), SC 15, Triple SC Dec (Body & Connect & Leg), SC 15, Dec (Connect & Body), SC, Sl St to beginning stitch, Ch 1 [86]

The "Connect" instruction refers to the next available stitch that was used to connect the Body and the Leg from Row 3. For example, when you work a Decrease into the Body & Connect, you will start the Decrease into the next available stitch on the Body and finish the Decrease into the next available stitch that was used to connect the Body with the Leg in Row 3.

Whenever you insert your hook into any leg in this row, you will be inserting your hook from the outside/right side to the inside/wrong side of the work. Do not crochet into any of the Sl St joins on the legs. Unless specifically instructed to work into/use one of the stitches used to connect the leg and the body, you will be working around the outside edge of the body and legs, and you will ignore the stitches used to connect the leg and body.

5. Dec, SC 15, Dec, SC 13, Dec, SC 7, Inc, Dec, Inc, SC 7, Dec, SC 13, Dec, SC 15, Dec, Sl St to beginning stitch, Ch 1 [81]

6. Dec, Inc, SC 13, Dec, SC 11, Dec, Inc, SC 5, Inc, SC 5, Inc, SC 5, Inc, Dec, SC 11, Dec, SC 13, Inc, Dec, Sl St to beginning stitch, Ch 1 [81]

7. Dec, Inc, SC 12, Dec, SC 11, Dec, SC 10, Inc, SC 10, Dec, SC 11, Dec, SC 12, Inc, Dec, Sl St to beginning stitch, Ch 1 [78]

8. SC 78, Sl St to beginning stitch, Ch 1 [78]

9. SC 2, Dec, SC, Inc, SC 10, Dec, SC 10, Dec, SC 6, Inc, SC 6, Inc, SC 6, Dec, SC 10, Dec, SC 10, Inc, SC, Dec, Sl St to beginning stitch, Ch 1 [76]

10. SC 38, <Dec>, SC 38, Sl St to beginning stitch, Ch 1 [77]

11. SC 7, Dec, SC 5, Dec, SC 47, (Dec, SC 5) x 2, Sl St to beginning stitch, Ch 1 [73]

12. SC 6, Dec, SC 4, Dec, SC 47, (Dec, SC 4) x 2, Sl St to beginning stitch, Ch 1 [69]

13. SC 12, Dec, SC 12, Inc, SC 9, Inc, SC 9, Inc, SC 12, Dec, SC 8, Sl St to beginning stitch, Ch 1 [70]

NOTE: *At this point, if you haven't already inserted wires, you can insert them now. If you make the wire circle the size of the hoof, it may take some effort to fully insert the wire all the way into the leg, but it can be done. After you insert the wire, you can optionally insert one glass gem each with the flat side down. And then you can stuff each hoof/leg.*

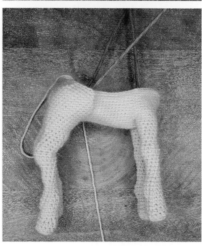

NOTE: *If you are using wire, at this point bend the back leg wire at a 90-degree angle toward the chest of the Unicorn. Make a bend at the same height as the current row level.*

14. (SC 4, Dec) x 2, SC 3, Ch 2, Skip 43 stitches, (SC 4, Dec) x 2, Sl St to beginning stitch, Ch 1 [25]

The stitch count includes the Ch stitches. Place a stitch marker in the 43rd skipped stitch to be referenced when attaching the yarn for the Neck.

15. (SC 3, Dec) x 5, Sl St to beginning stitch, Ch 1 [20]

16. (SC 2, Dec) x 5, Sl St to beginning stitch, Ch 1 [15]

17. (SC, Dec) x 5, Sl St to beginning stitch, Ch 1 [10]

18. Dec x 5, Sl St to beginning stitch [5]

Fasten off yarn with a long enough yarn tail to sew the hole shut. Stuff the body to this point medium-firm.

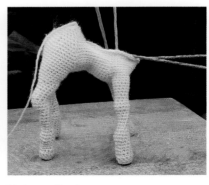

Unicorn Body

UNICORN NECK

With US size G (4 mm) crochet hook:

Starting with a long enough yarn tail to weave in later, attach the yarn to the marked SC just before the Ch stitches in Row 14 of the Unicorn Body.

1. Dec, SC 2, Dec, Ch 1, Turn [4]

The second leg of the 2nd Decrease should be into the 1st available stitch after the Chain stitches.

2–10. (9 rows of) SC 3, Dec, Ch 1, Turn [4]

11. SC 3, Dec, SC 31, Sl St to beginning stitch, Ch 1 [35]

If, for whatever reason, you are left with an extra stitch at the end of Row 11 (room for 32 instead of 31), make a Decrease into the final two stitches so that you come out of this row with the correct stitch count of 35.

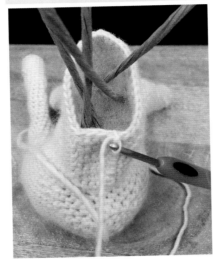

12. SC 3, Dec, SC 28, Dec, Sl St to beginning stitch, Ch 1 [33]

Starting with Row 13, do not slip stitch, Ch 1 at the end of the row unless otherwise noted. The stitch count is the topmost stitch count once the row is complete, not the cumulative number of stitches made in the row instructions. You will sometimes go beyond where the row began or where the previous row ended. Always work into stitches as normal; do not work into the side of stitches. Follow the instructions exactly as written. For a video demonstration on short rows, go here: https://www.youtube.com/watch?v=sh5T-idiwm8

13A. 2 Dec in 3 SC, Dec, SC 20, Ch 1, Turn

13B. SC 10, Ch 1, Turn

13C. SC 16, Dec, Sl St to beginning stitch, Ch 1 [30]

14. Dec, SC 5, Dec, SC 14, Dec, SC 5, Sl St to beginning stitch, Ch 1 [27]

15A. SC 7, Dec, SC 7, Dec, SC 4, Ch 1, Turn

15B. SC 12, Ch 1, Turn

15C. SC 15, Dec, Sl St to beginning stitch, Ch 1 [24]

16. SC 24, Sl St to beginning stitch, Ch 1 [24]

Keep stuffing with fiberfill as you go. At this point you can bend the wires that are sticking straight out from the rear legs so that they are now aimed upward through the neck.

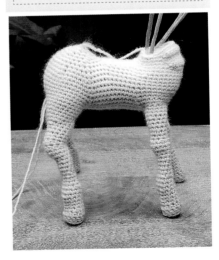

17A. SC 20, Ch 1, Turn

17B. SC 12, Ch 1, Turn

17C. SC 16, Sl St to beginning stitch, Ch 1 [16]

18. SC 12, Dec, SC 10, Sl St to beginning stitch, Ch 1 [23]

19. SC 12, 2 Dec in 3 SC, SC 8, Sl St to beginning stitch, Ch 1 [22]

20. SC 22, Sl St to beginning stitch, Ch 1 [22]

21. SC 12, Dec, SC 8, Sl St to beginning stitch, Ch 1 [21]

> At this point, without pulling on the wires too much, tape one of the rear leg wires to the front leg wire. And then tape the other rear leg wire to the front leg wire using thin strips of duct tape.

22. SC 12, Dec, SC 7. Continue in spiral. [20]

23. SC 20 [20]

24A. SC 8, Ch 1, Turn

24B. SC 10, Ch 1, Turn

24C. SC 9, SC/HDC Dec, SC 8, HDC/SC Dec, SC 18 [18]

25. SC 18 [18]

26. SC 12, 2 Dec in 3 SC, SC 3 [17]

27. SC 17 [17]

28. SC 3, 2 Dec in 3 SC, SC 11 [16]

29A. SC 12, Inc x 2, SC 11, Ch 1, Turn

> Stuff the neck firmly up to the open hole; you can fill this in a bit more as you affix the head to the neck.

29B. SC 8, Ch 1, Turn

29C. SC 8, Ch 1, Turn

29D. SC 8, Ch 1, Turn

29E. SC 8, Ch 1, Turn

29F. SC, Ch 6, starting in the 2nd Ch from hook, SC 3, HDC 2, continuing across the Unicorn Neck SC 6, Ch 6, starting in the 2nd Ch from hook, SC 3, HDC 2, in the last stitch available on the Unicorn Neck make a SC, Ch 1, Turn

> The "Ch 6, starting in the 2nd Ch from hook, SC 3, HDC 2" is the start of the Unicorn Ear.

29G. SC, Upper Ear (SC, HDC 2, SC 2, Ch 2, Sl St in the 2nd Ch from Hook, SC in the same stitch that you last Single Crocheted into, SC, HDC 2, SC), SC 6, Upper Ear (SC, HDC 2, SC 2, Ch 2, Sl St in the 2nd Ch from hook, SC in the same stitch that you last Single Crocheted into, SC, HDC 2, SC), SC, Ch 1, Turn

> The Upper Ear is created by crocheting up the side of the "Ch 6, starting in the 2nd Ch from hook, SC 3, HDC 2" that you made in 29F. The 1st four stitches (SC, HDC 2, SC) are made going up the side of those stitches. The next SC is made in the last available stitch; then you Ch 2, Sl St in the 2nd Ch from hook. The next SC is made in the 1st available stitch on the other side of the stitches from 29F. The last four stitches (SC, HDC 2, SC) are made down the other side to the end of the stitches from 29F to create the ear.

29H. SC, Skip Ear, SC 6, Skip Ear, SC

Fasten off with 24 in/61 cm long yarn tail.

UNICORN HEAD

With US size G (4 mm) crochet hook:

1. SC 6 in Magic Circle, Sl St to beginning stitch, Ch 1 [6]

2. (HDC, Inc) x 3, Sl St to beginning stitch, Ch 1 [9]

3. SC 3, Ch 2, SC in the same stitch as your last SC, SC 3, Ch 2, SC in the same stitch as your last SC, SC 2, Inc, Sl St to beginning stitch, Ch 1 [12]

> The "SC, Ch 2, SC in the same stitch as your last SC" is what creates a tiny nostril. Leave the chain stitches unworked and do not crochet into them in Row 4.

4. SC 3, Skip Ch stitches, SC 4, Skip Ch stitches, SC 4, <Dec>, SC, Sl St to beginning stitch, Ch 1 [13]

5. SC 4, Dec, SC 4, Triple SC Dec, Sl St to beginning stitch, Ch 1 [10]

6. SC 10, Sl St to beginning stitch, Ch 1 [10]

Top view, nose down

Side view, nose to the right

7. (SC 4, Inc) x 2, Sl St to beginning stitch, Ch 1 [12]

8. SC 12, Sl St to beginning stitch, Ch 1 [12]

9. (SC 3, Inc) x 3, Sl St to beginning stitch, Ch 1 [15]

10. SC 2, Inc, (SC 4, Inc) x 2, SC 2, Sl St to beginning stitch, Ch 1 [18]

11. (SC 5, Inc) x 3, Sl St to beginning stitch, Ch 1 [21]

12. SC 21, Sl St to beginning stitch, Ch 1 [21]

13. SC 3, Inc, (SC 6, Inc) x 2, SC 3, Sl St to beginning stitch, Ch 1 [24]

14. SC 24, Sl St to beginning stitch, Ch 1 [24]

15. SC 24, Sl St to beginning stitch, Ch 1 [24]

> Insert 18 mm–21 mm eyes between Rows 11 and Row 12, with 8 full stitch spaces between them.

16. (SC 4, Dec) x 4, Sl St to beginning stitch, Ch 1 [20]

17. (SC 2, Dec) x 5, Sl St to beginning stitch, Ch 1 [15]

18. (SC, Dec) x 5, Sl St to beginning stitch [10]

Fasten off with 18 in/46 cm long yarn tail. Stuff with fiberfill.

Using the hole in the back of the head, slide the head onto the protruding wire from the neck of the body of the unicorn. You want the wire to slide along the inside-top of the head, along the forehead and down to the nose of the unicorn. If the wire is too long, trim it or bend it back on itself and secure with duct tape. If the wire ends somewhere mid-head, that's fine. Stretch the back of the neck and ears up over the back of the head. Pin in place, sew in place. (I suggest whipstitches around the entire head everywhere it touches the neck.) If you are using wire, you can leave the final positioning up to bending the wire. If you are not using wire, you need to position the head in place exactly as you want it to be when you are finished.

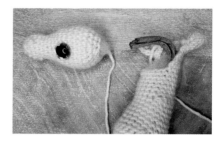

Unicorn Head

UNICORN PUFFY CLOUD MANE (MAKE 1)

Option 1

With US size G (4 mm) crochet hook:

I. Starting with a long enough yarn tail to weave in later, Ch 39, Turn, starting in the 2nd Ch from hook, Sl St 2, SC 2, Inc x 2, HDC Inc x 2, DC Inc x 30, Ch 2, Turn [72]

> The Ch 2 is a turning chain; you will not crochet into it. This applies to every row in this section.

2. DC 60, HDC 4, SC 4, Sl St, Ch 1, Turn [69]

3. Skip the Slip Stitch, Dec x 2, HDC Dec x 2, DC Dec x 30, Ch 47, Turn [34]

4. Starting in the 2nd Ch from hook, Sl St 2, SC 2, Inc x 2, HDC Inc x 4, DC Inc x 36, Ch 2, Turn [88]

5. DC 70, HDC 10, SC 3, Sl St, Ch 1, Turn [84]

6. Skip the Slip Stitch, SC, Dec x 2, HDC Dec x 4, DC Dec x 35, Ch 57, Turn [42]

7. Starting in the 2nd Ch from hook, Sl St 2, SC 2, Inc x 2, HDC Inc x 6, DC Inc x 44, Ch 2, Turn [108]

8. DC 84, HDC 14, SC 7, Sl St, Ch 1, Turn [106]

9. Skip the Slip Stitch, SC, Dec x 3, HDC Dec x 7, DC Dec x 42, Ch 62, Turn [53]

10. Starting in the 2nd Ch from hook, Sl St 2, SC 2, Inc x 2, HDC Inc x 7, DC Inc x 48, Ch 2, Turn [118]

11. DC 98, HDC 12, SC 5, Sl St, Ch 1, Turn [116]

12. Skip the Slip Stitch, SC, Dec x 3, HDC Dec x 6, DC Dec x 48, Ch 41, Turn [58]

13. Starting in the 2nd Ch from hook, Sl St 2, SC 2, Inc x 2, HDC Inc x 4, DC Inc x 30, Ch 2, Turn [76]

14. DC 60, HDC 8, SC 5, Sl St, Ch 1, Turn [74]

15. Skip the Slip Stitch, SC, Dec x 3, HDC Dec x 4, DC Dec x 29, Ch 39, Turn [37]

16. Starting in the 2nd Ch from hook, Sl St 2, SC 2, Inc x 2, HDC Inc x 2, DC Inc x 30, Ch 2, Turn [72]

17. DC 60, HDC 4, SC 5, Sl St, Ch 1, Turn [70]

18. Skip the Slip Stitch, SC, Dec x 3, HDC Dec x 2, DC Dec x 29 [35]

Fasten off with 24 in/61 cm yarn tail. Pin in place along the neck and sew to attach; weave in ends.

UNICORN PUFFY CLOUD TAIL (MAKE 1)

Option 1

With US size G (4 mm) crochet hook:

I. Starting with a long enough yarn tail to weave in later, Ch 62, Turn, starting in the 2nd Ch from hook, Sl St, SC 2, Inc x 3, HDC Inc x 5, DC Inc x 45, HDC Inc x 3, Inc x 2, Ch 1, Turn [119]

2. HDC 10, DC 90, HDC 10, SC 7, Sl St, Ch 1, Turn [117]

3. Skip the Slip Stitch, SC, Dec x 3, HDC Dec x 5, DC Dec x 45, HDC Dec x 3, Dec x 2 [59]

4. Repeat Rows 1–3 at least 3 more times

Fasten off with 24 in/61 cm long yarn tail. Pin in place on the rump and sew to attach; weave in ends.

Unicorn with Puffy Cloud Tail

UNICORN RUFFLE WAVY MANE (MAKE 1)

Option 2

With US size G (4 mm) crochet hook:

NOTE: A tighter tension produces a wavier mane.

---

1. Starting with a long enough yarn tail to weave in later, Ch 37, Turn, starting in the 2nd Ch from hook, Sl St 2, SC 2, Inc x 2, HDC Inc x 2, DC Inc x 28, Ch 1, Turn [68]

NOTE: For a simplified thinner, curly mane piece, of which you could make 2 or more whole pieces for a very full curly mane for the unicorn, just work the following rows: Row 1 (twice), Row 4 (twice), Row 7 (twice), Row 10 (twice), Row 13 (twice), and Row 16 (once), and all of the Chains that come at the end of the row just before these rows begin. Additionally, work all indicated DC stitches as HDC stitches (so all DC Increases will be HDC Increases).

---

2. (HDC, Inc) x 32, Sl St, Ch 1, Turn [97]

3. Skip the Slip Stitch, SC 86, HDC Dec x 5, Ch 47, Turn [91]

4. Starting in the 2nd Ch from hook, Sl St 2, SC 2, Inc x 2, HDC Inc x 4, DC Inc x 36, Ch 1, Turn [88]

5. (HDC, Inc) x 42, Sl St, Ch 1, Turn [127]

6. Skip the Slip Stitch, SC 116, HDC Dec x 5, Ch 57, Turn [121]

7. Starting in the 2nd Ch from hook, Sl St 2, SC 2, Inc x 2, HDC Inc x 6, DC Inc x 44, Ch 1, Turn [108]

8. (HDC, Inc) x 52, Sl St, Ch 1, Turn [157]

9. Skip the Slip Stitch, SC 146, HDC Dec x 5, Ch 57, Turn [151]

10. Starting in the 2nd Ch from hook, Sl St 2, SC 2, Inc x 2, HDC Inc x 6, DC Inc x 44, Ch 1, Turn [108]

11. (HDC, Inc) x 52, Sl St, Ch 1, Turn [157]

12. Skip the Slip Stitch, SC 146, HDC Dec x 5, Ch 41, Turn [151]

13. Starting in the 2nd Ch from hook, Sl St 2, SC 2, Inc x 2, HDC Inc x 4, DC Inc x 30, Ch 1, Turn [76]

14. (SC, Inc) x 36, Sl St, Ch 1, Turn [109]

15. Skip the Slip Stitch, SC 98, HDC Dec x 5, Ch 37, Turn [103]

16. Starting in the 2nd Ch from hook, Sl St 2, SC 2, Inc x 2, HDC Inc x 2, DC Inc x 28, Ch 1, Turn [68]

17. (SC, Inc) x 32, Sl St, Ch 1, Turn [97]

18. Skip the Slip stitch, SC 87, HDC Dec x 5 [92]

Fasten off with 24 in/61 cm yarn tail. Pin in place along the neck and sew to attach; weave in ends.

Unicorn with Ruffle Wavy Mane

UNICORN RUFFLE WAVY TAIL (MAKE 1)

Option 2

With US size G (4 mm) crochet hook:

NOTE: A tighter tension produces a wavier tail.

----

1. Starting with a long enough yarn tail to weave in later, Ch 62, Turn, starting in the 2nd Ch from hook, Sl St, SC 2, Inc x 3, HDC Inc x 5, DC Inc x 45, HDC Inc x 3, Inc x 2, Ch 1, Turn [119]

2. (SC, Inc) x 58, Sl St, Ch 1, Turn [175]

3. Skip the Slip Stitch, SC 164, Dec x 5 [169]

4. Repeat Rows 1–3 at least 3 more times

Fasten off with 24 in/61 cm long yarn tail. Pin in place on the rump and sew to attach; weave in ends.

Unicorn with Ruffle Wavy Tail

UNICORN SIMPLE HORN (MAKE 1)

Option 1

With US size G (4 mm) crochet hook:

1. SC 4 in Magic Circle, continue in spiral [4]
2. BLO [SC 4] [4]
3. BLO [Inc, SC 3] [5]
4. BLO [SC 5] [5]
5. BLO [SC 5] [5]
6. BLO [Inc, SC 4] [6]
7. BLO [SC 6] [6]
8. BLO [SC 6] [6]
9. BLO [Inc, SC 5] [7]
10. BLO [SC 7] [7]
11. BLO [SC 7, Sl St into the next available stitch] [8]

Unicorn Simple Horn

Fasten off with a 12 in/30 cm yarn tail. Pin in place on the head, sew to attach, and weave in ends.

NOTE: This piece does not require wire; you can sew to attach as is, which would be safest for a child, but the horn will be pliable and soft. If you want the horn to stand straight and firm, you can take one piece of wire about 9 in/23 cm long, fold it over on itself, and insert the bent end into the horn.

UNICORN ADVANCED SPIRAL HORN (MAKE 1)

Option 2

With doubled-up lace or sock weight yarn (a heavier yarn will make the horn too bulky) and a US size C (2.75 mm) crochet hook:

1. Start with a long enough yarn tail to weave in, Ch 54, Turn, starting in the 3rd Ch from hook, HDC Inc x 16, Inc x 10, Sl St 2, Inc x 10, HDC Inc x 14, Ch 1, Turn [102]

2. HDC 3, SC 35, Sl St 10, Ch 2, Skip the 2 Slip Stitches from Row 1, Sl St 10, SC 35, HDC 7, Ch 1, Turn [109]

3. Dec x 21, Dec x 5 around the slip stitches from Row 2 and into the same stitches that they were slip stitched into from Row 1, Ch 1, Slip Stitch around the entire piece encompassing the slip stitches from Row 1 and the Chains from Row 2, Ch 1, Dec x 5 around the slip stitches from Row

2 and into the same stitches that they were slip stitched into from Row 1, Dec x 19 [51]

Fasten off with 12 in/30 cm yarn tail.

At the halfway point of the piece you made, twist the horn together. It may take a couple of tries to figure it out, but it will work.

Unicorn Advanced Spiral Horn

Pin in place, sew to attach, and weave in ends. The horn will be soft to the touch (child-safe), but it should stand up on its own because of its shape.

ACKNOWLEDGMENTS

Special thanks to my husband and best friend, Greg, without whom I could not have accomplished all that I have. I love you.

And to my children, Riley and Harper. I am so proud of you. You inspire me every day.

Special thanks to my brother, Brendan Conway, who supported me through the process of creating this book, and to my wonderful sister-in-law, Grace Jacobson.

Thank you to my parents, Velma Conway and Richard Conway, and to my in-laws, Joy Lapp and Jim Lapp, for all of your love and support.

Special thanks to Jen Starbird and Sarah Constein for both being moderators for my FB group and helping to check over this book, test patterns, and make this book the best it can be.

Special thanks for additional crochet work and photography by Lauren Lewis in the previews for *Crochet Impkins*.

Special thanks to Kelly Bastow for capturing the Adult Dragon in her bookplate illustration.

Special thanks to my FB group moderators and friends:

Kat Bifield	Elizabeth Keane
Morgan Carpuski	Lauren Lewis
Shawna Dresslar	Laci Lynn Hall
Heather Flint	Laura Marshall
Amie Fournier-Flather	Jade Asli Muyan
Alix Frere	Laura Owens
Jeremy Leon Guerrero	Tammy Simmons
Dayna Lynn Inouye	Jennifer Steyn
Kate Jacques	Jasmine Winston
Daniel Jagoda	

Special thanks to my agent, Christi Cardenas.

PATTERN INDEX

CUTE CRITTERS

STANDARD SIZE

Available Now

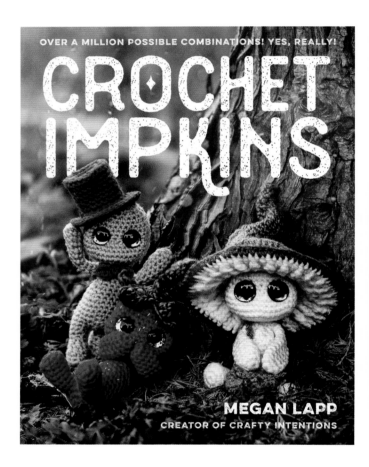

OVER A MILLION POSSIBLE COMBINATIONS! YES, REALLY!

CROCHET IMPKINS

MEGAN LAPP
CREATOR OF CRAFTY INTENTIONS

With more than 35 body patterns, you can mix and match options for thousands upon thousands of possibilities!

CROCHET MONSTERS

MEGAN LAPP Creator of Crafty Intentions